Joe Morgan

A LIFE IN BASEBALL

W·W·NORTON & COMPANY·NEW YORK·LONDON

Joe Morgan

A LIFE IN BASEBALL

Joe Morgan AND David Falkner

The text of this book is composed in Berling with the display set in Signum and
Rockwell
Composition and manufacturing by The Haddon Craftsmen, Inc.
Book design by Antonina Krass

Library of Congress Cataloging-in-Publication Data
Morgan, Joe, 1943–
Joe Morgan : a life in baseball / Joe Morgan and David Falkner.
p.   cm.
1. Morgan, Joe, 1943–   .   2. Baseball players—United States—Biography.   I.
Falkner, David.   II. Title.
GV865.M64A3   1993
796.357'092—dc20
[B]   92-40151

ISBN 0-393-03469-0
W. W. Norton & Company, Inc., 500 Fifth Avenue, New York, N.Y. 10110
W. W. Norton & Company Ltd., 10 Coptic Street, London WC1A 1PU
1 2 3 4 5 6 7 8 9 0

To the Morgan family
and Tom Reich

Contents

Three

THE BIG RED MACHINE

Four

THE LONG WAY HOME

Photographs appear following page 140

Part One

"A GOOD LITTLE PLAYER"

From the Booth:
Opening Ceremonies

When the Hall of Fame vote came up, I tried my best not to think about it. I had been out of the game for five years and it was the first time I was eligible. My friends said it was a lock but I wasn't so sure.

I had all the thrills a player could have through a career of twenty-two years with the Astros, Reds, Phillies, Giants, and A's: back-to-back World Series championships and consecutive MVP years with the Reds, playing with so many great players and a manager every bit as great as his players. We were the most written-about team of the 1970s.

But the most written-about player—in those years anyway—wasn't me, it was Johnny Bench. And then Pete Rose.

I had solid numbers, to be sure. But lots of guys had stats that were more impressive. I was never the home-run hitter Willie Stargell was; I never hit for average like Pete Rose or Rod Carew; I was a base stealer but never came close to the season marks of Lou Brock or Maury Wills.

Also, I'm a little guy and little guys often get overlooked. On the other hand, some big guys have told me that's really a blessing.

I was walking through the Oakland airport a few years ago with

Bob Lanier, the ex-NBA basketball player. Bob is 6 feet 10 inches and he can't go anywhere without people gawking at him. Like a lot of very tall people, he hunches his shoulders as if to hide his height. Our walk through the airport caused a lot of heads to turn. Bob said to me, "Joe, you're five-seven, an average person, you can get lost in a crowd. Big Bob, he can't hide anywhere. They all look at me like I'm a freak."

Of course, other big guys never miss an opportunity to rub it in. Bill Russell, the former Celtic great, is a very close friend of mine. We play golf a lot, often with Willie McCorey. One day at Willie's country club, playing a par-three 190-yard hole, I hit a shot straight at the pin. The ball disappeared over a little hill in front of the green.

"That ball just went in the hole," Russell said.

"Get outta here, you're kidding!" I said.

"If you weren't five-four you'd be able to see it yourself." He and Willie, who is six foot six, had a good laugh at that.

Bill Russell aside, being overlooked can actually be a tremendous advantage in sports.

I was in a celebrity golf tournament recently. The foursome I played with included some big guys who were heavy hitters: Mike Schmidt, Frank Gifford, and Michael Jordan. We flipped a coin to see who would hit on the first tee. I won and led off by smacking a drive right down the middle of the fairway. Schmidt was next and he hooked his ball into the next county. Gifford followed and sliced a ball to the county on the other side. Jordan, who has serious aspirations to be a professional golfer, hit his drive down the middle of the fairway, too.

As Mike and Frank went off to find their balls, Michael and I walked along laughing and talking. When we got to the first ball, he stopped and stood off to the other side. I also stood off to the other side. He looked at me, I looked at him. He said, "Are you gonna hit?"

"What do you mean," I said, "you're away."

He walked over, bent down, and looked at the ball. He looked up with an expression of pain and total disbelief.

"You little munchkin, you can't outdrive me!" he said.

"You're away, Michael," I said.

I've always been able to use my lack of height to advantage, especially in baseball where skill, not size or athleticism, counts most. From the earliest time, I worked to develop what skills I had, to become, through hard work and dedication, the best player I could be. I threw myself into the challenge of being a complete baseball player at the start of my career and I never looked back.

But the Hall of Fame on the first ballot? Even though I was proud of my numbers, proud of my career, you stack them up against other Hall of Fame players and it takes some doing. I think of Willie Mays, Hank Aaron, Ted Williams, and Babe Ruth—and I still find myself amazed to have joined them at Cooperstown.

In order to vote for me, a writer would have to see beyond numbers—even beyond the position I played. Second basemen are rarely big-time players; there are fewer second basemen in the Hall of Fame than players at any of the other positions. In fact, through all my years in the game, I thought of myself as a baseball player first, a second baseman second. I saw myself as a guy who wasn't necessarily the best at any one thing but did his best to win games any way he could—in other words, as someone who could be overlooked.

But I could not hide my excitement—and my worry—as this time of decision neared. Tom Reich, my agent, Roy Eisenhardt, the former executive of the Oakland A's, and others all assured me that I was going to make it on the first ballot. The more they encouraged me, the more I tried to turn it off. If I didn't make it, who was I to say that I *deserved* to make it and would therefore be put off if I didn't? What I did believe was that I had a chance for the Hall of Fame—but not on the first try. But if I didn't make it then, who knew what could happen. Nellie Fox, a great player and friend who had been instrumental in my career, missed election to the Hall of Fame by a fraction of one percent once. Nellie was a second baseman—like me. He was a little guy—like me. He was a complete, team player, who had a solid .288 lifetime batting average and an MVP award to go with it. He had a big tobacco chaw poking out from his cheek through nineteen great big-league seasons while he went at his business the way few others I have seen did—and he didn't make it. Turn down Nellie Fox, it was possible to turn down Joe Morgan.

As the time for the vote announcement drew near, I got more and more uncomfortable. Because my name had come up so often, I was too expectant and too apprehensive. I really wanted to be somewhere else, doing anything to keep my mind off the whole situation.

Meanwhile, Jack Lang, the president of the Baseball Writers Association, contacted me—as he did all the other candidates—to suggest I be in New York the day of the vote, just in case. I told Jack I wasn't sure I could make it.

My close friends—Tom Reich in particular—urged me to be on hand when the announcement was made. I kept resisting. In the end, not feeling at all good about it, I went along.

I arrived in New York with a small party of close friends—my new wife, Theresa, Tom and his fiancée, Trisha Williams, and Skip Korb, a friend from Cincinnati who was handling my media relations.

The candidates were all asked to stay in the one centrally located hotel. I checked into another, the Regency, selected by Tom Reich, and spent the time with these friends, as much as possible, doing the ordinary things—dinner, shows—that tourists do when they visit a place.

We were told the announcement would be made that night between nine and ten o'clock. We all went down to dinner and tried—without much success—to pretend nothing out of the ordinary was going on.

At eight-thirty we went back upstairs where we had a big suite and we all sat around silently—surrounded by bottles of unopened champagne—waiting and waiting . . . then the phone rang! I charged for it, tried to control my voice. But it was another call concerning something else. False alarm. Then, finally, at nine-thirty, *the* call.

Jack Lang's voice seemed to come from another planet, the words stilted and strange:

"Joe, from now on you will not be known as Joe Morgan any more, you'll be known as Joe Morgan, Hall of Famer," he said.

I just stood there smiling and then, suddenly, the room around me erupted. Champagne bottles were popping, people were hugging and kissing.

When I got off the phone we all raised a glass in celebration. Then I called my mother and father, who, more than anyone, imbued in me the values that sustained me through my entire playing career. I called my first wife, Gloria—who was very pleased and happy for me—and she in turn called our daughters to tell them. I called Sparky Anderson, my old manager with the Reds, who was family to me. And then I called Roy Eisenhardt, a special friend from my time with the Oakland A's, a great baseball person and a man who would make a terrific commissioner. Roy is a person of diverse interests and abilities who *loves* baseball (as distinct from just following it), and that love of the game, combined with his intelligence, would allow him to handle the business side as well as what happens on the field.

After I made my calls, I went out and enjoyed myself. We went to a local club to hear the Modern Jazz Quartet, a group I particularly like. Their music was perfect for the night, flowing and deeply tranquil. Wherever you are you wind up someplace else at the end of one of their numbers. Just what I needed. My wife, Theresa, not a jazz buff, was totally captivated; Tom Reich, a joyous person to begin with, couldn't have been happier. And neither could I. Milt Jackson, the great vibraharpist, recognized me in the crowd and came over to say hello. What an honor!

The next day, I went to a press conference in New York, the first of many, and its highlight for me was really a lowlight—there wasn't a representative from the National League there. My best years were spent in the National League. I was disappointed that

Bill White, the league president, had another engagement that day—and I let him know. Bill said he had commitments he could not break.

Jim Palmer was also elected to the Hall of Fame that year. At the press conference, Fay Vincent, the commissioner, said in his remarks that he was surprised to see two people who seemed to genuinely like each other elected to the Hall of Fame at the same time. He may have been referring to the fact that when Johnny Bench and Carl Yastrzemski went in the year before, Yaz had spent much of the time in a funk because he didn't receive the same number of votes Bench did and apparently resented it.

Palmer, for me, was and is a class act. And though we played most of our careers in different leagues, I retain a special memory of competing against him—one that does not particularly do me proud.

In my last year, when I played with the A's, we went into Baltimore for a series. Palmer was no longer the pitcher he once was—any more than I was the player I had been. He was brought in to pitch relief against us. We were leading 7–1 and his appearance was really a kind of humiliation—he was being used in a mop-up role.

Earlier I had been walked twice. In the at-bat against Palmer, I was about to be walked again. Palmer had fallen behind 3–0 in the count and he then came in with a pitch I took a rip at. I fouled the pitch off but the second I swung, I knew I had done something I would never normally have done to any struggling pitcher in a one-sided game. I was trying to kick a guy when he was down—and the pitcher happened to be Jim Palmer.

I went to Palmer in the outfield the next day during warmups and I found him playing catch, shagging flies. I told him what I had done and apologized. He asked why I was apologizing.

"Because I didn't make a career out of kicking people when they were down, especially someone I admire very much. I feel terrible about it and I just want you to know," I said.

"Joe, it's okay," he said. He was smiling and I could see all the years of pride and age in his face. Perhaps he saw the same in my eyes. The night before, I hadn't been able to sleep because of what I had done. The next night, after I apologized, I slept like a baby. The incident helped me realize that my playing days were coming to an end.

When I got to Cooperstown that weekend for the induction ceremonies, it was the first time I had seen the place. Cooperstown is a little, out-of-the-way village in upstate New York, very hard to get to, a perfect symbol of the game's roots.

The village and, particularly, Doubleday Field, a picturesque single-grandstand ballpark, take any visitor back. There are reminders here not only of baseball in its first days but of the games like Rounders and Town Ball that preceded it. You can almost feel the old ghosts of great players, walking out of their field of dreams on a line into that Hall of Fame.

The weekend began festively—and comfortably. Old friends were there, players and competitors I had not seen for a while. Friday, I played golf with Willie McCovey and two other friends. We were all staying in the Otessaga Hotel near the Hall of Fame and then the comings and goings, the asides with press and photographers, gained in intensity.

The hotel was beautiful, out on a lake, normally just a quiet, quaint, pretty place to spend a stretch of summer days. But now I felt a gathering sense of nervousness because what had only been a fantasy was hour by hour becoming real.

I worried about my speech, although I knew what I wanted to say. Then I had a tour of the museum and I saw all the plaques, all the players I would be joining—and it threw me.

There was a room set aside for Babe Ruth—a whole room. I understood that immediately. At the same time it struck me as peculiar that there was *not* a room set aside for Willie Mays. Willie Mays, to my generation, was just like Babe Ruth, had the same overpowering ability, the same charisma, generated the same excitement even when he struck out.

It was strange how, walking through that museum, these ghosts started to filter into my mind. I saw Jackie Robinson in his pigeon-toed lead off first base; I saw Stan Musial in his crouch, Ted Wil-

liams gripping and waving his bat, hitting the ball harder than anyone who ever lived. There was Ernie Banks playing two, actually
passing out in the second game of a doubleheader because he
would not, could not, get himself off the field. It was amazing how
these players and personalities, some of them long gone, came to
life again. John McGraw, Christy Mathewson, Satchel Paige, the
list goes on. I'll always have trouble saying Musial and Morgan in
the same breath. Mays and Morgan, Williams and Morgan? I can't
do it!

Ordinarily the schedule at the Hall of Fame begins with the
induction ceremony and moves on to a dinner for Hall of Famers
only. But it rained heavily and the induction ceremony was postponed to the next day. As a result I got to attend the Hall of Famers
dinner before I was officially a member.

I'm really glad that happened. Dinner with the Hall of Famers
really put a new perspective on my induction. The ceremony the
next day became much more memorable, and I know I gave a
better speech.

In that formal gathering the senior members of the Hall of Fame
welcome the inductees and give them a stamp of approval that the
fans and the writers can't.

For me, the biggest thrill was seeing Ted Williams. Williams was
one of my three childhood idols (Jackie Robinson and Nellie Fox
are the others). No matter who else is there, when Williams walks
into a room, that's when you know it is a Hall of Fame occasion. In
past years, Joe DiMaggio has not attended these festivities, nor has
Willie Mays. Williams *always* is there. He is the living embodiment
of the Hall of Fame and everyone there knows it. As old as I was, as
much as I had been through the wars, just seeing him was a thrill
and an honor.

I was giving an impromptu press conference one afternoon in the
lobby of the hotel and I failed to notice that Ted Williams had
moved into the crowd off to my side and was listening to my
remarks. When I finished he came up to me. I was surprised—and
elated. He told me that I had given exactly the right amount of

credit to others and to the game in answering questions about my-self. I felt like he had just given me my personal pass to the Hall of Fame.

I had this flashback of the first time I met him. I was with Nellie Fox in my first year with the Houston Colt 45s. It was in spring training and Nellie took me over to meet him. We shook hands, Nellie told him I was a terrific young player, someone he better keep an eye on, Williams smiled and shook my hand—I was a kid all over again. Years later, after I had won my first MVP award, Williams was asked what current players, if any, he liked.

"The little guy from Cincinnati," he said. "He hits for power, he hits singles, he knows how to take a pitch—he can do everything." I was just as excited by that as when I first met him, and as I was in this pre-induction moment.

It rained again the day of the induction ceremonies and we had to have them indoors. On the gym platform behind me were all the Hall of Famers who had come for the weekend. It was the proudest moment of my life. My parents were there, my second wife, Theresa, my oldest daughter, Lisa, my sisters, Patricia and Linda, and the friends and fellow players who had come to celebrate with me.

In my speech, I talked about old players and about caring for the game. I talked about who I was and where I came from, how hard it was for me and other black players to make it in baseball and in life. I thanked all the people who had helped me along the way. I thanked my first wife for putting up with me all those years and at such cost. I thanked my parents, my children, my friends, all who had supported and nurtured me.

I did not write out my speech. My friends Corey Busch and Bob Hartzell tried to help me formulate the right words. But when the moment arrived I let the words come as they would. I meant every-thing I said but, of course, I left out a lot of things—and thus the real purpose of this book.

I do not think the game is in as good shape now as when I received it as a young player. My story, which follows, is really about a life in the game and about the way the game is transmitted from era to era and how that may be breaking down. Is it possible today to put together a team that was like the Big Red Machine I once played for? Is it possible to maintain standards of excellence that assure the passing on of the game's secrets and skills? Is it possible in an age where, increasingly, money talks and everything else walks to really care for the sport? Is it possible, with so much at stake, to withstand the constant and growing antagonism of owners and players, the unresolved issues of drugs and free agency and arbitration and expansion and race? More than ever, the answers seem harder to come by.

On Hall of Fame weekend, at that pre-induction dinner, many of the old-timers are asked to get up and say something. It is a moving and impressive thing to witness—to watch as one after another of the old greats, Stan Musial, Willie Stargell, get up and say their few words, words that are really about how we pass on the game.

Ted Williams got up that weekend and he looked around the room where we had all gathered. Ted today looks and sounds like John Wayne. He more and more has acquired the look of an America that has already vanished. In more recent days, he has been ill. He is in his seventies now, and he will not be there forever to serve us in this way.

"I'd just like to say that it's great seeing so many of you back here again," he began. "I know you've been ill, Campy, and you too, Stan. It's wonderful to see you here tonight, and I hope we'll all be back together again next year. You are what the game is all about." Then he turned to Jim Palmer and me, and he said, "I want to welcome you, Joe, and you, Jim, to the greatest fraternity in the world."

It is the greatest fraternity in the world, and the thrill of belonging to it will never leave me.

I've always been conscious of the game as something that one generation passes down to another. When I was starting out, the older generation set a tough standard for me to emulate. I had to learn the game from the ground up and use every ounce and inch to make a life in baseball for myself. That made every achievement worth even more.

Today I'm poised between two generations in baseball, at a time when scandals and controversy can make it seem like standards don't even exist anymore. But they do, and they can still carry the great game of baseball forward. I hope my experiences, and the opinions I have come to as a result, can show something of how baseball got to where it is today, and the direction it should take tomorrow.

1

Childhood First

When you're a good little player (or just an energetic little guy), you overlook obstacles that get in your way. I think I've always had an ability to overlook what I didn't care to see. Little guy? I didn't think of myself as little. Whatever my friends could do, I could do just as well and better. When it came to choosing up sides for anything, I expected to be chosen first—and often I was. And when I wasn't, I thought to myself, That's their mistake, they're in for a surprise.

I was born in a small town, but I never saw it as small. Bonham, Texas, in 1943, had just over 7,500 people. But Bonham, through the five years I lived there, seemed like a big place. My memories of it are that it was almost like a mid-sized city, though obviously it wasn't.

We lived in a black area of town—except that I didn't know anything about segregation then and consequently never experienced anything that might have left lasting social or psychological scars. In fact, the first sense I had that there were real lines between black and white came later, when I moved to California, when those lines began to break down.

My early memories had nothing to do with segregation but with the closeness of my family, being a favorite because I was the firstborn child. I remember black and white living areas only in the sense that they seemed to touch each other, a block apart.

My grandfather was a home builder. He built homes for white people, built homes for black people. I used to go with him on his job rounds. He'd negotiate, stop, and spend easy time with white people. He was a respected man in a town living just the way it always had.

I have no recollection of deprivation and injustice—though obviously they were everywhere. My father served in the army and had a tough time because, while he was fighting for his country, his country was maintaining a segregated army—and my father resented it deeply.

He had three years of college, but not the fourth that would have given him his degree. Instead, he got married. My dad tried in every way he could to make sure his family got what it needed. That meant that he nearly always was working at two jobs, just so I might retain the memories I have now. I can't recall ever being without. When I wanted a bike, I got a bike; when I needed shoes and clothes, I got them right away. The most shining gift I ever received was the sense given to me that I had a right to the joy of my own childhood.

From the start, I was something of a daredevil as a little kid. One time, when I was five, a group of friends and I were climbing around, playing follow the leader—and I was the leader. Bonham was a flat, dusty place with lots of areas of scrub brush and Texas pine. There were places to hide, to play games. I led my friends through an obstacle course of underbrush and rocks. I got to the bank of a rather large creek that ran behind my house. There was a big and obviously dangerous jump to make to get to the other side. My friends wanted me to turn back. Instead, I jumped—which was just the dumbest thing I could have done. I landed wrong and broke my leg.

Because I was just a kid and didn't know any better, I assumed it was no big deal, that I'd be fine in no time. Instead, I was laid up for the next several weeks. My leg was elevated by a portable pulley contraption that was fixed to the end of my bed. It was awful.

The fracture was in the worst place possible—in the thigh bone—so my hip-to-shin cast also involved a lot of tape which had to be changed regularly. The doctor visited me daily and kept changing the tape on my leg. The only problem was that every time the tape was changed, skin from my shin went with it (I still retain the scars). It was only my grandfather, Joe Cook, who saved me from this torture chamber.

Though he was a stern disciplinarian, he was a very kindly person as well. He could not tolerate the idea of pain in children—particularly if they happened to be his grandchildren.

My grandfather found an old high-laced boot and, after removing the foot portion of it, tightened it around my shin in place of the tape which was being used to keep the cast secure. Instead of daily changes of the tape, there was shoeleather which the doctor really could not quarrel with.

My grandfather also found a way around the doctor's absolute command that my leg at all times was to remain elevated in those pulleys. The problem—which my grandfather understood—was that after a while I was in agony with my leg elevated. Each day, against the strenuous objections of my grandmother, my parents, and the doctor, he would settle a couple of pillows on the bed and then lower my leg onto them, easing the pressure and the pain for an hour or two.

My grandfather looked after me then, just as he would later on. He was always interested in my baseball game, and he sent me my first pair of steel spikes when I was fourteen. One of the highlights of my rookie season in the major leagues was that I was able to go out and hit a home run for him the first time he came to see me play. That was in the Houston Astrodome, and it was the first major-league game my grandfather had ever been to in person.

The rest of my family also helped me when my leg was hurt. I played cards for hours on end with my grandmother, Bessie Morgan, played checkers with my father, listened to my mother read me stories—until I was finally well again. Curiously, with all the attention, the activity that took up most of my time was solitaire. I lost my pain in the cards over and over again.

I took advantage of my position as the favorite in the house. The year before I broke my leg, an uncle of mine invited me out to ride on his bicycle with him. I couldn't have been more than four at the time. He said, "Go inside and ask your mom if she'll let you ride with me."

I ran into the house but my mother was not there; she must have been out shopping or doing chores. I came back outside and told my uncle, "Yeah, she says it's okay, I can go."

As I tried to get set in position behind my uncle on the bike, my foot got caught in the spikes of the rear wheel and I severely injured my Achilles tendon. If my uncle had put his feet on the brakes of the bike the tendon would have been completely severed. If that happened I might never have walked normally again. I might never have been a professional athlete.

Every family has its own story and every person usually finds some explanation within that family history for who they later became. My strength comes from my family.

My mother and father, grandparents, uncles, aunts, cousins, their friends, their relatives did things together. In my family, one of the unwritten but absolutely unwavering laws was that we supported one another. I had the benefit for a while, as the firstborn, of really being pampered. But ultimately, long before there were six brothers and sisters (three and three), our home was a place of mutual respect and shared obligation.

My mother and father were clear about the need for all of us to pitch in and help. We did our chores, we were expected always to do our best out in the world—at school, at church, at chores. On the other hand, it was never chores come first, you come second.

I loved sports from an early age. I worked hard at home, cutting the lawn, cleaning the yard, doing whatever errands needed to be done. But if ever I had a game or a practice to get to and it conflicted with a scheduled time to cut the lawn, the lawn cutting was automatically canceled or transferred to someone else who would in turn receive time from me when they needed it.

Whenever one of the children had something special going on, the family cheering section turned out. My youngest sister, Patricia, is a violinist. From her earliest years, all of us encouraged her as if her activity was the most important thing in the world. We were a regular churchgoing family and different family members sang in the choir. Whenever and wherever the choir went to sing, the Morgan family, all of them, went along—same as on Sundays. None of this had anything to do with what activity we were involved in and everything to do with supporting one another. This sense of mutual support eventually formed some of my core thinking about the way teams, not individuals, win baseball games.

My whole family was under the gun in those Texas years. Making ends meet turned out to be just too hard. One by one our large family started moving up and out of Bonham, looking for better places to live and work.

My father had a brother who moved to Columbus, Ohio. He was the first.

Once a year, my mother and father and I went up to visit my uncle Herman in Ohio. We got on a train in Bonham and traveled two nights and three days across huge stretches of the country. I'd sit at the window and watch the farms, the houses, the hills roll by, the little tank towns and the distant shapes of the big cities, and it was like I was in a dream, in a cocoon of adventure all my own. I loved those trips and never once saw them through my parents' eyes.

One of my mother's brothers—Homer—moved up to the Oakland area, then another brother, James, and his children went along. When I was five, we moved to Oakland, too.

James junior, my cousin, was three days older than I was, and my sister Linda was three days older than James's second son, Charles—so right from the start the Oakland area became more than an outpost for us. My father and his brothers-in-law all got work for the same company, Pacific Tire and Rubber, and the children were all into schools and churches and Sunday dinners together.

My dad, as well as working hard, was a ballplayer, too. In Texas, he played semi-professional ball on the weekends on a team that included a number of my uncles. I don't remember much about those games I was taken to, other than being made the batboy for the team and going with them crowded into one of the cars that traveled to a neighboring town when they had a team to play. My dad was a tall man (tall by my standards), around 6 feet, had a thin build, could run, and had good reflexes. He pitched, caught, played shortstop. His big thing, though, was being a complete player, doing everything well.

Our move was from the "segregated" South to the "integrated" North. The strange thing was that this made race a "problem" in a way it hadn't been before. In Texas, because segregation had been there forever, trouble between the races was just not visible, at least through a boy's eyes. Things were understood, unspoken, and because unspoken, unseen.

We were one of the first black families to move into our new neighborhood. Soon after our move, the neighborhood, sure enough, became all black. They didn't call it redlining then, and no organizations protested, but this was the all-too-common pattern that developed in northern cities. Oddly, in those early boyhood years I remained color-blind.

I don't know why, but I was just slow to pick up on color differences, though clearly they were already there in my life. I know I played with both black and white kids then. Once, however, I got into an argument with a white kid. When I got home later, I told my mother about it. I made a point of saying that it was a white kid I'd wrangled with.

"Would you be upset if it was a black kid who argued with you?" she asked.

"Yes," I answered.

"Then why does it matter that he's white? You deal with people not color," she said, as strongly as she could.

My life has changed since then. I am no babe in the woods anymore but I have never deviated too far from my mother's teaching. There have been assassinations and riots since then but my mother's words have stayed with me.

My best friend at that time was black, a kid named Benny Whitfield. I met Benny when I first moved to Oakland, and we remained friends from grade school right through high school—and for a while beyond that after we went our separate ways.

Benny and I shared a love of sports and spent a lot of time in each other's houses. Benny was a great athlete, great football player, a track star, he could do virtually anything on a playing field. He had trouble in school, though. He went on to the University of Arizona on a football scholarship but could not cope with the academics. He ultimately dropped out and back into the pool of ill-prepared, underskilled men whose lives become an increasing and constant struggle for everyday survival.

I had a couple of other close friends in those early days—Amos Tingle and Willie Collins. Amos and Willie lived on the same block I did and so we'd invariably go off to school together in the mornings, come home together in the afternoons, hang around as much as we could. In between, we were into sports, sports, sports. We went to movies together, went swimming, even played golf together on local public courses. Most young kids don't play golf, but we did. Our dads had golf clubs, and we were allowed to use them (my dad's right-handed clubs made it inevitable that I learned to play golf right-handed).

We also had a schoolyard game among ourselves—Army Ball, a popular West Coast stick-and-ball game that was supposed to have originated on one of the many conscription bases in the area. The game actually helped me later on as a ballplayer.

Army Ball was a three-man game—that is, one batter, a pitcher, and a fielder. The field was spread from any makeshift backstop to any tall "portable" (temporary wooden school building, barracks, whatever). The "portable" had different levels. If you hit the building above one level it was a double, another level a triple, and the roof or over, a home run. Because there were only three players in the game, you could not hit the opposite way. This was strictly a pull-hitting game—hence the need to get the bat into the hitting zone quickly. (We used a regular baseball bat and a hard rubberized ball, an indoor ball they called it, for this game.)

There were an awful lot of home runs hit in Army Ball. I had 800 one year (we all were fanatical recordkeepers), but Willie hit more—in the thousands! Another feature of this game was that there were no walks. You stayed at bat until you hit or struck out. That might seem beneath Little League, but it actually served to make hitters wait for desired pitches. You learned from this what you could and couldn't handle, where your strength was, where it wasn't. I see many hitters today, hitters with real talent, who simply never learned that most elementary component of good hitting and suffer for it accordingly.

I am not sure if it was Amos or Willie who told me one day that I might hit for greater distance if I choked up on my bat, but I took the advice. I found then that I could hit harder, farther. I was ten or eleven years old at the time. I choked up on my bat from then till the last day of my major-league career.

My friends were certainly taller and, I guess, stronger than I was, but the curious thing was that I never felt deprived. When I got to high school, I had trouble making the football team but I made it. I knew what I could do. I was always good at sports, usually better than anyone else around. What did it matter if someone was a head taller if I could hit a ball three times as far, shoot over the best defender, put my head down and drive through a wall of beefy linemen? Because I always wound up surprising opponents by what I could do, I have always regarded my size as an asset, not a liability. I never allowed other people's assumptions to hold me back.

In school, I wasn't a great student, but neither did I have academic difficulties. I got C's, B's, and occasional A's. I knew school was important, and I took care of business—so I could then get on with sports. My parents made me understand that I would one day have to go out and earn a living. I accepted that. I learned math in school and thought I might one day use it in business. I paid attention to other subjects not because I liked them but because I knew they might one day come in handy.

Closeness continued to dominate family life. Sports in Oakland provided lots of extra time for us to be with one another. We lived a few blocks from the old Oakland Oaks ballpark. There was no major-league ball then on the coast. The Pacific Coast League Oaks, full of former big-league players, was the only game in town.

We went to the ballpark, my sister Linda, my father, and I (my mother wasn't into baseball), literally every night. The Oaks played anywhere from 40 to 50 home games a year, and we saw most of them. It was a ritual for us.

My dad got home from work, I had done my chores and my homework, early dinner was on the table, and then, afterwards, while it was still light out, we walked up the block toward the park. We approached the park, this big old wooden structure with advertising on the walls, and entered a gate near the far right-field corner of the field and we always got seats along the right-field line down close to the action.

The park then was colorful in ways other than the outfield fences. There was a little section down along the right-field foul line where a bunch of men, nearly always the same cast of characters, used to sit. They'd talk and argue, busily exchanging sheets of paper and notes among themselves. These men were local gamblers and they took to ball games like they were the ponies.

Of course I was a baseball "fan" then but, mainly, a Pacific Coast League fan. The Oaks were my team but I was also into the league. My big-league heroes, Ted Williams, Nellie Fox, and Jackie Robinson, were one thing. But my truly favorite players were Coast Leaguers. There was a clear distinction in my twelve-year-old mind then—and now—between heroes and favorites. Favorites had nothing to do with how famous or even how talented a player was. There was just the sense of liking him. My "favorite" was Jim Marshall, who went on to have a brief major-league career as a player and a somewhat longer one as a manager. I liked Jim Marshall not because he was the best on the team but because he was a new player whom I happened to catch on his first day with the ballclub. He also happened to do exceptionally well that day.

These trips to the ballpark, as much as they were part of a family ritual, were really part of my baseball education. I count my father as among the handful of really important teachers I had.

We talked about the different players. My father knew all about them. He'd tell me that one player could hit but not field, or that another player was fast but didn't know how to use his speed; he'd point out that one guy could bunt, that another could throw. What he'd emphasize over and over again was the value of being a complete player—one who could do it all. He stressed how much a complete player added to his team—and how much he took away when parts of his game weren't there. "You get a guy who can drive in a run for you but who goes out in the field and gives that run back because he can't pick up a ground ball or turn a double play and what do you have? You got a guy who robs Peter to pay Paul."

We also went to football games—across the bay, to watch the 49ers. A Texas uncle of mine, Terry Cook, came out of the army and was invited to try out with the 49ers and so moved into our house when he was getting his shot (he was a halfback—and didn't make it). The 49ers then had their "Million Dollar Backfield," consisting of Y. A. Tittle, Joe Perry, Hugh McElhenny, and John Henry Johnson. So we all became 49er fans. These were the days before specialists took over, of course, so the value of a player who was consistent in many aspects of the game was easy to see. My father insisted that a complete player—whether in baseball or football— did not ever have to be a record setter in one area but that if he did all things well he had a better chance of helping his team win. My father's perspective was crystal clear: players belonged to teams. The single objective of teams in any competitive sport was to win.

I had been playing ball since I was four or five years old, every chance I could get. But until I was thirteen I had never played in any kind of organized setting. Till then it had always been wherever and whenever, with whoever was around. For years, my father took me across the Bay to Golden Gate Park. We loved to visit the park because it was a beautiful place to go on weekends—and because there was an elementary school nearby where the kids had choose-up games.

I didn't think then too much about playing in a real league with a real team because I was just happy to have the chance to play wherever I could.

Then one day I read in the paper that there were going to be tryouts for the Babe Ruth League, a league for thirteen- to fifteen-year-olds, at McConnell Field in Oakland.

McConnell Field was far from my house but I was intrigued by the announcement and, not knowing what to expect, tried to talk some of my friends into going up there with me. None was willing to go. I told my father and mother that I wanted to go anyway and they let me. I don't remember if I biked there or got a lift that first day.

The field was probably ten or fifteen miles from home and at the time it felt like ten or fifteen hundred miles. I didn't know anyone there. I had no idea what to expect, even what a "tryout" was. Tryout for what? There were an awful lot of kids there when I arrived, nearly all of them bigger than me, all of them looking as though they knew exactly why they were there, as though they had all been through it before.

The tryout was set up in the way major-league tryouts were run in those days. You took turns hitting, running, throwing. From an initial group, a smaller group was drawn, and from that group teams were picked.

When the coaches running the tryout got around to me they asked what position I played and I told them I played shortstop. I was sent out there and then for what seemed like only a brief stretch, they hit ground balls to me. I had no idea then what I was doing. My dad's training had basically been to allow me to follow my own instincts. I had no technique whatsoever, no idea about the way ground balls were supposed to be played other than catching the ball, straightening up and throwing. What I had, though, was good hand-eye coordination, some zip on the ball when I threw it. I was quick, my first steps were quick, everything I did was quick. When I hit, my bat was quick.

I wasn't better—or worse—than anyone else at the tryout. I just did what I could and was glad to have the opportunity. There was a kid there who saw how inexperienced I was. He, too, was a short-stop but had been moved over to second base when I had my chance in the field. After watching me take a few ground balls, he came over and suggested that before each pitch I should bend down and put my hands on my knees—that I would have a better chance of getting to a ball from that position. I welcomed the advice. Till then, all I knew was to just stand there waiting for the next ball to be hit. If someone had mentioned the word "fundamentals" to me I would have assumed they were into spelling bees.

I survived the cut that day—a Saturday—and was asked to come back the following day, when I was chosen for the area team.

For the next three years, I played Babe Ruth, and each year we did well enough to get to the playoffs for the state championship, though we never won. For me, though, the competition and the chance to play were everything. I did really well. I was an all-star each of the years I played (which meant the chance to play in all-star games) and, it turned out, small as I was, I was the best player on our team.

But all of that was a prelude to playing high school and then junior college baseball. In my area, schoolboy and college sports regularly produced players who later went on to big-time professional careers. The list of ballplayers included the likes of Frank Robinson and Curt Flood, not to mention Willie Stargell, the DiMaggio brothers, Ernie Lombardi, Cookie Lavagetto, and hosts of others. But when my time came, I was totally surprised. All the way through high school and on into junior college, I had become increasingly convinced I would never get the chance to play pro ball, much less actually make it to the majors. So far as I knew, no scouts were interested in me, no one ever offered a contract or even an invitation to a tryout. Whenever someone had something kind to say, there was nearly always a double edge to it: I was known as a good little player—with emphasis on the second of the two adjectives.

2

School Daze

I was fifteen years old when I entered Castlemont High School. Compared to the grade school I went to, which was mixed but still predominantly white, Castlemont was so white that black faces were a rarity.

I was never bothered by that, though, because I felt accepted, able to get on with my life and with my friends, many of whom were white. I'm sure I was blind to a lot then. At least I was so focused on wanting to do well and wanting to get along, I just didn't take in what I didn't really want to see.

I had a close friend in those days, Jim Lamp. He spent time at my house, I spent time at his. His parents seemed to accept me as my parents accepted him. I assumed the question of color never even crossed the minds of my friend and his parents—until one day in our senior year, Jim told me he had been accepted at the college of his choice: Brigham Young. Of course I knew that Brigham Young was a Mormon university and that Mormon teaching regarded black people as inferior. Feeling really foolish, I asked my friend:

"Are you . . . are you a Mormon?"

"Sure," he said.

Sure? That was news to me. I mentioned the understanding I had about the Mormon view of black people.

"What does that have to do with me?" Jim asked.

Sensible. I couldn't begin to answer that—but in the years following we drifted steadily apart. Whether it was the natural course of our lives, moving us in very different directions, or there was an undertow of racial assumptions I simply had been unable to pick up, I never knew. But we eventually stopped being friends.

I have always paid a price for a tendency to focus almost exclusively on what I'm interested in at the time. In baseball, where concentration is called for, that's been a plus. But in life, where a wider view is demanded, I have sometimes been hurt.

I have always been susceptible to moods where I just shut out the world. In school, if one of these moods hit me, teachers would ask me things and I wouldn't reply. Classroom participation was normally something I entered into willingly and cheerfully, but they might as well have been talking to the wall.

My mother mercifully handled these moods in a low key. "Let him be," she'd say. My father was willing to let me have some space—so long as it was not around him. "You go to your room till you're feeling better," he'd say. And I did. I'd sit in my room, feeling dead and down, not knowing what had come over me. My moods rarely lasted more than a few hours at a time—though their recurrence continues to this day—but I have never been able to figure out what might be behind them.

I wanted to do well in school; in fact by the time I reached high school, I was determined to be successful at whatever I did. My goal then—as now—was not geared to any one thing so much as to just be out front, to work at things harder, longer, more thoroughly than others so that I might make something of myself.

I pursued sports as vigorously as ever. Baseball, by then, clearly was number one for me. I made the varsity squad in my very first year, when I was just fifteen years old. Making the varsity at Castlemont, one of the schools in the powerful Oakland Athletic League, was no mean achievement. I was not overly impressed with myself, though. I knew our team was a good one—but not a great one. I soon saw that I would not learn much in the baseball program because our coach was not an especially good teacher. I did learn as

I went along—but mainly from a couple of coaches in basketball and track, John Nordhausen and Nick Garedakis.

Nordhausen emphasized the virtues of quickness; Coach Garedakis, who really knew very little about baseball, encouraged me to apply basic principles of track to base-stealing. In getting my jump, he said, it was important to drive hard off the back foot so as to be at full speed almost instantly. He taught me to run low to the ground, to compress rather than to spread my weight. Use your arms, he said. The rhythmical, precision pumping of the arms aided foot speed.

I had trouble my first year on the team—but not, as it turned out, because of what I did, or didn't do, on the field. As far as that went, I was one of the better players on the team. It was just that I was headstrong. Our coach wanted me to commit to playing American Legion ball through the summer months to sharpen my skills. I told him I was already committed to playing for a Babe Ruth team (Legion teams are for older and more experienced players). Our Babe Ruth team then had a real chance to go to the state championships—and I was not about to miss the opportunity. I told my coach that I did not want to let myself or my other teammates down in that way. My coach replied if I wanted to play for the varsity that year I would have to play American Legion.

I stuck to my guns and, sure enough, was demoted to junior varsity. Our Babe Ruth team was knocked out of a chance to go to the Nationals by another area team led by a future major-leaguer, Walt Williams. But within a season, because I was doing well wherever I played (I was a Babe Ruth all-star, then the MVP in the next Babe Ruth all-star game), I was again selected for varsity. The Castlemont team I played for eventually went on to win an Oakland Athletic League championship in my senior year.

I was certainly a good enough ballplayer in high school to be serious about playing. Because I played as much as I did and at such a good competitive level, I dreamed about going on to play pro ball. I didn't fool myself, though. It was apparent to me that scouts who regularly watched our high school games talked to other players rather than to me. For me, the absence of interest only made me work harder.

Baseball and baseball practice took up most of my hours. My school friendships were mostly with other guys who played ball. We worked together, played together, walked each other home at dark after practice.

One of my closest high school baseball friends was Rudy May, a year behind me in school, who from day one was the player everyone in our area assumed would make it to the majors. Scouts were always there when he pitched. And why not? Rudy, as a schoolboy, was big, powerful, left-handed. He had a major-league arm by the time he was a tenth-grader.

I was a star. I played second, short, hit for average and power, stole bases, but I might as well have been playing in Little League.

The surprise for all of us came when Rudy actually was signed. There was another kid in our area the scouts had been following—a left-handed pitcher named Frank Battania—and recently Battania had been signed for about $100,000, a really big sum in those days. All of us thought Rudy would do better. Battania, a soft-throwing control pitcher, wasn't nearly as talented as Rudy, but when it came time for Rudy to sign, he was offered only $8,000—which he accepted, against all kinds of advice from friends and family.

But Rudy knew, what many of us knew without wanting to admit, that there was a relationship between skin color and bonus money. There was nothing he could do about it if he wanted to play. He accepted the deal he was offered—which also included a brand-new Chevy Impala 409, one of the fastest, flashiest numbers on the road. The car was a pride and joy to Rudy—and, it turned out, an immediate source of trouble, which I learned about firsthand.

Because Rudy and I were friends, we regularly spent time at each other's houses. Usually, we idled away evening hours playing cards, watching the tube, just hanging out. When Rudy got the car, however, our horizons immediately broadened.

In high school then, drag racing was a regular, if questionable, form of teenage amusement. One night, we got a challenge from these other high school guys. We went out in Rudy's new car to a little-used East Oakland road where unofficial races were held, lined up with these other guys, and, *whoosh*, took off down the strip.

Rudy lost control of the car and it skidded off the road, slamming into a pole, crunching the vehicle beyond repair, though neither of us was hurt.

The loss of the car, within days of getting it, was bad enough. But having to go home and tell his parents what had happened was even worse. How in the world could something like this be explained. That, in any case, was what we tried to work out as we made our way back to Rudy's house. When we got there, we had worked out a solution.

Rudy called the police and told them his car had been stolen. How? the cops wanted to know. Oh it was terrible, Rudy said, it was given to him by a major-league team that had just signed him to a baseball contract and here he was sitting in his own house, playing cards all night with a friend, and then when he went out to give his friend a ride in the car, it was missing. It was just terrible, Rudy said. He carried on and on. His objective really didn't have to do with diddling the cops but to keep his father from finding out what had actually happened. That meant death as far as Rudy was concerned. Eventually, without anyone the worse for wear, the car was replaced through an insurance company.

My senior year in high school was a dividing line for me. The team couldn't have done better. We won the Oakland Athletic League championship, and I was right at the center of it all. Only it was clear to me that my baseball future, like my high school career, was ending rather than beginning. Rudy went off to play professional ball, I busied myself with plans for college—that is, junior college. My idea was to go to Oakland City College (the name has since been changed to Merritt College) and then on to a full four-year school if I did well enough at City.

When I entered college the following fall, I knew why I was

there and what I needed to do. I majored in business, took accounting courses, typing, and shorthand. I was determined to learn as much as I could, as quickly as I could, so that I would be prepared for the workaday commercial world which would soon be upon me. I lived at home and had an afternoon job as a local playground director, setting up basketball and other recreational activities for kids. At night, I hit the books. I did well in school, a lot better as a college student than I had as a high school student. My limited social life, which had been typical California—some backyard parties and movie dates—was never very wild to begin with and was becoming less so now.

In high school I had two steady girlfriends. (I actually had met both of them at the same party, going out with them alternately through the last couple of years.) Now I was down to one girlfriend—and she was really turning out to be far more than a girlfriend. Though marriage wasn't yet in our immediate plans, it was clear to both Gloria and myself that we were heading there, pending this coming period of getting a college education and then going out in the world to make a real living.

I played baseball that spring for my college team, and we won the league championship in our division. I was the team's second baseman, leading hitter and base stealer, and was, within our competitive range, clearly one of the top players in the league. But by then I had more or less come to accept the fact that my baseball career, such as it was, was not going to extend to the pros. From high school on, the scouts had been around, had seen me play, had drawn whatever conclusions they were going to draw about me. Cookie Lavagetto, the former major-leaguer who lived in the Oakland area, had been impressed with me and had tried to get the local Mets' scout to sign me. There was interest, I was told, but I was never approached directly and nothing ever came of it. I had also heard, again indirectly, that one other team, the New York Yankees, had been thinking about me—again without anyone actually contacting me. Whenever I did have a conversation with a scout—which wasn't often—the same phrase kept coming up

again and again. I was "a good little player," they said. I always knew
what that meant. I had no future.

All that changed during my first spring in college. Bill Wight, a
scout from an expansion team, the Houston Colt 45s, approached
me one day and told me, "You're a really good player." There was
no qualifier relating to my size—and for that alone, I was grateful
and overjoyed.

When I told my mother and father that I had been talking to a
scout from the Colt 45s, they had a mixed response. My father was
excited. My mother, though a supporter of her son's dreams, did
not want to see me give up on my education after just one year of
junior college. We went back and forth on that for a while until I
assured my mother that I would continue my education no matter
what.

"You won't be able to, once you're a professional ballplayer," she
said.

"I promise you I will finish college. I will graduate and get a
degree," I said. My mother remained skeptical. But I meant what I
said. It took me twenty years to get my degree. So I'm glad I didn't
promise Mom a schedule.

The day finally arrived when Bill Wight said that he wanted to
sign me to a minor-league contract. I vividly remember the night I
brought him home to meet my parents and to negotiate my contract. It was Halloween, the perfect setting somehow.

My dad thought—and I did, too—that I should have gotten a
signing bonus of around $5,000. Mr. Wight was offering $2,000, a
good little bonus for a good little player, you might say. It didn't
compensate much for the insufficient salary I would be getting—
around $500 a month. No matter what was being said, it was clear
that what the Colt 45s were offering was as close to rock bottom as
an offer could be.

My dad, though, seemed to like Bill Wight, and he was secretly
pleased that I was going to have the opportunity to play ball—
which was really all I wanted. The truth of the matter was that I
would have paid to play if it came to that, but fortunately it never
did.

At the outset of our meeting, my dad offered Bill a beer, which was gratefully accepted. And then he offered him another, and another after that. In fact, once my dad discovered that Bill loved his brew, he took me aside and had me go down to the corner store and get as many six-packs as I could carry. None of us were drinkers so we didn't join Bill. My father, remaining clear-eyed to the end, managed to bump the signing bonus from $2,000 to $3,000.

"Listen Joe," Bill said, turning to me, "you can be a great player— you can make $35,000 a year one day." I was nearly struck dumb.

How times have changed. Some players make more than that a day now. But as funny as all that seems, the reality was never about money but about playing pro ball. In the end, this Halloween night was not a negotiation but a celebration, without masks but, at three thousand bucks, with more treats than tricks.

3

Southern Comfort

My first stop in the 45s' organization was Moultree, Georgia, where the minor-leaguers had their camp and instructional program. Moultree in 1963 was completely segregated. The handful of black players in the minors were housed together; the club went out of its way to shield us all from the world beyond the outfield fences.

Because I was not a top prospect, I could easily have been passed over in this setting but, fortunately for me, the 45s ran a special kind of camp, one where I had a lot of playing time.

Rather than drilling ever day, they ran games: eighteen innings a day, sometimes more. All of us had the chance to show what we could do in competition.

The main thing was the opportunity to play, which made any obstacle secondary. I mostly played shortstop in these games. When the camp was over and the different ratings came out, I was told that I was second among all players in arm strength. I had good ratings in speed, range in the field, and so forth. More important, I hit regularly and with power. That was a surprise for all of them. I had games where I'd go 5 for 8, 6 for 9; I hit a couple of balls out of the park; I drove in a ton of runs.

Till then, I had been ticketed for the lowest level in the minors, but now there was talk of jumping me ahead. The problem the organization people had was twofold. One, moving me up meant leapfrogging me past many other players with higher bonuses. There were guys there whose monthly tax bill was higher than my monthly salary. Baseball people use the phrase, "big-money body." This is a scouting and organizational term which is used to project a minor-league player's professional prospects. A player signed for $3,000 really isn't supposed to do that much. The dollar sign on my body turned out to be incorrect.

Another complication: Any time a player exceeds his expectations, especially when he is unknown, the need arises to hide him so that other organizations won't pick him off in the annual minor-league draft where only so many players are allowed to be officially protected. Because baseball is really a tight little island, this is easier said than done. The 45s initially targeted me for one of their lower-level farm teams in Modesto, California. Ironically, it was the Modesto Reds. The Modesto manager, Dave Philly, had a great saying to inspire young players: "There's a pot of gold to be made in this game. All you have to do is go out and work hard and get it.

I didn't hear him say it too often; in a month I was gone. I did nothing special in that month—I hit around .260, had four or five home runs, but it was enough to attract attention. The fear was that unless a situation was found for me where I could get the seasoning I needed, I would be picked off. The best way to keep me hidden, the 45s reasoned, was to throw me in over my head, to let me play in a league where I could not really do well. One month into my first season, I was shipped from Modesto to the 45s' affiliate in the Carolina League, the Durham Bulls. I was a Durham Bull long before Susan Sarandon and Kevin Costner hit town.

I did not want to leave Modesto so soon. Durham was not only a big step up competitively, it was also on the other side of the United States, in a setting and on a team where it would be very hard to feel at home.

I was the only black player on the team. The day I arrived was probably difficult for everyone. I was told at the ballpark when I got there that I would not be playing that night, to just sit and relax and watch the game. There was a certain amount of nervousness in the clubhouse because my arrival had been advertised for the past few days and the Durham players and executives, I later was told, had been hearing about it from their fans. I, too, could hear the words coming from the stands during warm-ups that first night. Nigger this, nigger that—there was nothing loud or disruptive, but the undertow was steady and unsettling. I looked out at the action during the game, taking in the double-decked wooden fence full of advertising, the strange haze the lights threw over the field, the factory building looming beyond the right-field wall. As much as possible, I tried to make myself feel comfortable—but I couldn't.

I was lucky that I was not thrown into the starting lineup that night. My guess is that if I had been I would have fallen flat on my face, overwhelmed by nerves. A bad start creates its own momentum and with what I was up against, I did not need that.

I credit Paul Richards, the 45s' general manager and one of the smartest baseball men in recent memory, for taking into account what I would be facing. He suggested to Billy Goodman, our manager, that I sit that night. I credit Billy Goodman not only for going along but also for sensing when he could throw me into action.

He called on me late in that game—in the ninth inning, when we were down by a run with one runner on and one out.

"Take a bat, Joe," he said, as though I had been there for months, "I'm gonna hit you next." Over the course of the game, I had slowly, imperceptibly, eased up, so that when Billy called on me, I wanted to hit. I was into the game rather than into my situation.

Once again, luck was on my side. I happened to get a fat pitch that night. In my first at-bat in the Carolina League, I hit a game-winning home run. Whatever was being said in the stands changed immediately to wild cheering, which gave me goosebumps as I circled the bases. In one swing of the bat, I went from being the only black player on the team, nigger this and nigger that, to being just one good player. That one at-bat created another kind of momentum for me. I wound up having a great year at Durham. I hit

.332, had 13 homers in just over 300 at-bats, and was, above all, really popular with the hometown fans. The most satisfying part of the whole season was that in the closing days, I finished second in fan balloting for the team's most popular player.

But as lucky as I was, as well as I did, my first year was anything but easy. Because I had such a spectacular start, I had little problem focusing on playing ball at first. As usual, I shut out everything around me that I did not want to see.

I had no social life of any kind. The organization arranged for me to live with a black family, the Spauldings, who were most kind and generous to me. I spent time with no one, however. I occasionally ate dinner with the Spauldings, I always left them tickets for our games, I very often walked home with them afterwards. But that, and an occasional solo movie, was the extent of my social life. I had no girlfriends, didn't spend time with teammates. The Spauldings suggested I might like to keep company with a young friend of theirs. I declined. I was there for baseball. It was as though I had unconsciously put this wall up around myself, as if anything other than baseball would be just too much.

In a way I was right.

I had been with the Durham Bulls for a week or two when we went out on a road trip. We all piled into a bus, the everyday means of transportation in the minors, and set out for Winston-Salem.

When we got to the motel in Winston-Salem, I started to get off the bus with the rest of the players. The bus driver, the only other black person in the organization, called me back.

"Where do you think you're going?" he said to me.

I pointed and he just smiled. "Come on back," he said. "We don't stay here, we stay somewhere else."

It was strange. Till that moment, I had somehow tricked myself into believing I was living in just another place. Even though I saw the "colored-only" signs at the ballpark and on the streets every day, I had managed to miss them. It had been like standing in the sun and not noticing that it was light out.

We went to a motel in the black section of town. There was no air conditioning, the place was run down and gloomy—but the food was great and that was enough for the moment.

Then we went to the ballpark that night and that was really strange because, once again, I didn't see anything even though this time the signs and divided facilities were literally right under my nose. I dressed with my teammates, as I usually did, I was in my normally cheerful mood, then I picked up my glove and bats and started out for the field, walking out among the fans to a runway that led to the field. Then, for some reason, my eyes fixed on one sign: COLORED DRINKING FOUNTAIN; then another: WHITE DRINKING FOUNTAIN; then another: COLORED BATHROOM. At first I just went blank. I had no feeling, no awareness other than feeling numb.

I turned a corner, followed a ramp to the field, and the first thing I saw was a section of the right-field grandstand fenced in like a cage, the section reserved for black people. Then it all hit me. I had been in North Carolina all this time *never once having seen or acknowledged* that it was segregated. The fans in the right-field stands rose and began cheering as I walked out on the turf, perhaps wanting me to feel their support and their warmth. But all I could think of was that they were in a cage.

All during batting practice it ate at me and ate at me to the point where, even during the game, I couldn't think of anything else. I thought not only was this intolerable but also that I shared responsibility for it because I was taking part. When I got back to the motel that night, I decided to quit. I told my friend the bus driver what I was going to do, he tried to talk me out of it, but I wasn't about to listen—or really to spend time with him. I stayed in my room, thought about how I would have to make plane reservations and then what it would be like going home and telling my parents what had happened. That is what finally brought me up short and made me change my mind.

It would be nice to be able to say that I changed my mind because of the example of earlier black players who had it far tougher, like Jackie Robinson. If I needed inspiration, those first black pioneers in the game surely offered it. But my decision came from my own sense of shame and embarrassment. When I thought of facing my father and telling him that I had quit—I simply could not go ahead.

I don't know if my father would have actually said a word to me or not (my guess is he would have supported whatever decision I made), but I do know that on that summer night in 1963, when I was within hours of ending my professional baseball career even before it began, it was only the image of my father's face and nothing so high-minded as "commitment" that turned me around.

I got up the next day and went to the ballpark, determined to just block out of my mind and out of view, as I had before, the sights and sounds of the ugliness that was everywhere. I intended to say nothing and to just go on as before.

The bus driver, though, went to our manager, Billy Goodman, and told him what had happened. He told Billy about the conversation we had had and that I had actually decided to jump the team. Goodman called me aside and we then talked a little bit.

"Joe," he said, "there are people in this world who think this way but your teammates don't."

I had no counter to that because it struck me as true. In the time I had been with the Bulls there had been no run-ins, no hostility, outward or masked, from the other players that I could detect. Only baseball. Billy Goodman, in just a few words, reminded me of a home truth I have since never lost. You didn't have to like someone to get along with him, or to work together as a team.

For the rest of the season, I spent every available hour at the ballpark. I was always willing to take ground balls, extra hitting, to hang around the clubhouse, the batting cage, the dugout, going over things with my teammates, my manager.

Billy Goodman was the first of several baseball people who became really important in my development as a player. He was a former American League batting champion and was also a former teammate of Ted Williams. I am not sure which was more impressive to me, but when Billy talked I listened.

Very early on, Billy came up to me after an at-bat I had in which I flied out on a first pitch. I had been going really well and the last thing I had in mind was that I might not be using my at-bats to full advantage. But that is just what Billy confronted me with. I had no idea then that swinging at a first pitch, especially in the initial innings of a game, was almost always a mistake. Why? Billy explained what he had picked up from Ted Williams—this was authority doubled, to be sure, but also good practical advice—that by swinging at a first pitch, you deprive yourself of an advantage that comes from being able to measure a pitcher through his repertoire. The more pitches you take, the more you see what he has. The more you see what he has, the more prepared you are. Even more important, Billy pointed out, you might need to have this information for later in the game if, say, the pitcher was still in there in the eighth or ninth inning and you had a chance to get a big hit off him. So, even when you might feel you had a guy measured early in the game, it was still advisable to wait through as many pitches as possible, so that you might better answer for yourself that first question that every batter asks his teammates: "What's he throwing?" That's *your* responsibility to find out, Billy told me. And, of course, he was right. I wound up walking 1,865 times in my career, third behind Babe Ruth and Ted Williams. I took my first learning steps right there in single-A Durham.

I had something of a dream year on the field, which scrambled the 45s' plans for me. Where they had wanted me to develop slowly (I'm convinced now that placing me on a southern team where I was the only black was one additional way of furthering this design), there was no way they could keep me back any longer. At the end of the season, when major-league rosters were expanded, I was brought all the way up. I played my first games as a major-leaguer at the end of my very first year in pro ball.

Just the idea of making it that way still seems like a dream, although 1963, only the second year of the Colts' existence, was another era entirely in the game.

We played our games then in Colt Stadium, an old minor-league park in Houston, a single-decked, horseshoe-shaped grandstand with small outfield bleacher sections in right and left field. It was a flat, open space with terrible lighting. It attracted a constant swarm of the deadliest mosquitoes north of the Rio Grande. The year I came up people were actually falling sick from the mosquito bites. There were outbreaks of encephalitis attributed to the mosquitoes and the ballpark reeked with the stench of insecticide. Beyond the danger to life and limb from flying things, there was the oppressive and unending Texas heat, the bad stadium lights, the ruts and pot-holes of a minor-league field. I couldn't have been happier.

In my first game, I was sent in as pinch runner in the seventh inning of a game against the Phillies. Then I stayed in the game.

The Phillies were fighting for the pennant at that point, three games out—and we went to the ninth inning of the game, all tied. We went to the bottom of the ninth still tied and I was scheduled to hit fourth.

When we got a man on with two outs, I was in the on-deck circle telling myself I would be removed for a pinch hitter. I wasn't. The peculiar thing was that I kept standing there in the on-deck circle, waiting to be lifted, until someone yelled to me from the bench, "Go on up there and hit!" I went up to the plate almost in a daze.

The Phillies' pitcher was Johnny Klippstein. He worked the count on me to 2 and 0, and then he tried to come inside with a fastball. I grounded a base hit to right, scoring the winning run from second base!

Following the game, the Phils' manager, Gene Mauch, went wild in the clubhouse. Big-league teams all have some kind of food spread waiting for players at the end of games. In recent years, there has been all kinds of attention to healthy snacks like fruit and vegetables. In those days, the tables were laden. Norm Gerdeman, our clubhouse man, had the best spread in the league: barbecued ribs and steaks. Other teams usually had varieties of "heavy" foods out there as well.

Mauch swept the Phillies' food table onto the floor; he raved and ranted to his players, cursing them for allowing someone who looked like a Little Leaguer to beat them. His tirade made *Sports Illustrated* and so, by proxy, did I. Not a bad start to a big-league career!

Because the 45s now had to force-feed me or risk losing me if they didn't bring me along quickly, I was sent to Instructional League that fall, following the regular season. I joined a combined Red Sox–Houston camp in Florida and, over the next two months, even though I was bone tired and down to 130 pounds from a full season of more than 150 games with three teams, I underwent a baseball cram course which more resembled marine boot camp than Florida vacation time.

Each day, I had to take 100 ground balls before a game. Then I had to turn 50 double plays. Then there was the game, and the organization, because it was rushing me, had me play every day. I couldn't do a thing. I had come through a season where I had hit .332, but here I never got my average above .190. I was a star in one place, and just pathetic in this situation. I remember the Red Sox instructor, Eddie Popowski, kidding around, came up to me and said, "Joe, I hear you hit .332 in the Carolina League?" I said, "Yeah, that's right." He said, "What do they do, pitch underhand in that league?" I didn't think the joke was all that funny but neither did I want to cop a plea by saying how tired I was.

In fact, I didn't mind the fatigue that much. I liked the company I was keeping. The Red Sox in those days had some real young talent and it was a pleasure to watch them: Tony Conigliaro, soon to launch a brief but spectacular home-run-hitting career that was cut short by a tragic beaning; Rico Petrocelli, who would be an anchor at two positions on the left side of the Red Sox infield for the next twelve years; and then there was a guy named George Scott.

When I got off the plane in Sarasota, I gave the cab driver the address of the team hotel. The hotel was one of these old places with ceiling fans and potted palms in the lobby, and a wide porch running across the front of the building. The day was typically humid and lazy, the kind where everyone would be at the beach or hiding out in some air-conditioned bar, but there was one guy out on the porch when I arrived, this huge black man who eyed me steadily as I made my way up the stairs. He was seated in a chair on the veranda with his feet up on a railing and as I made my way past him, he suddenly stood up. Towering over me, he said, "My name is George 'Long Tater' Scott from Greenville, Mississippi, and don't you forget it, because I'll be hitting a lot of long taters in the big leagues one day." I was so taken aback that all I could do was freeze on the spot. "Yessir," I said. I thought I was talking to an escaped Caribbean dictator.

The very next day, he came up to me, wrapped an arm around my shoulder, and introduced me to his teammates—as though I was his long-lost brother. We have been friends ever since.

He made good on his promise, by the way. But all the long tater home runs he hit as the Boston Red Sox first baseman brought him a new nickname, "Boomer."

The most memorable part of this camp, for me, really had nothing to do with baseball. We were at the ballpark one day, just having finished lunch, when someone walked by me and said, "They just shot the president."

The news was shocking and incomprehensible in this baseball setting, as it was everywhere else in the country. I said something like, "Is he all right?" but got no answer. Things just seemed to go into slow motion then. There were no radios around, no one seemed sure of anything, and then about ten minutes later, someone came along who told us that the president was dead.

For the next two days, we didn't do much. We practiced in the morning but our games were called off. There was talk about whether we should play but in the end the games were canceled. Whatever others felt, I know this was especially hard on me and the other black players in camp because, at that time, we had regarded JFK as a hero—he was the first president in our experience who had shown any sensitivity at all to the evils of racism. The black players on both teams hung out with one another and I remember that through those next days, at every meal, every spare hour we had, that's all we talked about. Baseball had ceased to exist. At least for a time.

I began the following season with the San Antonio Bullets, our double-A affiliate in the Texas League. I was rested, heavier, full of confidence. As in Durham, I knew why I was there, what I had to do. San Antonio, in a social sense, was not nearly as trying as Carolina. The town was cosmopolitan and had less overt segregation than Carolina. Also, there were other black players there with me. I had guys I could talk to, share a meal with, see an occasional movie with.

We had a really great team, too. Sonny Jackson and I were the middle infield combo; Brock Davis, Aaron Pointer, J. C. Hartman, Von McDaniel, Chuck Harrison, and Leo Posada, all eventual major-leaguers, were teammates.

Lou Fitzgerald was our manager; Clint Courtney, the old major-league catcher, was a coach. Courtney had a reputation for hard-nosed (and sometimes dirty) play. They called him "Scraps" for all the fights he had been in. We called him "Scraps" because he was always after us to hustle, play hard, give everything.

Because I was coming off the year I had at Durham, I was now considered the rising star in the organization. But I hit the ground standing still, not even crawling. I went 0 for my first 20 or more at-bats. I was wound tighter than a drum. The more I failed, the tighter I got. I felt as though I should be hitting the pitching I was seeing, I wasn't particularly intimidated, but I just couldn't do anything. Lou Fitzgerald, finally, took me aside. Before he could say a word, I told him just how badly I was playing and that I would eventually play myself out of it if I had the chance. I'm not sure I believed it.

"Hey, kid, don't worry about anything," he said. "You're here for the whole season even if you don't get one hit. So just relax and play."

It was funny how much that meant to me. Sometimes the simplest things work—and that did. It was like the slight twisting of a lens where a picture that was fuzzy suddenly becomes clear. Nothing on the field changed—but my thinking did. From then on, I had an outstanding season. I finished the season hitting .323, driving in 90 runs, hitting 12 homers, stealing 47 bases. I was voted Texas League MVP that year.

At the midway point, the Colt 45s came down to play the Texas League all-stars in our stadium. I was selected for the all-star team, and I had a really good game against the Colts—2 for 3, hit the ball out, the whole thing. We actually beat the 45s and, afterwards, Scraps Courtney told the local newspaper that if I wasn't in the big leagues next season then he didn't know anything about baseball. I could play, he said, it was as simple as that.

In terms of opportunity, I played about as much in the final month as I had the previous year—I had a handful of at-bats, with not much to show. The games were by then without meaning; the days and the hours till the end of the season were on many players' minds. But this was a different experience for me. I was not nearly as nervous or as uncertain as I had been the previous year. I knew that I had an excellent chance to make the team the following year. For the first time, I began to think of myself as a major-leaguer.

The team's manager then was Harry Craft, as nice a person as you will ever find in baseball. Paul Richards probably felt that to survive last place and to be continually exposed to the Texas heat and to all those mosquitoes, it was really necessary to have a patient and easygoing person in the dugout who was willing to suffer fools and, especially on our team, foolishness.

I wasn't quick to pick up on it the previous year, but this time around I could not help noticing that the Colt 45s had more than young and inexperienced players on their roster. Like most expansion teams, they had a number of players left over from other rosters. Some of these players had been shipped to the heat and dust of Texas because the asylums were full elsewhere.

We had a guy on our team named Dick "Turk" Farrell, who earlier in his career had been the unofficial leader of a group of players on the Phillies called the Dalton Gang. This group of five earned their name by being homicidally notorious. They would go into bars and beat up people, they'd tear clubhouses apart with their practical jokes, they would do anything anytime. Turk, and another gang member, Jim Owens, had been exiled to Houston and, as far as they were concerned, not a thing had changed except their uniforms.

One day, I came to the ballpark and Turk was in an argument with a coach who had told him he was going to be pitching the following day.

"No," Turk said, "I don't pitch in daylight."

"What?"

"You heard me, I only pitch at night."

In the twilight of his career, Turk didn't trust his fastball to the sharper, clearer light of day. He knew himself well enough to know that he was another kind of pitcher in the gloom and darkness of the lights at Colt Stadium.

"Listen, Turk, you're *scheduled* to pitch tomorrow afternoon, you understand?" Turk didn't say a thing and that's where the matter was left until the next day when, with game time approaching, there was no Turk Farrell.

At first, it was like he had been overlooked and then people began to get frantic. They called his home, called the front office, did everything but put out an APB on him—but no one located him and another pitcher was pressed into service for the game.

When we had finished the game and were sitting around in the locker room, about five o'clock, in walks Turk Farrell. Needless to say, Harry and the coaching staff were livid. If the team had had any other manager, Turk might have been barred from entering the clubhouse—but in he walks and they get all over him.

"Turk, where the hell have you been?"

Turk, the total innocent, looking as wide-eyed as a kid at Communion, says, "Huh? I come to pitch."

"Whaddaya mean you come to pitch, the game's over."

"Game's over, whaddaya mean? Game doesn't start for another two and a half hours."

Then when Harry and the coaches got hot with Turk, he got

angry back as though he wasn't going to put up with anyone questioning his sincerity.

This went back and forth for a good ten or fifteen minutes but at the end of that time, there were no fines, no suspensions, no penalties of any kind. In fact, what did happen was that Turk was then penciled in to pitch our next game, the following night (which he won).

All of this would have seemed like the Bad News Bears in the Swamps, except for the fact that the 45s had many good young players coming up, a top-flight baseball guy in Paul Richards, and plans for the future that literally everyone in Houston from the ballboy to local cab drivers could see with their own eyes.

All through that season, in 1964, as the team battled the mosquitoes and the Mets to stay out of last place, a new ballpark was going up across the way from Colt Stadium. Uncompleted, the roof not yet attached, the Astrodome, called the "Eighth Wonder of the World," rose up beyond the outfield wall like an Egyptian pyramid, representing power, accomplishment, style, the ultimate image of the future.

The only problem was, the building, like the team it housed, didn't quite work.

Part Two

LIFTOFF

FROM THE BOOTH:
In the Eighth Wonder of the World

When I go into the Astrodome today, it is sometimes hard to remember what it represented when I was first breaking in. I broadcast a game recently between the Astros and the Giants. As a matter of course, I noted that the Astros' outfielders played deep and hunched up, leaving plenty of room down the lines. That was because on Astroturf the ball moves with such speed that defensive players have to yield. They can't play in for fear of a ball kangarooing over their heads, and they can't play the lines for fear of the ball speeding through the gaps.

The Astrodome was the first of a series of new and larger stadiums built in the '60s and '70s that opened the way for a different kind of player. Busch Stadium in St. Louis was opened in 1966, as was Atlanta's Fulton-County Stadium; the expansion Padres began play in the new Jack Murphy Stadium in 1969; Three Rivers in Pittsburgh came on line in 1970, along with Riverfront in Cincinnati; the Vet in Philadelphia opened for business the following year.

Players like Andre Dawson, Jose Canseco, Barry Bonds, and Eric Davis combine tremendous power hitting with unbelievable speed—the speed necessary to cover large turf-covered sections of outfield. Until these players came along, the term "30–30 man" (30 home runs, 30 stolen bases) was almost unknown (Willie Mays, the first "30–30 man," never heard the label). With Canseco, baseball today has a "40–40 man." Wide spaces and Astroturf demanded players like these.

But in the mid-sixties, it was hard to associate the Astrodome with more than the unanticipated problems it produced. Some of those problems, like the roof and the playing surface, now seem laughable—but then they were something else.

I made copy as soon as I set foot inside the Astrodome. Before a pitch was thrown in my rookie season, I took one look at the roof and began saying to anyone who would listen that there was going to be a problem with the sun shining through the overhead glass. I mean it was obvious, you didn't need to be a rocket scientist or even a brash rookie to point that out. No, I was told, the problem had been taken care of, nothing to worry about. The next day, the papers gave my remarks headline space: MORGAN CHAL-LENGES ARCHITECTS. The gist of the story wasn't about the Astrodome but about me. Who was this smartass kid telling the experts they didn't know what they were doing?

Soon after we began testing the actual playing conditions inside the stadium, my smartass remarks didn't seem so foolish. The first time a batter hoisted a ball above the level of the infield in a day game, it disappeared against the glare of the translucent paneling. Unfortunately the space agency wasn't in charge here, so that first fly ball was just the beginning of what turned out to be a year-long vaudeville.

Management's answer to the problem of these beanballs from space was sunglasses. When they finally understood that all players who played in the Astrodome, not just the expansion Astros, couldn't see, they decided that specially prepared sunglasses—shooting glasses—would solve what all those prestigious architects had somehow overlooked in their plans. The sunglasses turned everything into a seagreen mush where it was still impossible to pick out a fly ball against the roof. It seemed like we then went through eighty different kinds of shooting glasses or whatever they called them before reality took hold—and then it wasn't reality either. Someone thereafter had the really bright idea that what sunglasses couldn't accomplish, paint would. I don't know how many hundreds of thousands of clear tiles there were on the roof of the Astrodome, but all of them were then painted—allowing the players, at long last, to track the trajectory of any ball lofted skywards. The only problem was that while the paint allowed us to see, it allowed the grass to die.

Over the weeks following the paint job, the grass wilted. The entire field turned into one of these rock-hard high school playground fields where every ground ball came at you like a ricocheting bullet.

The same working minds that had turned to sunglasses and buckets of paint tried to deal with the subsequent problem of dead grass. The solution was another winner—more paint. The field at this point had occasional patches of wilted grass along with huge islands of dirt. The whole mess was painted over with layers of green gunk so that from the stands it all looked like fresh grass. Down on the field it was murder.

Ground balls inevitably picked up topspin and kicked up sheets of green dust. Your life was literally in danger as these cannon shots came at you. I remember one time I got in the way of a monster shot hit by the Phils' slugger Richie Allen. I thought I was dead, for sure. The ball simply exploded off Allen's bat. It was hit directly at me on a line but with tremendous topspin so that it dipped into the dirt before me. By reflex I did what I was trained to do, put my body in a position to block it. If the ball had taken a true bounce, I think I would have been on my way home in a box. Fortunately, it kicked up and over my shoulder.

The following season, when the Astros got around to laying down Astroturf, they institutionalized what they had blundered into. Little did they know it, but they had revolutionized the game, though it took a while for the rest of the baseball world to catch on.

In 1968, early in the season, I was seriously injured on a play at second base by Tommy Agee of the Mets. Agee, like a lot of other guys in the league, always played hard. On this one play, I was stretched out at second base, receiving a double-play throw. My body, especially my leg and knee, was fully extended and rigid. Agee came into me full force with a body block that tore the mediate cruciate ligaments in my left knee. I did not know I had been seriously injured. I wasn't particularly in pain and I could walk. When my leg later began to stiffen up, I became worried enough to ask the trainer about it. It was a bruise, he said, nothing more. When I was finally operated on, Doug Rader, my teammate, wise-cracked to our trainer, "I see where they cut the bruise out of Joe's leg today."

It turned out that my injury, which sidelined me for the rest of the season, was a blessing in disguise. With time off, I had a chance to study. I made it a project to go to every single home game the Astros played. I took a seat directly behind the plate, and I literally went to school.

I had no lesson plan, no curriculum that I mapped out for myself. I was intent only on learning by observing. The first thing I noticed, looking out at the field, was just how big the Astrodome was. I had played close to 200 games there already, but looking at the field from the stands made me appreciate just what the oversized dimensions of the park meant.

I looked at those parts of my game where I could better utilize my speed, particularly base-stealing. Till then, I hadn't done much. Twenty-nine steals was my best and I had accomplished that the year before.

With notebook in hand, I studied pitchers, catchers, infielders. I observed little subtleties I missed as a player. The very first move pitchers made, the imperceptible, easily overlooked tics of movement made by a catcher, the variation in those movements that occurred when pickoff moves or pitchouts were made. Don Drysdale (who had a great pickoff move) bent his knee in a funny way when he went to first; Bob Veale, another great pitcher, didn't come to a complete stop in his motion.

From these idiosyncrasies, I learned something I carried with me for the rest of my career: The telltale movement was a red light or green light when it came to stealing. When I returned to play, I thereafter always stole on the "green light–red light" signal I got from reading a pitcher's first movement. Lefties were easier to read because they faced me, but right-handers also gave themselves away in their first movement—if I could see it clearly.

When I had fully recovered, my base-stealing totals immediately skyrocketed. My sense of who I was on the field was totally different. Far from feeling like I was a little guy up against it in cavernous new stadiums, I realized I was a player of the future, ideally suited to these new parks. When 1969 rolled around, I was a graduate of my own school. My baseball education till then was down on the field, in the school of hard knocks.

4

A Baseball Education

I arrived as a full-time major-leaguer in 1965 with a lot going for me. Because of the MVP year I had in the Texas League, I was jumped to the big team without having to go through a year of triple-A and, on top of that, because the Astros were an expansion team, the way was open for me to play full time.

If all of that sounds easy, it wasn't. For one thing, the game in 1965 was as different from today's game as bare-knuckle fighting was different from fighting with oversized gloves and helmets—well, almost.

Rookies, especially rookies who played middle infield, had to prove themselves. There was no way to avoid that. In those days, for example, there were no rules covering the way runners came into second base to break up double plays. Today the so-called McRae Rule (put into effect following an especially flagrant take-out of Yankee second baseman Willie Randolph by Hal McRae of the Royals during the 1980 A.L. Championship Series) prohibits any kind of mayhem. Back then, a runner could slide, throw cross-body blocks, roll into a guy with the intent to break him in two (Ty Cobb in an earlier era used to file his spikes to a razor edge before he went after base runners). The only rule that mattered to anyone seemed to be the general one about winning—anyway possible, no holds barred.

Because I was both small and a rookie, playing second was a little like being a moving target in a shooting gallery. Players tested me all the time. I got hit so many times I couldn't begin to cite the instances, the players, the situations. I never was bothered by guys knocking me around, only by those who came in with their spikes up. On the other hand, I learned early to aim my relay throw right between the eyes of the incoming runner. I never drilled anyone but I did get these guys to hit the dirt, which gave me the chance to complete double plays.

There were guys who were especially nasty coming in to second in those days. Curt Flood was a terror. So was Frank Robinson. The first time I saw Frank on the field, I tried to talk to him. We were both from Oakland and I thought that would count for something. He was standing with Vada Pinson, another Oakland-area player, and, even though I was a rookie with the Astros and they were regulars with the Reds, I thought hometown allegiances would somehow soften the fact that we wore different uniforms.

Frank didn't say much, was neither cordial nor chilly, but when the game started, the first time he came into second base, he hit me with a thunderous body block. I shook it off because that was the way you played the game. The first time I played in St. Louis, Curt Flood and I talked. He was quite friendly, smart, well-spoken, very easy about consorting with an "enemy" player. When it was game time, all of that went out the window. He nearly destroyed me on a play at second base. Unlike Frank and some of the other big guys who seemed to take a special pleasure in bouncing a little guy all over the field, Curt was fast and quick. He got down to second base on a play and flipped me right up into the air so that I came down hard. He never so much as gave me a glance afterward.

Very early on, I made a vow to myself that I would nail guys like Frank and Curt. But somehow they always got down in time whenever they saw I had that extra second on a relay throw.

Roberto Clemente was another one I wanted. During the first

weeks of that season, we were in Pittsburgh. It was in the eighth inning and we were tied. There was a ground ball to short and Clemente was running from first. The throw from short was right on the money, and the result should have been a routine double play.

Instead, Clemente came in standing up waving his arms at me. I tried to keep from hitting him—you know you don't want to hit a Roberto Clemente in the head—and I threw the ball away. And we lost the game. So from then on, Clemente was on my list, too. Whenever I could, I would always try to hit Clemente, Frank, Curt (and a few others)—but I never did. And I don't remember anyone ever seriously hurting me aside from Tommy Agee, and that was part of the game.

I am probably coming on with a little too much swagger here. I was not an especially tough guy, I certainly wasn't a know-it-all. On the contrary, I was acutely aware of what I was up against when I broke in.

For beginners, the position that was supposedly "open" for me was already being held down by Nellie Fox. What an irony that when I got to the big leagues to stay, an idol of mine was there as a teammate—and a rival.

I was more than uneasy about knowing that I was being brought up to the big club for the purpose of replacing Fox at second. Nellie was clearly in the twilight of his career. He had come to the Astros the previous season after having played most of his career with the White Sox. He was going on thirty-eight and everyone in camp knew that he and I were vying for the same position. Neither of us was going to be moved to another position; one of us was going to spend a lot of time sitting.

My uneasiness went beyond Nellie Fox. Veterans generally are wary of rookies; they get on them if they see anything like laggard play or an indifferent attitude. They are quick to suspect rookies of thinking too much about themselves while not being experienced enough in the skills they need to help their team.

It is really difficult to convey to anyone outside the game what the resistance of older players can mean. There is an unwritten rule among veteran players that they protect each other. Particularly in those days when players had little bargaining power and there were always younger horses backed up in the minors ready to come on strong, it was just assumed that older players would do everything they could to make sure a young player went through it before he was accepted. When Pete Rose was trying to take Don Blasingame's job in Cincinnati his first year, none of the veteran players would talk to him. When he got to the batting cage, they'd yell at him, "Get outta there, rookie." He got shortchanged in everything. Ultimately, two veterans on the team—Frank Robinson and Vada Pinson—helped him. He was lucky. But I was even luckier.

I remember the first conversation I had with Nellie. It was very strange. He came up to me in the dugout, put an arm around me, and walked me out to the field, into the midst of a group of older players. With his arm around my shoulder all the while, he casually joked with these players for a bit, then when he was sure they were aware of my presence, he said,

"Listen, this guy is really special. I'm gonna do the best I can to help him and I want you to do the same."

I was so dumbfounded that when the other players wandered away and Nellie and I were standing there, I said to him, "Look, I understand the situation and I just want you to know that if this wasn't late in your career none of this would be happening."

"You're wrong," he said, without even skipping a beat, "you have twice as much ability as I ever had." I'm sure it was not easy for Fox to say any of that, but nevertheless he was intent on letting me know there was no contest between us, though surely there was.

One of the first things that happened was that Nellie, Bob Lillis, who has been a manager and a coach in the big leagues for the last thirty years, Eddie Kasko, who is now director of player personnel for the Boston Red Sox, and some of the other older players came out to the park early to work with me on making the double play. Nellie knew, as only a second baseman could, just how vulnerable I would be if I didn't learn how to turn the double play correctly and he saw right away that I was making a fundamental mistake in what I was doing.

My problem, he pointed out, was that I came across the bag with the wrong foot. I hit the bag—the way I had been taught—with my right foot, then I took a step and threw off my left foot. But while that felt comfortable it added time to the play, thereby giving the batter a better chance to reach first and the incoming runner a better chance to wreck me.

Nellie and these other veterans would hit me dozens of double-play ground balls. There would be runners out there for me, someone would play short. And over and over again, I'd work on hitting the bag with my *left* foot so that I'd be almost ready to throw as my foot was planted. The runners were instructed to come in as hard as they could, to do everything possible to put pressure on me so that I would have no time to think, just to use my quickness and my footwork as reflexively as possible.

Nellie and Bob got me to watch Bill "No Touch" Mazeroski, the great Pirate second baseman. Mazeroski didn't have the range I had and didn't have the arm that many other second basemen had. But he turned double plays better than anyone. They called him "No Touch" because of the way he seemed to get rid of the ball in the very motion of catching it. Watching him on a double-play relay it seemed like he barely made contact with the ball before getting it on to the first baseman. He was able to do this because his hands were so quick and sure, because his footwork was absolutely perfect, and because he wore possibly the smallest glove of any big-league player in modern times.

Nellie made sure I understood, Mazeroski *never* cheated. This "no-touch" technique allowed him to get to the bag and get rid of the ball without ever having to take an extra step. He'd hit the bag with his left foot and the ball would be on its way, he'd be turning the play without giving an inch to the runner. The little glove allowed him to receive and get rid of the ball without ever losing it in the webbing or the depth of the pocket. While the play looked like magic, what it was really about was making sure that that second out was going to be recorded. Next time you're at the ballpark or watching a game on TV, study the way second basemen do it today—they're "profiling," as the guys say now. But notice how many take that little extra step away from the runner. The play looks good, but the runner going to first will somehow just beat the throw. That little bit of cheating (or sloppy technique) is actually the difference between winning and losing. On top of everything, the rules today make it *easier* for second basemen because runners coming into the bag can hit the fielder only if they can make contact with the bag in their slide.

Where Nellie had been/was a bona-fide star, Bob Lillis and Eddie Kasko were veteran utility infielders, guys who had had to scrap and fight to do all the little extra things that make so much difference. Both these guys were extraordinarily smart players and they continued to work with me after Nellie left the following season, especially Bob Lillis.

I cannot emphasize enough what Nellie and these other older players gave to me. From them, I learned not only technique but a kind of artistry that only comes with a real love of the game. Catch the ball with two hands, they emphasized. I did. Pop-ups, grounders, anything I could naturally get two hands on. "Feel the ball," they'd say, "feel the ball." Nellie would emphasize this over and over again. If you teach yourself to feel the ball you will be making your hands better; the better your hands, the better your chances of making plays you never imagined you could make.

I noticed that Nellie, like Bill Mazeroski, also wore a very small glove. It was an old, brown mudcake of a glove that had been turned into a slimy mess from years of tobacco juice which Nellie spit into the pocket. The glove had no thongs between the fingers the way nearly all gloves did. The idea was that the less the glove did the work, the more your hands would. I soon got around to thinking about the kind of glove I should be wearing and then, with Nellie's help, I started designing my own.

The glove was to be small, very small. I wanted a stiff thumb and one long finger that I could shape anyway I wanted—and then I did *not* want any stiffness or padding in the heel, where most gloves are usually protected. Nearly all gloves were (and are) made with heel padding because the heel is an especially delicate part of the hand, but I felt that if a ball kicked off the stiffened heel portion of the mitt it would tend to kick farther away. I didn't want that. Nellie's point was not that I build a glove like his but that I build it my way so that it really conformed to my hand. And that I did. It was a glove that answered the original and simple need that had been drilled into me: "Hands on the ball!"

While I was lucky in my "teachers," I also came along at a time when teaching in the big leagues was part of the everyday order of things. Older players would turn their backs on rookies, but they never did so quietly. Chatter, bench jockeying, conversation, and just plain hanging around were regular features of the game at a time when players roomed with each other on the road, when they had time on their hands and no headsets on their ears. The teaching came from many directions, including ribbing and taunting.

One time in a game at the Astrodome that first full season, we were losing by a run or two to the Pirates in the late innings. I came up and hit a smash through the middle that the pitcher somehow snared on one hop. I was so dejected I just wound up trotting to first. When I approached the bag, Donn Clendenon, the Pirates' first baseman, yelled at me, loud enough for everyone in the field, on the benches, in the first couple of rows of the stands to hear: "Run the ball out, rook!"

At first this shocked and embarrassed me, then I got mad. I glared at Donn as I went in to the bench—and Lillis came right over to me.

"He was trying to help you. You looked like a dog running down to first!"

It took a moment but I finally understood. I went to the edge of the dugout and yelled at Clendenon, "Thanks!" He nodded and we went on.

What I understood was that while Clendenon surely was not looking out for me he was trying to help me. Not for my sake but because we *both* were on the same field. It was the game. Recently, Carlton Fisk, in his final years with the White Sox, maybe the last of a breed, got a lot of ink when he started screaming at Deion Sanders, then with the Yankees, for not running out a ground ball. People wondered what that was all about. It was simple. Fisk, coming from another time in the game, had certain standards he was not about to see compromised. He couldn't have cared one way or the other about Deion; it would have mattered less to him if he did or didn't become a good player. But he didn't want the game they shared to be taken down a notch. That was all.

During that first full season in 1965, we regularly played in ballparks that teams had played in for the better part of the century. Stories, traditions, and, most important, particular skills were associated with these parks. Some of my teachers in these ballparks also turned out to be players from other teams, who knew their turf like masters.

I remember the first time I went into Cincinnati, when the Reds were playing in Crosley Field. There was a noticeable incline in left field going up to the fence and outfielders had to learn not only what to do with their feet but what would happen to a baseball if it came into contact with the slope. It would hit the wall differently if its first bounce was on the slope, it would kick off another way if the ball was hit with any slice or hook.

The field itself had the oddest configuration I had ever seen. It was 320 feet down the left-field line. And then going into left center field there was a huge scoreboard, flush to the field at an odd angle. Dead center field was only about 380 feet away, the alley in right center was 358, but then down the line in right it was 360. It was a genuinely weird ballpark. It was a great hitter's park because it had all these nooks and crannies that forced the outfielders to play out of position—not to the hitter's strength but to the ballpark's weaknesses. They played down the line in left, for example, because they knew they had the scoreboard in left center, but they played away from the line in right because there was so much room. That was a special invitation for me.

In one early game I played there, I hit what I thought was a sure home run with the bases loaded. Because I was being played over into right center, I tried to pull. I lined a high drive down the line—but the wind was blowing in and there was all that distance to the fence. Frank Robinson went up over the wall and took my sure homer away.

As he was trotting in from the field and as I was taking my place at second base, he yelled over to me, "Hey kid, if you took a regular swing, you had a grand slam!" Right. He taught me a basic lesson about not letting the park I was playing in alter my hitting style.

I picked up another of these lessons in Connie Mack Stadium— Shibe Park—in Philadelphia. This was a ballpark, though more spacious than the others, that had all kinds of wonderful oddities which challenged some skills, enhanced others. It was double-decked all the way across left field, like Ebbets Field or Tiger Stadium, but in right field there was a double wall, fifty feet high, broken in right center field by a scoreboard that went up from the base of the field to a height of around fifty feet.

The lesson came when I hit a ball off the *top* of that scoreboard. It was a shot that felt like a home run when it left my bat and would easily have been one to *either* side of the scoreboard. But the ball struck the scoreboard and dropped straight down into the waiting glove of an outfielder. Because I had eased up, I was lucky to get a double out of it. Richie Allen, a home-run hitter if there ever was one, called over to me from third base. "Home runs can be doubles in this park, kid." I understood exactly what he meant. I never again failed to go all out on any ball I hit until I saw it disappear over a wall or until I saw an umpire circling his hand above his head.

My "education" was experience. A guy who took time to tell you something could help so much but then you were on your own. As a hitter, no matter what you were taught, you had to stand alone. The learning process was facing major-league pitching.

No one could prepare me for my first at-bat against Sandy Koufax. It was early in the season, in Los Angeles. I can't say that I was nervous about facing Koufax—even though my teammates had told me more than enough about him to put me on notice.

Actually, just because he was so feared and admired, I ached to face him. In the weeks before our trip to L.A. I found myself slipping into these fantasies about hitting against him. I wanted to stand in and show what I could do. I looked forward to it. By the time we got to L.A. it was almost all I could think about.

As a kid growing up, I had seen him any number of times going against the Giants at Candlestick. All the while, I'd listen to the radio and they'd tell me over and over again just how great and unhittable he was. And so there I was face-to-face with a legend and with my own pumped-up belief that I could handle any pitcher any time, anywhere.

When I stepped into the batter's box at Dodger Stadium that first time I felt I was where I wanted to be: that is, until Koufax threw his first pitch.

I never saw it. I literally heard it go by me. I couldn't believe anyone could throw that hard. I did see the next pitch—but only barely. I swung at it and missed by a lot. The third pitch, like the first two, was a high fastball which was by me before my bat was halfway toward the strike zone. I struck out on three pitches—as I did the second time up. And then the third time up, I fouled one off. I told myself then, "I got him now." I struck out on the next pitch. But, coming back to the bench I told the guys, "I got him, I got this guy." They looked at me like I was crazy. But the next time up I did not strike out, I popped up. And thereafter, I wound up hitting Koufax pretty well, including home runs in Dodger Stadium and the Astrodome that same year. Koufax, first of all, was a lefty and it was usually easier for me to see lefties open up than right-handers. Also, Koufax threw nearly over the top. His release point was easy to spot. After a while, when I got used to him, I actually could see (as well as hear) his pitches.

To be sure, my teammates helped me a lot in adjusting to major-league pitching. The first time I faced Vern Law, the Pirates' top righty who led them to a world championship in 1960, I hit him hard. When I came back to the bench, I sat down next to Howie

Pollet, the pitching coach on our team who looked out for me. He told me to make sure when I went up next to look for the ball inside, and then to hit him hard because he would be looking to see if I could handle a ball there. Howie was absolutely right. I went up next *looking* for the ball inside. I got a pitch there and drilled it. I hit Law and other sinker/slider pitchers like him who could be forced to give up the inside of the plate.

The first time I faced Juan Marichal, he made me look silly. He threw screwballs and I couldn't handle them. I had never seen a screwball before then and his and Mike Cuellar's ranked with that of Carl Hubbell, the Hall of Famer, who put on a spectacular strikeout show with that pitch in the 1936 All-Star Game.

When I came back to the bench, Howie told me that I had been looking for a screwball, that I could never hit that way. The way to prepare, he said, was to look for the fastball and *adjust* to the screwball. He's setting you up with the screwball so he can get you with fastball inside, Howie said. If you're ready for his fastball inside, he'll stop throwing the screwball. Right again. When I was ready for the fastball, I was better able to handle the screwball, to take it up the middle or the other way rather than trying to jerk it. Because the screwball is a slower pitch than the fastball, there is more time to adjust to it, if you have set yourself for a fastball. Marichal adjusted to my adjustment, and eventually stopped throwing me screwballs.

So much of what I was learning about hitting had to do with psyching pitchers out. The battle was not so much about physical ability, which I had, but about acquiring the kind of experience that would enable me to successfully duel with pitchers.

In the minors, Billy Goodman told me how Ted Williams had psyched a pitcher out of his best pitch. The toughest pitch to hit, Williams claimed, was a slider because it came in like a fastball, not allowing you to pick up the spin on the ball, and then it moved at the last second. Up against a tough left-hander from Detroit who had gotten him out on sliders, Williams came back to the bench after one at-bat and told Goodman, "I'm gonna hit his slider up on the roof." Next time up, though, he took three straight fastballs right down the middle. The time following, he took two more. Then this pitcher threw him a slider and Williams hit it out of sight. The point was that he knew he was in a duel and there was only one way for him to win it. He had an idea at the plate—and he had the discipline (and ability) to follow through.

Through the first part of the season, I was not doing well. My batting average hovered around the .200 mark. No matter how much I applied myself, I was not quite doing it. There was a young player on the ballclub, John Bateman, a reserve catcher who one day was cut and sent to the minors. Bateman came to me before he cleared out his locker. Coming up, we had played together. Rookies stuck together.

"They're sending me down, Joe," he told me.

"Damn, that's too bad," I said, trying to be as supportive as I could.

"You'll be coming right behind me," he said, knowingly. He was trying to keep up the camaraderie. I felt sick because, unfortunately, I was all too ready to believe him.

Then a very peculiar thing happened. In early July in Milwaukee, we played an extra-inning game against the Braves. In my first at-bat, I homered against Tony Cloninger. I homered in my second at-bat as well.

When I hit the second home run, I had a weird and uneasy feeling running around the bases. Something had happened to me and I didn't know what it was. When I rounded third base coming home, I realized the Braves pitcher, Tony Cloninger, had actually been following me, walking toward each base as I made my way. When I got to the bench, he was standing on the foul line staring at me. One of our players, Arthur Lee Maye, got up on the dugout steps and screamed at Cloninger, "And he's gonna hit another one off you, too."

Fortunately, Cloninger was out of the game before I came up again. But what I was experiencing had nothing to do with Cloninger's mind-set. In these first at-bats, I was seeing the ball differently. Instinctively, I had cut out a lot of preliminary hand and head movements at the plate. Suddenly I saw the ball as I had never seen it before. It was as though the ball came at me in slow motion.

I have since learned, by talking to a lot of different athletes, that that happens at a particularly high level of concentration. Magic Johnson, for example, has said that, when moving at full flight, he saw everyone else on the court moving in slow motion. Ted Williams—in that All-Star Game and all through his career—was able to slow the baseball down to the point where he could actually pick up the spin on it. That is what happened to me.

I wound up going 6 for 6 in this game (tying a modern record later broken by Rennie Stennett of the Pirates, who had 7 hits in a game in 1975).

We won our game and went on to New York where I hit two more home runs in the very next game. Howard Cosell asked for an interview with me. Howard would go on to make the analyst's job in sportscasting more important than the play by play. But then he was an unknown. He had me meet him on a streetcorner near his home in the East 60s. Standing there in the middle of traffic, he wasn't curious about what I might have been eating for breakfast. He wanted to know what it felt like to be a great young player surrounded by a bunch of mediocrities. Typical Howard Cosell.

I replied that my teammates were all good, that far from being a great player, I just felt grateful to be in the major leagues. In the back of my mind, I was thinking about John Bateman.

In the summer of 1992 I had lunch with Howard. Even though he was ailing he still had the spirit to remind me, like he always does, of how he got me started in television.

5

Baseball Education,
Part II

If you watch a professional team going through an airport, checking into a hotel, boarding a team bus, you will probably be able to guess that you're looking at athletes. The guys are all young, most of them are taller than average, they walk with a certain swagger and dress like they've just come back from Hawaii.

The look of our team was a little different, even to me. I was struck on the very first roadtrip we took by how many of the guys carried attaché cases with them. That's interesting, I thought, these guys look more like businessmen than players. Being a rookie, I didn't ask too many questions, I just tried to keep up. I went out and bought an attaché case, too. I didn't quite know what to put in it. Sometimes it was empty. But it looked good, like everyone else's, and that's all I really cared about. It took a while before I figured out what the attaché cases were for.

Our team was full of characters. Because we were an expansion team, not only did we have a mix of aging and untried players, we also had a number of "problem" players, unwanted anywhere else.

For beginners we had the remnants of the Dalton Gang. "Turk" Farrell and Jim Owens, after being banished from Philadelphia for setting fire to a hotel room, had a group of new recruits who now ran with them in Houston.

I didn't notice anything resembling the Wild West when I broke in, though. I just noticed a bunch of guys in business suits carrying attaché cases.

One day, I observed one of the guys on a team flight open his attaché case and take out a small flask. He opened it, poured himself a stiff drink in a plastic cup, then replaced the flask in the attaché case. I didn't think much of it till I saw another player on another trip do the same thing. Then I started asking questions. It turned out everyone on the ballclub was carrying liquor in their attaché cases. In those days there was a regulation against drinking on planes. Our guys, led by Turk and Jim, weren't about to be put off by anything as mean-spirited as regulations.

I didn't ever carry a flask because I didn't drink. As much as I wanted to be accepted, that was not a price I was willing to pay. But for appearance sake, why not? (It's funny. I have never been as personally offended by booze as by drugs. That has more to do with my own sense of values than common sense, I'm sure. Drinking has been part of baseball for as long as anyone remembers. It doesn't make it okay, but you think of Babe Ruth, you think of home runs and then booze. Same with a lot of players, some whose careers were destroyed by alcohol, others who got along just fine. Booze, for better or worse, has been part of the lore of the game, part of the lore of the country. If it doesn't do damage, I don't mind it; if it does, I do.)

There was a story I remember from my rookie season, told to me by Don Drysdale, a guy who has been known to hoist a few. The Dodgers were playing us in the Astrodome on a getaway day and Drysdale was scheduled to pitch not that day but the following one, opening up in another city. After he worked out, he went into the clubhouse to relax and have a beer—because he knew he wasn't going to pitch that day.

I am not sure how many brews he downed, but somehow the game turned into one of these marathon 17-inning affairs, with both bullpens thoroughly depleted—and the Dodgers wound up having to call on Drysdale to hold on to a 2–1 lead.

He came in to pitch to me with two out and the tying and

winning runs on base. He said when he got the call and had to come downstairs, he was "feeling real good." He took the mound and proceeded to end the game by striking me out on three pitches, throwing three fastballs on the outside corner. It wasn't booze that did it—I couldn't hit Drysdale then or ever—but booze apparently did nothing to slow him down then, or ever. The Big D had a long and honorable Hall of Fame career.

While I desperately wanted to be one of the guys, I knew I wasn't. Not just because there was nothing in my attaché case but because the old Dalton Gang members were hard to cozy up to. These desperados were genuinely, dangerously crazy. To illustrate— there was a Houston beat writer, Mickey Hershkowitz, who had written several unflattering stories about the Gang and its leader, Dick "Turk" Farrell.

We were on the road, in Philadelphia, when a particularly harsh article about Turk Farrell was published. We had a long flight from Philadelphia to Houston. The attaché cases flew open on the bus to the Philadelphia airport and opened again as soon as the plane lifted off for Houston. On the bus from the Houston airport back to the stadium, the desperados were at full gallop.

I was sitting in an aisle seat on the bus, really not paying much attention to what was going on around me. I failed to notice that Mickey Hershkowitz was sitting next to me by the window. Somewhere en route, I heard the hoofbeats.

"Where is that little motherfucker?" a voice cried out.

I was startled out of my reverie.

I assumed I was the one being referred to. The voice belonged to Jim Owens, who was sitting directly across the aisle from me. Shit, I thought to myself, what have I done now? I couldn't imagine what it was but I was the only guy Jim seemed to be looking at. Suddenly he lunged across the aisle, right past me. He grabbed five-foot, 105-pound Mickey by the throat, lifted him out of his seat, and dragged him over me into the aisle. Then he raised him straight up by the neck right off the ground. Jim's face was demented. Mickey's was turning crimson.

"If you ever write anything bad about my friend Turk again, if you ever say so much as one bad word about him, I'll kill you, you understand?" Mickey tried to answer, I guess, but with Jim's hand around his throat he could only get out a few squeaks.

Turk Farrell came barreling through to grab Jim, yelling, "Let him go, Jim, he's not worth it!" "No," Jim said, "I'm gonna kill this mother." And Turk said, "Let him go, Jim, or I'm gonna hit you." And still Jim held on so Turk actually began pounding him, "Let him go, man, let him go."

It took a couple of guys to pull Jim off and when they finally did, Mickey dropped straight to the floor.

"He can't breathe, man!" one of the guys said.

I looked down from my seat. I felt awful. The sight of this poor guy made me feel even worse. I reached out to him, unsure whether he was going to live or die. I had never seen anyone before who had literally had the breath choked out of him. Fortunately, Mickey revived and, aside from the shock and fright of it, was not really hurt. But incidents like this made my first months very jumpy, until my own relationship to the Gang became clearer.

It turned out I needed the Gang more than they needed me.

In those first months, like any other rookie, I was up against it. Making my way around the league, I had my baptism of fire. I was confident but I also had good reason to be worried. Managers like Gene Mauch and Leo Durocher were adamant about testing rookies. If they could win a game by intimidating a rookie batter, they did. As a result pitchers around the league then knew how to frighten hitters, not necessarily to physically punish them. Today, there are only a handful of pitchers who know how to pitch inside. Batters, assuming they won't be hit, stand closer to the plate. The result is probably that more, not fewer, batters are hit by pitches and when they are, brawls ensue. Even close pitches today are liable to raise the possibility of a class-action lawsuit.

It would have been a joke if I had ever complained about the working over I got when I began. There was one game against Larry Jackson of the Cubs. I fouled a pitch off my foot during an at-bat and hobbled around for quite a while before I stepped back in the batter's box. After the game, Jackson walked up to Nellie Fox and said: "Tell Morgan he'll pay for breaking my rhythm." The next time we faced him, I spent most of the afternoon flat on my back.

There was another game where I got buzzed on a 3–0 pitch. I thought it was unnecessary, but I didn't say a word. Afterwards, one of our coaches told me a story about a "memorable" game several seasons before. Pitching for the Dodgers, Stan Williams was set to walk Hank Aaron intentionally. When the count got to 3–0, Williams hit Aaron in the helmet. Asked later why he did it, Williams said, "He was going to get to first anyway so why not give the guy on deck something to think about?"

Then there was Bob Gibson. He was an education all by himself. Gibson was a notoriously fast worker as well as a ferocious competitor. If you so much as fiddled with the bill of your cap during an at-bat you were in for it. A fellow rookie on our team named Aaron Pointer once fouled a Gibson pitch off his foot. When Pointer stepped out, Gibson didn't make a mental note to relay word to him that in the future he better watch out. Even though the count then was 0–2, Gibson drilled him in the ribs with the next pitch.

Bob Aspromonte, another player on our team, broke Gibson's rhythm in one game by briefly stepping out on him. Gibson hit him in the back with the next pitch. It sounded like a cannon shot. Aspromonte was out for almost a month. Gibson games lasted less than two hours—and the main reason was that no one was ever willing to stand in against him one second longer than was absolutely necessary.

Early in my rookie season I went to bat for the first time against him, in St. Louis. I happened to have been having some problems hitting then and I remember before the game talking to the Cardinals' first baseman, Bill White (later the N.L. president). White was another of these older players who was willing to be helpful to young players who wanted to learn. The problem I was having, I explained, was in staying back long enough before I started my swing. In committing too soon, I found myself too easily fooled by pitches, opening up too quickly, getting out on my front foot with my power neutralized before I had my bat on the ball.

Bill suggested that I go to a heavier bat and he offered me one of his for the game, a big, 36-ounce war club.

"Choke up on it, it may help keep you back," he said.

So I took his bat and followed his advice. That was where Bob Gibson came in.

First inning, I come to the plate and Gibson stares down at me like a bug he's going to squash. Gibson did not socialize, did not so much as exchange words with players on other teams, he said, because any time they were in the batter's box he needed the freedom to knock them down.

After taking a pitch or two in close, I connected off a Gibson fastball. I ripped the ball just to the right of the mound. Because Gibson's follow-through motion carried him naturally to his left, leaving him off balance, he was in the way of a line drive—which nicked his ear sharply enough to draw blood.

When I was standing on first, Gibson turned to me before he resumed pitching. It seemed like a full minute, though surely it was less, but he just stared at me. That stare had intimidated a lot of players. It was Gibson's trademark, as it is for Dave Stewart today.

I later came around to score but when I got back to the bench, the usual round of congratulations was missing. In fact, there was complete silence. My teammates actually made a point of avoiding me. They knew what I, unfortunately, also knew. I'm a dead man, I told myself, a dead man who had to go out and face the firing squad at least two more times. My teammates were not ribbing me either, as though I were a flyweight hitter who accidentally hit a home run. They *knew* that Gibson was going to kill me, that was all—and knowing that, I was no longer a teammate, just a guy who unfortunately happened to be wearing the same uniform.

In my next at-bat, I stepped up fully expecting to be done away with. I don't know why exactly, but I wasn't afraid. I had never been afraid on the field before, and I wasn't then. Maybe I was just as crazy as Gibson was supposed to be but I was there for only one purpose: to hit. And I did.

Gibson did not throw at me. I swung at his first pitch and

grounded out. In my next at-bats, no knockdown pitches, no high and tight ones. In fact—this was the strangest part of all—in the ten years we were in the league together, Gibson never hit me with a pitch, never knocked me down. He would occasionally nod to me before games, but there were no conversations. He never in any way indicated that he liked, respected, or in any other way regarded me as human. It got so that I eventually began feeling really funny about it. It was not until years later, my last season in Cincinnati ('79), when Gibby finally did say his first words to me—and then I was nearly bowled over.

At the time, I was living in the downtown Stouffer's Hotel. It was late one night. I was returning to the hotel, and Gibson, who was then in his final season with the Cardinals, was in the lobby with Lynn McGlothen, whom he'd taken under his wing.

"Hi, Joe," he said as I walked past him. It was like he had stuck one up under my chin. I stopped dead in my tracks.

"Huh?"

"Hi, Joe, howya doin'?"

I was looking into the face of a very friendly man. I didn't know what to make of this. He said, "Wanna have a drink with us?"

Now this actually unsettled me. I said, "Yeah, sure," but I was as wary as I had ever been in the batter's box as we went upstairs to the bar.

For the next several hours we sat there and just talked baseball. It was one of the most pleasurable evenings I have ever had in my life. I found Bob Gibson knew as much about hitting and the rest of the game as he did about pitching. I had never closed a bar before or since, but we closed the Stouffer's bar that night. However, I couldn't bring myself to ask him about the silent treatment.

Much later I was talking with Curt Flood one night, and I brought up the story about how I had once hit Gibson on the ear.

Flood told me that a little later that first season, just prior to another series between our teams, they had one of these team meetings where they go over the way they want to pitch the batters on the other team. Gibson was pitching that night and when they came to my name, he said, "You guys just scatter out there, the little asshole's going to get his hits no matter what."

All those years and I never knew! That line drive off his ear stayed with him the same way a ball against my skull would have stayed with me!

The odd thing is that Bob Gibson was the only pitcher who really knew how to pitch to me. Because I stood close to the plate, everybody thought I liked the ball inside. I didn't. I crowded the plate because I didn't want the ball away from me to be unreachable. Gibson knew the way to get me was to fire the ball over the inside corner of the plate. But it was hard even for Bob Gibson to be successful with that strategy, because I didn't swing at bad pitches.

If I have made Bob Gibson out to be peculiar, he wasn't. The whole point was that he was just the fiercest of competitors. What seemed forbidding in him was only part of the game, part of what I had to go through as a rookie.

Everywhere I went, I got the same treatment. Joey Jay in Cincinnati, Don Cardwell in Pittsburgh, Tony Cloninger in Milwaukee, guys who made a living making you eat dirt. They were nasty—and expert—and for some time during that first summer, I never believed I could do a thing to stop what was happening other than to stand in and hit without backing down. If teammates of mine said anything at all, it was usually something lame like, "You're a rookie, you have to go through this." The only guy who came to my defense in those first months was, again, Nellie Fox. We were playing in the Astrodome one day and the Cub pitcher, Bill Faul, nailed me on the wrist with a pitch. Nellie went crazy. It was okay for someone to knock me down, but not to hit me, not to possibly put me out for a season or a career. Nellie, small as he was, started yelling at Faul. I thought he might go after him—and if he went I would have to go, even though I had no trouble taking my medicine.

Finally, my second time around the league, Dick Farrell came to my rescue. We were in Philadelphia again. Chris Short was going against us and I knew I was going to be in trouble, because the first time I had faced him a couple of months before I had gone 3 for 4.

So in the first inning, I got knocked down with a pitch right at my head. On the next pitch I lined a base hit to right field. I got to first base and Dick Stuart (the slugger whose nickname was "Doctor Strangeglove") sort of laughed at me. "Way to go, kid," he said, "don't let them intimidate you." Next time up, of course, I was back in the dirt. Well, after that time, Turk Farrell came over to me on the bench and said, "Okay, you've proved you belong, we're gonna put a stop to that shit. Who do you want?"

At first, I didn't know what he meant. But Turk made sure I understood exactly. Every time when he was pitching and a pitcher on the other team threw at me, he would nail a batter on that team. In fact, what he actually said was, "I'll get one for you—and one for me."

Then, just as he said, in our next game, when I got sent to the dirt again, Dick was pitching and he came over to me and asked:

"Who do you want?"

"The catcher," I said.

"Good, the catcher is yours, the motherfuckin' pitcher is mine."

Sure enough, Turk drilled them both. The next day, before we played our getaway game, the guys on the other team were telling me the same thing Turk had told me: that I had earned my rookie spurs and that no one was going to be after me from then on. That, however, was just the beginning.

Wherever we went, Turk was my protector. And, for me, welcome as it was to be taken into the club, that "protection" was always a mixed blessing. One time we were playing in San Francisco and Turk decided his target after I had been knocked down was going to be Orlando Cepeda. Cepeda was every bit as mean as the Turk or anyone else who ever played. When Cepeda came up that time, Dick hit him above the knee. Cepeda was a guy who was alternately mean and friendly, he could be very helpful to other players, but he could also turn into Mr. Hyde in a flash. When Farrell hit him, Cepeda didn't move. He just stood in the batter's box and stared out.

The Turk finally yelled at him:

"What the fuck are you looking at?"

Cepeda, in his fractured English, said, "I'm not gonna say nothin', Turk, but I'm gonna come up there and kick your ass."

Farrell walked to the front of the mound and yelled right back, "Well, either get up here or get your ass down to first base, it doesn't make any difference what you do but do something. You're holding up the game."

Cepeda decided he would go to first base but from there he screamed these wild obscenities, in Spanish, at Farrell, having to do with his parentage and what substances his body was made from. The whole scene was insane, I kept wondering to myself what was wrong with these guys. But now I was one of them, a member of the fraternity who had apparently paid his dues. It was a wonder I ever made it, because all of this was natural and normal. Pitchers, lots of them, would as soon kill you as look at you. They threw at you, around you, near you, and no one got too worked up over it. It was just part of the order of things. Pete Rose told me later on that he was in a game when Gibson was pitching against Tony Cloninger (then with the Reds). Gibson threw close to Tony Perez's head. On the next pitch, Perez flied to right and when he trotted back across the field, he cursed Gibson as he passed by.

As soon as the teams changed sides, Cloninger went after Lou Brock. Cloninger aimed a pitch at his helmet. Brock spun out of the way at the last second, sprawling into the dirt. Brock got up screaming and yelling at Cloninger, who motioned for Brock to come forward. "Hey Lou, I can't hear you, come a little closer and say it, why don't you!" Brock glowered at Cloninger, Cloninger glowered back, the umpire removed his mask and walked out in front of Brock, but that was it. No fights, no dugouts emptying. The game resumed, because nothing really out of the ordinary had happened.

When I talk about what I was learning and how I was getting along, I cannot avoid coming back to the fact that I was a black player at an earlier and different period in the game. Of course, there were many black players in the game then, as there are now, but it had been less than twenty years since Jackie Robinson broke in and the whole question of race and color was still very much an issue.

On my team, with all the help I got from guys like Nellie Fox, Bob Lillis, and Eddie Kasko, the black players on the team were able to help me in ways that white players simply could not have. It was the accumulated experience of being black and in the big leagues that helped so much.

Arthur Lee Maye, who had come up with Milwaukee, was a good player on our team. He hit .300 a few times, he could run, wasn't a good outfielder, but he was a solid player nevertheless.

Joe Gaines was basically a utility guy, but he worked hard and everybody liked him for that; Walt Bond was supposed to be the next Willie Mays, though he wasn't. He was a big guy, around 6 feet 6 inches, very strong, a player everyone thought would shatter all kinds of home-run records, though that never happened.

Collectively, these guys had been around the majors for a long time and when they talked, I listened.

We were sitting around one time, we weren't talking about anything intense or special, and suddenly, out of nowhere, Joe Gaines said to me, "I want you to make sure that you do everything that everyone asks of you and then some, because I don't want to see you end up like us."

"Whaddaya mean?" I said.

"We're just hanging day to day, man, can't you see that? When your time comes I want you to be able to walk away from the game and have money."

What I was being told, in translation, was that marginal white players could hang on year after year but black players had to be starters.

On another occasion, I was in the batting cage, having a good time, and Arthur Lee Maye was standing around. I was mouthing off like a smartass rookie telling him how well I could hit. Arthur Lee didn't laugh, didn't even smile. "Let me tell you something, kid, you just try to stay in this game as long as I have and then you can pop off."

I said something smart back, "Well, maybe I don't catch the ball the way I should but the way I hit they can't catch it either." There was no way Arthur Lee was going to make a joke of this. He also wasn't about to start sermonizing. "No," he said, simply, "that's not the way to look at the game."

There were so many ways these older black players were helpful to me. They understood, in ways that others could not, what kind of opportunity there was in playing in the majors. They, better than others, knew just how hard and how tenuous it all was.

One home game against the Dodgers in that first year, we were up against Sandy Koufax. No matter how confident I felt personally, whenever we faced Koufax we knew it was David versus Goliath. We were always looking at games where we were lucky to score a run and where he'd have 15 strikeouts.

On this particular night, Don Notterbart was pitching a great game for us. We went in to the ninth inning in a scoreless tie. The Dodgers got a man on, advanced him to second, and then to third with two out. On what should have been the final out of the inning, I let a ground ball go right through my legs, allowing the run to score. We were at home, before a packed house, and 50,000 people booed me.

When I came up to hit in the last of the ninth, John Roseboro, the Dodgers' catcher, saw that I had tears in my eyes.

"Hang in there, kid, you're gonna have a lot of good days," he said. I was much too upset to be comforted by what was obviously a gracious and caring remark from an opposing player.

My teammates tried to help me too. Nellie came over after the game and reminded me that the year before he had blown a no-hitter for Ken Johnson, a pitcher on our team, by making a two-out ninth-inning error. One of the coaches came over and reminded me that one play doesn't win or lose a game. "You didn't put that guy on third base, you didn't do any of the things that led up to his being able to score, did you?" None of it mattered because all I could think of was the hurt I felt. But it was Walt Bond who straightened me out.

Walt is dead now. He died just a couple of years later from leukemia, without reaching the power numbers some had predicted for him.

"Let's go have a drink, kid," he said.

"No, I want to go home," I said.

"You're going with me," he said. Walt was a very gentle guy and I was surprised by his forcefulness. All 6 foot 6 was behind this "request" of his. There was no way I could have turned him down.

So we went out and drank. Actually, because I didn't like drinking, we just sat around in this place for a couple of hours till I calmed down, which was what Walt was after. He didn't want me to go out and drown my sorrows in alcohol.

It was funny in a way because I never would have done that. I probably would have gone home, watched some TV, and felt very sorry for myself.

But Walt, with his gentleness and his compassion, got me out of the dumps. He, too, wanted to make sure I understood that I could have a long career.

"You have a full season, you make mistakes," he said. "You have a long career, there'll be many mistakes." He told me what others told me, that I'd have good days and bad days. Then he said something else:

"You're a good player so you're gonna have far more good days than bad ones and the thing about good players is that they always bounce back."

Next day, I made three great plays in the field and got a couple of big hits as well.

I believe, absolutely, that a single game can make or break a player because of what he carries away from it. I might have been derailed by that Koufax game. My moods ran that deep. But Walt Bond instinctively knew that and saved me from myself.

FROM THE BOOTH:
Living Color

When I broke in, though all I ever wanted was to be just another player, I was a black player. I came along at a time when integration was not yet law in all parts of the United States, when baseball itself had been integrated for a little over a decade and a half. In my time, the mid-sixties, there was a literal social revolution sweeping the country. It was the time of Martin Luther King and Malcolm X. You could not be a black player breaking in without some awareness of who these men were and what they stood for.

Likewise you could not help being aware that no matter how fairly others tried to treat you (never a guarantee) it was always a struggle to go from town to town, hotel to hotel, restaurant to restaurant. Even in those places where black people were allowed, there was still an underlying sense of being out of place. It was as though, without anyone ever saying it, a black player could just feel the silent judgments and objections to his presence. When you stayed in the same hotel with your teammates, when you went to a bar or a restaurant, there was always that unvoiced question, "Why is he here?"

The racism young black players today are up against is much more subtle. Because of that, all too many of these young players seem to be almost oblivious to the past they have come from.

In my first years with the Astros, we had a game in San Francisco that was going to be nationally televised on NBC. The NBC announcers that day were Jackie Robinson and Pee Wee Reese. Though there were far more black players in the game then than a decade before, it was still a special thrill to see Jackie Robinson. In fact, I was approached before the game by the NBC staff and asked if I would consent to be interviewed. I agreed, realizing that the interviewer might be Robinson. I waited nervously in the dugout, not knowing what I might say, but hoping that Jackie, not Pee Wee, would be the interviewer. Then I saw Pee Wee walk over from the other dugout with his mike. So after the interview, I walked over to Jackie anyway. I introduced myself, as nervous, as awestruck as any rookie. I did not know what to say, other than wanting to convey to him in some way what debt of gratitude I owed him. He was a large man, larger than I realized from the many pictures I had seen of him. He was heavier and also older-looking than his years. His hair was prematurely white. I didn't know it, but he already was battling major health problems that eventually shortened his life.

"Thank you," was all I could get out of my mouth.

Robinson smiled. His eyes, ever so slightly, seemed to brighten for a second. Then I just walked off to do my business.

Too many players today, white and black, don't know anything about Jackie Robinson. Young black players, in particular, come into the game taking too much for granted. Because they can come and go, stay in the same hotels, eat in the same restaurants with their white teammates, they really have little sense of what it was like just a few decades ago—when Jackie Robinson broke in. As the song goes: "A people without knowledge of their history is like a tree without roots."

A black player today can command a top salary in the game but his blackness still sets him apart. He can make his way and his money like a white player, but he cannot avoid the fears, the assumptions, the judgments that lurk just beneath the smiling masks of easy acceptance. And beyond the pretense of equality, in the case of private country clubs, many businesses and labor unions, there is hardly an effort at pretense.

Not long ago, I left the office one afternoon to catch a flight to Tucson for an LPGA celebrity golf tournament. I go there every year to help raise money for charity. I left Oakland about 4:30 in the afternoon and had to change planes in L.A. When I got off at L.A.X. and walked from one gate to the other, it was announced that the plane I needed to catch was delayed. So I sat around in the lounge area talking to people, signing autographs. All of this was very friendly and cordial. Perfect strangers, who knew me from TV, told me how much they liked my baseball telecasts—until some guy came over and said that the delay was going to be longer than anticipated. I then excused myself because I needed to go and call ahead to Tucson to let them know that I was going to arrive late. I went to the phone booth just beyond the lounge area, leaving my bags right where they were.

As I was dialing my number, a guy put his hand on my shoulder and forcefully whirled me around.

"Hey, what's your problem?" I said, looking into a hard, hostile face.

Without identifying himself, he said: "You're a drug dealer and you're coming with me."

"I don't know what you're talking about," I said. "I just got off the plane, I'm not with anyone."

"You're coming with me," he said.

"I don't want to go with you. I haven't done anything."

He said, "You have identification?"

I told him that I did and I turned to start walking back to my bags. Before I could take a step, he grabbed me. Now I started to get upset.

"Hey, what's your problem, man, let me get my bag and I'll identify myself." The guy had never asked who I was and didn't seem interested in finding out now. Just then, one of the people in the lounge area who happened to be at the next phone tried to intercede.

"That's Joe Morgan, the broadcaster, the baseball star," he said. "I was on the plane with him from Oakland."

"Get the fuck away from here or I'll take you in with him!" the guy said. My witness left.

By this time I was getting a little shaky because it was slowly dawning on me that there was nothing I could do to identify myself or save myself from what was going to happen.

"Okay," I said, "what do you want me to do?"

He pointed over my right shoulder, indicating that he wanted me to go that way. When I turned, he pinned my arms behind me, put his knee in my back, and knocked me to the ground.

"Why are you doing this to me?" I cried out. I couldn't think of anything else to say.

"I'm an authority figure. I'll show you what authority is, you've been up against us before." I did not know what he meant then or now. I thought he was crazy.

When this cop's partner walked up, he said to him, "D'you see him take a swing at me?"

The other cop said, "Yes."

Over the next hours, the nightmare deepened, and it was all because I was just another black man. No longer protected by celebrity, as anonymous as any other black man, I was exposed to whatever undeserved fury was going to be meted out.

I was cuffed, taken into custody, held for some time in a security area of the airport. Here there were no witnesses, no one to stand up for me. Anything could happen, I realized. Finally, a woman walked in, perhaps an official of some kind, who seemed to recognize me. She left, the two cops huddled for a while, and then the arresting cop came over to me and said, "Well, maybe you're who you say you are."

I wanted to say, "I never told you who I was, I never had the chance," but instead, I just kept quiet. In no way did I want to be provocative. He said, "If I let you go, you promise to forget about this?" I didn't immediately answer, because I wasn't about to forget it. He repeated his offer. This time I said, "You do what you have to do, I'll do what I have to do." "Tell you what," this bright light said, "I think I'll call the newspapers and tell them we're holding Joe

Morgan on a drug investigation, how do you think that'll play?" I said nothing. After another standoff, the cop looked at his partner and between them they decided to take the cuffs off and let me go.

As soon as I was out of there, I went to airport security and told them what had happened. They told me their people weren't involved, that it was the LAPD. Learning that, I went to the nearest LAPD substation and tried to file a formal complaint.

The night was by no means over. I was not allowed to file a complaint. As I was in the process of requesting information on how to file, the two cops who roughed me up turned up again and began screaming at me. I felt lucky just to get out of there. This incident happened without any press fanfare. A couple of years later, the experience of a motorist, Rodney King, told the rest of America that Los Angeles was not a place for a black person to fall into the hands of the police.

Because I had been unable to file a complaint, I filed a lawsuit against the LAPD, which I eventually won. But in no way did that change my sense that the struggle begun by such pioneers as Jackie Robinson still remains only a promise. The reality, far more deadly, is that too many people, black and white, have simply settled into newer, safer forms of the old thinking. It is therefore doubly painful to me to see young people, especially young black people, without real memory of the past. Maybe so many people flocking to the movie *Malcolm X* means things are about to change. I certainly hope so.

Some might counter that I have nothing to complain about, that I have achieved worldly success far beyond what most white people in this country achieve. That is, as my experience in Los Angeles showed, quite beside the point. Charles Barkley, the basketball star, raised a lot of eyebrows when he told a roomful of media people that although he was habitually treated with smiles, friendliness, and respect, the real question was how an anonymous black person would be treated by the same people. Charles is usually outspoken, but his words often hit the mark. This time, he was a little off. I'm a celebrity and that didn't help me a bit.

6

Friends: Black
and White

To be young and an Astro in those days was more than I ever could
have imagined when I signed my first pro contract. I came close to
winning the Rookie of the Year Award in my first season, losing out
to Jim Lefebvre of the Dodgers. Jim did not have the numbers I had
and there were people who said the choice was a matter of color:
He wore Dodger Blue.

I had an even better second year. I hit .285, and became the first
Astro ever selected to start an All-Star Game. That first All-Star
Game, though I was unable to play because of a fractured kneecap,
remains one of my special memories.

I was given a locker next to Willie Mays. To either side of us
there were guys who had been heroes and legends to me from the
time I was a kid: Willie McCovey, Roberto Clemente, Juan Marichal. As we got dressed, Willie recalled how brash I was in my first
year. He made an incredible catch off me in one game, coming over
from right center field all the way to left center where I had hit a
long line drive. He made a tumbling catch, rolling over on his neck.
I was already at second base when he made the catch and I couldn't
believe he had gotten there. I yelled out to him:

"I hope you broke your neck!"

The guys on the field said, "Hey, that's Willie Mays you're talking to."

I said, "So what?"

Willie laughed about it now. I laughed with him. I couldn't believe I was side by side with him. I was a little kid—but I was a pro, too. I remembered an at-bat of his during my first year. Claude Ramon, the Montreal broadcaster, was pitching for us then and he threw as hard as anyone in the league. We had a one-run lead in the ninth inning of this game and Willie was the last player Ramon had to get. Everyone in the park knew what Willie was up there to do. From the first pitch Ramon threw, Willie was leaving the earth swinging for a home run. The count went to 3–2 and then he fouled off six straight pitches, swinging at each as hard as he could. On the seventh pitch, he hit a game-tying home run.

He was the greatest player who ever lived. For this one game, he was my teammate.

My Astro teammates, young and mostly unknown, made my everyday baseball life just as exciting. When I look back on those early Astro teams, I am amazed that we did not have immediate success. Some of the players who were there during the seven years I was on the club were Rusty Staub, Jimmy Wynn, Bob Watson, Doug Rader, Cesar Cedeño, John Mayberry, Denis Menke, Jesus Alou, Larry Dierker, Don Wilson, Mike Cuellar, Jack Billingham. We were simply brimming with young, superb talent. Yet, we didn't win. It turned out that there were reasons for it, beyond the simple facts of youth and inexperience.

I knew by the end of my first full season with the team that I was there to stay. In no way had I taken anything for granted, in no way had any of the success I had gone to my head. The only thing that had become certain for me was that I now could go out and play every day the way I wanted to: which was to do anything I could to help my team win. Nellie Fox said to me: "Joe, the players who stay in the league longest are the players who do the most to help their teams win." I always lived by that code.

In my first full season, we finished in ninth place, 32 games behind the Dodgers. We were out of it early but we kept at it as if we were in a race of some kind, and maybe we were. We did not want the Mets to beat us out—and they didn't. The Mets finished dead last that year, 15 games behind us. The following year, we finished eighth, but were only 23 games off the pace.

Because I was one of many young players, I made friends on the Astros in a way I never did elsewhere. One of the first close friends I had on the team was Rusty Staub, still a friend today. Rusty was a southern white, I was a black from Northern California. Our habits, our upbringing, our ways of looking at the world were totally different.

I lived in the black section of Houston, Rusty lived in a white suburb. We used to go to dinner all the time, we used to go to each other's houses regularly on Friday nights when the team was in town. Rusty would come to my house, bringing other friends of his along, and I'd go to his house bringing friends of mine. We simply enjoyed each other a lot. Each of us had in his makeup something that enabled the other to connect and feel comfortable across barriers.

One of the guys who came along with Rusty to my house was Chris Zachary, then a rookie pitcher on our team. We hung around playing cards that night and then when it was time to go home, Chris came running back inside all upset. His car, which had been sitting out in front of my house, had been put up on blocks, and all his tires had been stolen.

Thanks to Rusty, an unpleasant surprise was turned into laughter and not anger in general toward black people. That turned out to be the only time there was ever an "incident" in my neighborhood but what really mattered was that these Friday nights went on as before.

I used to play golf with Rusty a lot. He belonged to a segregated country club but I was so frequently there as his guest that I wound up leaving my clubs there along with his. One day, of course, Rusty was told that he could no longer bring me there. Rusty did not quit the club, though I am sure he did what he could to get an allowance for me. I never blamed Rusty for continuing to play there because I knew he had a good heart.

The day he wound up telling me we could no longer play at the club together he literally spent the whole day working himself up to say what he had to. When he finally got around to it, I could see how bad he felt.

"Hey, man, forget about it," I said.

So I was more than surprised when, one day, I discovered that Rusty was involved in an entirely different kind of controversy. I got to the park early and I noticed that there was a tense atmosphere in the clubhouse. I asked someone if anything was wrong and I was told all hell had broken loose. When I asked what had happened, there was just a shrug. No one would say anything. It was really weird—but I wasn't about to push, so there the matter lay until Rusty walked over to my locker.

"I got to talk to you," he said.

"Sure, what's up?"

We went off to one side, away from the rest of the players.

"You know, I really made a terrible mistake today and I don't know what to do about it."

I could see that he was upset and I was genuinely concerned for him.

"What do you mean?" I said. "What's happened?"

"Well," he said, "you know, I'm from New Orleans, I grew up there—in New Orleans. If a black guy was a good guy he was a good nigger, you know?"

I could feel myself tighten.

"Yeah?"

"You know I was having this talk with Aaron Pointer," he said, "and I happened to say to him, 'You know, I like you, you're a good nigger.' Well, Aaron hit me and we started fighting right there. The worst of it is that everybody thinks I'm prejudiced and I'm not."

I didn't know what Rusty wanted from me. If he had said that to me, I would have hit him, too. I continued to believe he wasn't prejudiced, but there was no way I could help him out.

"You just don't say things like that, man," I said.

Somewhere between then and game time Rusty figured out that he was the only person who could help himself in that situation. He called all of the black players on the team together. There were no other white players there to back him up or lend moral support.

"I'd like to say something to all of you," he explained, slowly and quietly. He told us all what he had told me and then he said: "I've apologized to Aaron and I hope he accepts that. But I also want to apologize to each and every one of you. I know that what I did was wrong, but I hope you'll accept my apology and let who I am and the way I behave speak louder than my words."

I admired Rusty for that apology. It took courage and decency. Rusty for his part let his behavior speak for him though I think it was impossible to repair the relations within the team that he had damaged. Aaron had one more year with the club and was sent to the minors; Rusty, at the end of 1968, was traded to the Expos.

Another early friend of mine was Jimmy Wynn, the Toy Cannon. Jimmy was my roommate in those first years and became the closest friend I ever had in baseball.

Unless you saw him play, the record books will not tell you that much about Jimmy. They'll show that he was a power hitter, 291 career home runs, didn't hit much for average, lifetime .250, drove in a hundred runs twice. But Jimmy was a great talent. He had far more ability than I did, he could do anything on a baseball field— and do it spectacularly. In the beginning, Jimmy not only hit the long ball, he flat-out hit. He struck out a little too much but he was a patient hitter, he led the league once in strikeouts, but he also led the league twice in walks.

Jimmy was fast. He could have been a base-stealing champion if he had ever wanted to be. He stole 43 bases in his rookie season but then decided that that was not what he was going to concentrate on: The long ball was his meal ticket, his assurance of staying up in the big leagues, and, for Jimmy, the big leagues represented the ultimate. He reasoned that he was only going to live once and that he was only once going to be in this place that provided him such a high and beautiful time.

In that way, Jimmy and I were an odd couple. I wanted to have a good time, too. I think I did. But I know I was all business. I wanted to be just one of the guys but, as Bob Aspromonte said, I probably never could have been a "rookie" or any other kind of wide-eyed, fun-loving type. My whole concept was to play baseball. I wasn't there to be a Goodtime Charlie, to go out drinking with the boys, none of that. But Jimmy was still my closest friend.

We liked a lot of the same things. We were both addicted to Western movies. *High Noon, Fort Apache, She Wore a Yellow Ribbon* were flicks we could watch endlessly. Let somebody tell us about a "modern" Western like *Bad Day at Black Rock*, we'd both take a pass. We had a mutual passion for golf—and for steak. A steak a day was our diet on the road, although Jimmy had his own, special variation: He ate apple pie simultaneously with his steak. A forkful of steak *and* a forkful of pie in one big mouthful. I said to him once,

"Jim, why do you eat steak that way?"

He didn't bat an eye. His mouth was too full.

"Good, room," he mumbled.

Jimmy, along with Cesar Cedeño and Ken Griffey Jr., had more ability than any young player I have seen. It is simply impossible to adequately describe what Jimmy could do on a field. I said he was fast and could steal bases. But that isn't the half of it. In that first year when he stole 43 bases, he was thrown out twice! Forty-three steals in 45 attempts! And the two times he was thrown out, it was by the two worst-throwing catchers in the league, which meant that Jimmy wasn't concentrating then, a problem he had throughout his career.

Jimmy's speed enabled him to cover ground the way other outfielders could only dream about. He had the kind of arm that drew raves from other players. We were in Candlestick one day and Jimmy ran down a ball in deepest right center field, caught it, and, in the same motion, wheeled and threw all the way to home on the fly, nailing a Giant runner trying to score. Willie Mays said it was the greatest throw he had ever seen. He should know.

Jimmy could do all of that. He was Willie Mays at the same age, but he just had a different agenda, and because of that he never progressed.

It used to bother me a lot that Jimmy wouldn't work to nurture his talent. I'd talk to him about it but it never mattered and I never pushed it because I liked him too much and who was I, anyway, to tell anyone what they should or shouldn't do with their careers. It may be that Jimmy had the right idea and I had the wrong one about what a life in baseball was all about.

Jimmy, in so many ways, epitomized the old ballplayer, the guy who came along before the portfolios, the agents, and the business managers. When he said he was going to put aside most other things and concentrate on home runs, he was really saying he didn't want to work at those other things. The home run, he knew, would keep him in the majors. One year, he hit 37 homers and was tied with Hank Aaron for the league lead going into the last day of the season when Hank hit one for the crown. Afterwards, Hank said that as far as he was concerned, Jimmy was the home-run champion because he played in the Astrodome—and no one could be expected to have home-run totals like that playing there. The size of the place and the dead indoor air, made heavier by air conditioning, drastically reduced the chances of hitting one out.

Jimmy would give you the shirt off his back, which is not a good way to be if you're a ballplayer because there are always people willing to take that shirt and then some. Whenever Jimmy was in a bar, he'd always wind up buying drinks. He didn't care, not about money, not about his own talent, just about enjoying himself.

Of course he was a competitor. He and I, as roommates, as fellow rookies, wound up trying to outdo the other on the field. We were in Chicago once, standing around the batting cage, and Ernie Banks came up to us and started in with his talking. It was the usual stuff, you know; "The Cubs are going to win the pennant and you guys are going to help us do it." Then he stopped and got serious: "You wanna know something," he said, "you two guys have the greatest thing in the world going. You both push each other to greater heights."

He was right but I also know there was more. If only that had been all of it. Because I came to know Jimmy so well, I soon lost the sense of being challenged by him. As soon as I caught on to him, I just became his fan: I wanted him to hit 40, 50 home runs, I wanted him to steal those bases, make those plays, do anything that would get him to decide that he was going to take his talent as far as he could. As Jimmy had no regrets for his career, neither did I—and the truth of the matter was that I enjoyed and admired him too much to ever wish it had been different.

Here's a typical Jimmy Wynn story: Whenever we were in Pittsburgh, we'd all go out with Willie Stargell. Willie was from Oakland, a hometown guy, and the warmest, friendliest, most generous soul in the world, as well as the sort of player who exuded leadership in everything he did on the field and in the clubhouse.

We were in Pittsburgh during 1966 for a day game on July 3rd with a July 4th doubleheader scheduled to begin the next morning at ten. After we finished the single day game, Jimmy and I, along with Jesse Gonder of the Pirates, went over to Willie's house. Jesse, like Willie and me, was from Oakland, so it was like old home week. We ordered a huge mountain of barbecued ribs from some local restaurant and we just sat around all afternoon, talking, eating ribs, having a great time. About nine o'clock we decided to go out to a club and have a drink. Then after we were at that place for a while, we went on to another, and it was clear that there would be more stops to follow.

I went along for a while but this type of evening was just not for me. When the time came to move on to the third bar, around midnight, I said, "Man, we gotta doubleheader beginning at ten in the morning, we gotta get some rest." Stargell, Jimmy, Jesse, and whoever else was there just laughed. Willie put a big arm around me and said, "No, no, no, man, we're going to just a few more places and it won't kill you, you can come along."

So we hailed a cab, packed ourselves in, and set out for the next nightclub. When we got to the next joint, I told the guys I'd pay the cabfare. After they all climbed out, I ordered the driver to take me on to the hotel.

Shortly after midnight, then, I was in bed, asleep, and those fools were out till whatever time they were out, doing whatever, having a high old time, with this midsummer meatgrinder waiting to eat them alive in the morning.

The team bus left for the ballpark at eight in the morning and as I was making my way across the lobby, I saw Jimmy—coming in from that long night out. What was worse, his hand was bleeding.

"Man, what happened to you, did you get in a fight or something?" I asked.

"No, no," he said, "no fight, nothin' like that. I just cut my hand, that's all." I couldn't tell whether he was hiding anything or he was just oblivious to what had happened to him.

I asked Jim if he was going to be able to play.

"Sure," he said, "why not?"

And play he did. In the first game of the doubleheader, Jimmy went 5 for 5 with two home runs; in the second game he got two more hits—a total of seven hits for the afternoon! And that was not even the half of it. That whole sleepless, mile high crew stole the afternoon. Jesse Gonder got three hits in the first game, didn't play the second; Willie Stargell, well never mind. All Willie did was go 4 for 4 in the first game (with two home runs), and 5 for 5 in the second while I, playing both games on lots of rest and a full tank of natural energy, scratched out one bunt single.

Between games, Willie sent a note to me from the Pirate clubhouse. All it said was "You should have stayed with us last night." Jimmy, meanwhile, needled me for seven hours and then, just to rub it in, asked me if I might not want to go out that night.

I am sure that Jimmy could have made it to the Hall of Fame if he had wanted to, just as I know that there are other players who might have if they had cultivated the superior talent they had. But Jimmy's choice was clear. Maybe there should be a Hall of Fame for all those guys, too, the ones who decided that life at the top was about enjoying yourself to the fullest while you had the chance. I went another way. And I can measure that way not only by the numbers I put up, by the awards I got, but also by all those hours sitting alone in hotel rooms, watching TV, not enjoying myself very much, but doing what I wanted to do nevertheless. For better or worse, I was a man with goals. For Jimmy and I both, beginning in 1968, we needed all the resources of ability and spirit we possessed simply to survive in Houston.

7

Harry Walker

In the years I played for the Astros, we had four managers, Harry
Craft, Luman Harris, Grady Hatton, and Harry Walker, the brother
of Dixie. The four of them were as different as could be.

Harry Craft and Lum Harris were easygoing, tolerant, and very
good baseball men from the old school. They knew what they
wanted from their players, gave them room to get it, and then
offered them full credit for whatever they accomplished. They
were not much on discipline, however, and there was feeling in the
front office that that was what was needed to get us going. Grady
Hatton was supposed to fill that bill but it turned out we fared no
better under him than we had under Harry or Lum. So, on our way
to a last-place finish in 1968, Hatton was fired and in came Harry
Walker, the ultimate disciplinarian and possibly the biggest fool I
have ever known in the game.

Harry had credentials. He played eleven years in the big leagues,
won a batting title in 1947, the year Jackie Robinson broke in.
(Harry hit .363 that year, but was traded in midseason from the
Cards to the Phils, which might suggest he had some problems—
batting champions usually don't get traded in midstream.)

Harry didn't like black players. In fact, during '47, he and his brother Dixie had sought to lead a boycott of major-league players against Jackie Robinson. At the time, Happy Chandler, then commissioner, interceded to break it up. He told the Walkers that if they went ahead with their boycott, they and everyone who joined them would be permanently banned from the game. Chandler, who himself was an old-line southerner, was one of the unsung heroes of the game.

Harry and Dixie knuckled under but, as they say, you can take the man out of the redneck but you can't take the redneck out of the man. There were a hundred little ways Harry made clear his feelings about blacks. There were any number of times he called team meetings when we weren't going well and singled out only the black players on the team for criticism; black players, to him, somehow didn't have discipline or while they were good athletes they just didn't think; he would bait and humiliate black players without even realizing he was doing it; he'd invariably go through hoops whenever he used the word "Negro" in conversation. "Blah blah blah Negro, oops, I mean black," he'd say. If he'd use an expression like "It was a black day," he'd go, "Oh, I didn't mean that, I meant bad day." This probably sounds crazy, but in all the time I knew him I never saw Harry Walker in a pair of black shoes. Now, obviously, that may have been coincidental, but after being with the man for as long as I was I'm not so sure.

I was warned in advance about Harry by Bill Mazeroski. I had developed a friendship with Maz, who was one of the game's special good guys. He was another one who looked out for younger players, talked to them, encouraged them, spent time with them. We regularly swapped stories and small talk before games whenever our teams met. Late in 1968, when we went into Pittsburgh for a series, Maz took me aside. "Joe, I feel sorry for you, Harry Walker's gonna be your manager next season." I was surprised. Grady Hatton hadn't been running the team that long, it didn't seem likely that a change was in the offing.

But Maz insisted. Walker had recently been fired as the Pirates manager and, Bill said, had signed on as a special assignments scout with the Astros. He had it from Pretty reliable front office sources that Harry was soon going to replace Hatton. And Maz, who never had a mean word to say about anyone, said, "Joe, I know the guy and he's gonna be your manager, and he's a bad guy."

Sure enough, Harry was named our manager in midseason and, as if to underscore what Maz had said, when the Astros completed a deal with the Expos sending Rusty Staub to Montreal for Donn Clendenon, Donn, who had played for Harry in Pittsburgh, refused to report to Houston and Rusty, once in Montreal, refused to return to play under Harry Walker.

Though he was hardly the game's only bigot, Harry Walker represented that side of the old school that absolutely had to go. But even before he was a racist, Harry was a fool because he undermined his team. As player, though he won batting titles, he was the kind of guy who would bunt for a hit with two out and a runner in scoring position, just to pad his average. In other words, he was a guy whose thinking could get in the way of winning.

Harry thought he was smart and, in some ways, particularly in those ways of getting to players and undermining them, he was. He would do little things, seemingly unrelated to race or personality, to needle players. I think he felt he had power over a player so long as he could upset him, and he tried, again and again, to do just that.

Jimmy Wynn was a special target. But so were others, Don Wilson and Jesus Alou, any black player who made the mistake of being provoked into showing Harry their feelings.

Don Wilson, a pitcher who I believe had the gifts of a J. R. Richard, was temperamentally just unable to play for Walker. Don was a madman, an original. No one messed with him, no one dared to figure out where he was coming from. He was fun to be with, but also extremely dangerous. On opening day in 1971 we were playing the Dodgers at home. Don was by then one of the league's top pitchers. He lost that day, 2–1, on a hit by Bill Buckner, then a rookie. Afterwards Buckner was quoted in the papers as saying that if Don Wilson was one of the best pitchers in the league he was going to do very well. Don read that and his eyes just told you there was going to be big trouble. "Man, why did you say that?" I said to the image of this poor rookie I had in my mind.

Next time we saw the Dodgers was in L.A., where they sold out every game. With 50,000 people out there, Don called up the Dodger clubhouse and told Buckner he wanted to meet him outside, wanted to "talk" to him. Buckner stayed in the clubhouse. All the while, Don sat quietly on the bench waiting for him, but Buckner never showed his face in the dugout until the game began.

Now it was around the fifth inning. In those days, pitchers used to throw between starts (that's not done anymore). Don got up after the side went out in the fifth and started out to the bullpen, ostensibly to do his throwing. He started walking toward right field, where Buckner was playing and where the visiting bullpen was situated. Buckner was taking his warm-ups with the other outfielders and suddenly Don broke and went after him. In full view of the entire stadium, he chased him all over the outfield until we went out there to restrain him and walk him away!

Another time, we were playing the Reds and they were killing us. Despite their big lead, Johnny Bench kept calling for 3–2 curveballs and whatnot. After the game, Don, who did not pitch that day, called over to the Reds' dressing room and got Bench on the phone. He told him he'd better watch out, that he'd see him in Cincinnati. Weeks later, when we played the Reds again, he drilled John the first time he came to bat.

Don could be just as ferocious with his own teammates. Once, when we were in New York, he came within a hair of killing Jimmy Wynn. It happened in our hotel.

I was showering and through the door I heard Jimmy and Don arguing in the living room (about what I could not tell and afterwards I never asked). When I got out of the shower Don was holding Jimmy upside down, by his heels, out a window. We were up on the twentieth floor and Don was dangling him over the pedestrians and traffic far below.

I tried to step in and get Don to listen to reason. Don was screaming, "I'm gonna drop the motherfucker, I'm gonna drop him." To make matters worse, Jimmy was screaming right back, "Go on, drop me, I don't care, drop me! I dare you, drop me!" I think all that prevented Don from letting go was that he really liked him. He once interceded for him with the Dodger pitcher Bill Singer. Jimmy feared Singer because he had been beaned by him in the minors. "If Jim Wynn so much as gets a dirt mark on the heels of his shoes leaning back from a pitch of yours," he said casually to Singer one afternoon, "I'll bust your head open." Singer never threw a pitch close to Jimmy again.

In any case, Jimmy, despite his loud challenge, was not dropped and life went on. Don, still at large, ultimately and far more seriously, got around to Harry Walker.

The first real run-in between them occurred following a game we had in Los Angeles. Don was pitching that day and because L.A. was his hometown he was really pumped. He carried a 3–1 lead into the eighth inning and had the game well under control. But when Don walked the first batter in the eighth, Harry went and took him out of the game. Of course, we wound up losing, with the winning run scoring on a bases-loaded walk.

As soon as we got to the clubhouse, Harry wiped the food table to the floor and started ranting and raving. "We're a bunch of chickenshit losers," he shouted. "We get a goddamn lead and can't hold on to it. You wanna know why that is, I'll tell ya why: Starting pitchers on this team don't have a damn bit of guts."

I don't think Don heard this because Harry seemed to be looking around for him when he said it. Then he said it again, even louder: "I said, I don't think the damn starting pitchers on this ballclub have any guts, they're always looking for help from the bullpen." This time, no mistaking it, Don heard him.

Don rose up from his locker stool as though he had been launched.

"I'll show you who has guts," he thundered, propelling himself across the room toward Harry. When I saw what was about to happen, I pushed a table into Don, slowing him for a second. The other guys jumped up and grabbed him. Harry went into his office and slammed the door shut.

The clubhouse then was frozen. I mean, nobody moved or said a word. A few minutes later, one of the coaches emerged from Harry's office and asked me to go in there with him.

I was ushered into the office, which was locked behind me. Harry was sitting there, visibly upset but clearly hoping the incident was over.

"Joe, I called you in here because I want to thank you for what could have been an ugly scene out there," he said.

What a farce.

"Harry," I said, "I didn't do that for you. I did that for Don. Don's my friend. If he kills you, he can't play baseball." I turned and walked out of his office.

But that was not the end of it. With Harry Walker these incidents multiplied because he was who he was. Hellfire could break out any time, any place.

We were, again, in Los Angeles, when Harry went after Jesus Alou. It started when he approached him and asked—that is, demanded—that he switch bats and use one of the models Harry had used when he was a player.

Now the reason for that, as far as I was able to figure, was because Harry had been unable to get under Alou's skin and this was the best way to do it. Alou was a terrific hitter, having an outstanding year for us. He was neither in a slump nor sliding into bad batting habits at the time. Harry simply wanted to assert his authority.

Jesus Alou also happened to be the sweetest guy in the world, funny, easygoing, impervious to guys like Harry Walker. Alou used to refer to himself all the time in the third person and by his own initial. "The J. Alou is feeling like he has three hits in his bat today," he'd croon, or "How come the J. Alou don't hit fourth, nobody in this league can get the J. Alou out, give him a chance, the J. Alou drives in as many runs as anybody." It was funny and good-spirited and the whole team got a kick out of him—except, it seemed, Harry.

When he told Alou he wanted him to put his bat aside and use his, Alou refused.

"No, no, the J. Alou has a lifetime batting average of .285, he likes his own bat," he told Harry, "he's used it all his life and the J. Alou's bat still has a lot of hits left in it."

Harry did not say anything and we went out to play that afternoon. In the first inning, Alou made the third out by hitting a fly ball to left field. After we retired the Dodgers in the bottom of the first, we came back in to hit again and Alou's favorite bat was missing from the batrack. It was discovered halfway up the runway broken in two.

Alou said, "Who did this to my bat?"

Harry replied, "I did. If you don't want to use mine, you don't play." Alou continued to use his own bats and Harry never benched him—but that wasn't the point.

The thing was that Jesus Alou just didn't get mad at anybody. But now he was mad. He held his anger in until the next team meeting, a few days later. In this meeting, Harry started going on about how certain players (all of them black) just didn't have it in them to play smart, how they might have the moves but not the brains. The same old crap. He was always fond of meetings where he could chew out his players, particularly if he could use a black or Hispanic player to illustrate something he wanted to say to the whole team. In the middle of this, Don Wilson, sitting over in one corner, muttered under his breath:

"Be consistent."

Everyone in the room heard Don but no one was quite sure what he meant. Meanwhile Harry continued to rave and rant and then Don spoke up louder:

"Be consistent!"

At that point, Harry couldn't ignore Don.

"What did you say, Don?" he asked.

"I said, 'Be consistent,' motherfucker," Don roared, leaping up and charging Harry. Doug Rader tackled Don before he could get to Harry and then it seemed like there were four or five guys holding Don down. Don was screaming, "Lemme go! Lemme go! I'm gonna kill the motherfucker!"

"No, Don, you can't do that, nobody's gonna letcha!" he was told. Don struggled anyway.

"It doesn't matter how long you hold me down. Sooner or later you'll have to let me go and when you do, I'll get him then!"

I don't know how long it took to calm Don down but when he finally was quiet, Jesus Alou started up. Just as Harry was about to continue the meeting, Alou jumped up and said: "I'm sick of ya, I'm sick of ya!"

The sight of Jesus Alou in a fury—I mean this man *never* got mad—was so startling everyone in the room held their breaths.

"The J. Alou don't bother nobody," he shouted, "nobody! I just wanna play baseball. You don't let me play baseball! You're always picking on the J. Alou. You don't mess with these other guys. You don't mess with Morgan, you don't mess with Rader, you mess with the J. Alou. Well, the J. Alou is going home." He was at the peak now: "I go to the Dominican, I can't stand this anymore! The J. Alou is going home!"

The problem was that everyone in the room was laughing. We were laughing not because of his anger or his way of expressing it but because he was such a nice guy his outburst seemed totally out of character. All the guys on the team came around him and talked with him and reassured him about how much he was needed, and all the while he kept protesting: "The J. Alou can hit, the J. Alou can really hit and I don't let this guy do this to me anymore."

Meanwhile there were at least two guys making sure that Don had no place to go, while Harry, who had seen and heard enough, once more barricaded himself in his office.

Harry got a double victory out of that incident because two players that he didn't like lost their cool right in front of him and the rest of the team. That was what Harry really was after, that was the way he got you. Once you cracked, he had you, he had shown you up, demonstrated that he was somehow smarter than you were. And I believe right at the heart of Harry's bigotry was this undying belief that he was simply smarter than any player who was black or Latino.

Harry came after me in the same way. I believe he did everything in his power to get me to crack, to blow up and out in front of him.

"Damn that Wynn. I tell ya, Joe, these people are stupid and lazy. I just don't know how they learned to tie their shoes, ya know what I mean?"

"No, Harry, what do you mean?"

"Why are these people lazy? I mean, look at 'em. Watson, Cedeño, Wynn. They just don't have the capacity to concentrate. Are they born that way or something?"

"You'd have to ask them, Harry."

"It'll be a black day before I—woops, didn't mean to say that, pardner, ya know what I mean, though, huh? Ha! ha!"

Because I played hard all the time, because I would never give an inch to this man, I know he wanted me, I know I frustrated him because I would never give him the satisfaction he was seeking. I didn't have to say it but what Harry got from me every day was the sense that I was smarter than he was, smarter than his games and his cruelty.

One time he almost got me. It was close—because Harry in this instance had devised a way to pit Jimmy Wynn against me, and Jimmy, unable to take it, nearly blew it for both of us.

What happened was that we were locked in a tough, tough game against the New York Mets. Jimmy wasn't playing this day but I was, and I had gone 5 for 5. Tug McGraw was pitching for the Mets then and I had gotten my last hit off him two innings before. The game was tied at that point, we were in the tenth inning, and we had a runner at second base with two out. I was in the on-deck circle, watching McGraw, thinking only about what I needed to do in that situation, when, suddenly, there was a walk and it was my turn to hit. I was called back to the bench. Harry and Jimmy were glaring at each other. I was being pinch-hit for, I was told, and Jimmy was refusing to go up and hit for me.

I walked Jimmy off to the side of the dugout. My own emotions were churning because the game was on the line.

"You tell your friend he hits or he gets fined and suspended— and believe me I'll make it stick," Harry yelled towards me. I wanted to punch Harry then but I could not let myself do it.

"Go up and hit for me, man," I told Jimmy.

"I'm not doin' it," he said.

"You've got to," I said. "Don't let him do that to you."

"He's doin' it to you, man. If he wants to fuck you let him get somebody else."

"Jimmy, you just go on up there and win the game for us. Believe me, I can take care of myself. Don't do it for him, do it for the rest of us, win us a game!"

I believe Jimmy's career was in jeopardy at that moment. He went up to hit, not because he sensed danger to himself but because a friend was imploring him. He could tell I needed him not to buckle under at that moment and he went to the plate. Jimmy did not get a hit, we did not score, we eventually lost the ball game. It was all so shabby.

After I was removed, I went back to the clubhouse, passing Harry as I went. I knew if I ever challenged him about why he had done that he would come back at me with some bull about percentages but he knew it would never wash. I hit left-handers even better than I did right-handers. But if I questioned him, I would have given him what he really was looking for. Instead, as I passed him on my way out of the dugout, I said very calmly to him, "You know, you're not trying to win."

And from then on, I knew my days on any team Harry Walker was managing were numbered. I got the reputation of being a troublemaker, although I wasn't then or ever. But a "reputation" in baseball is as indelible as a birthmark.

For my part, I wasn't about to alter my behavior. I didn't confront Harry then or afterwards, I never let myself blow in front of him. He went to the front office and complained about my "attitude." I said nothing. Houston and the Astros were where I wanted to be. I came up in the organization, I made my way through the ranks, I was part of an emerging team that would one day be a contender, if people like Harry Walker didn't ruin it. But I knew then, from the moment it was understood in the front office that the team's manager considered me someone he couldn't get along with, that my days in Houston were numbered. And that bothered me. Houston, far from being just a stop along the baseball trail, had become my home.

During my Houston years, I had gotten married. My wife, Gloria, and I had settled here, made friends, become comfortable. Also, I had increasingly become committed to community work, putting in whatever spare time I had during the season, all my time during the off-season, to working with disadvantaged kids who had had trouble with drugs and/or the law. It was the least I could do to pay back the tremendous good fortune I had had being a major-league ballplayer. It was a time of commitment and I was committed. I came from Oakland, California, home of the Black Panthers. I casually knew some of those people, believed that their programs, no matter how maligned, were about something. I was no revolutionary, but I wanted to do as much as I could within the system. When I saw politicians, I argued with them, tried to get them to see things differently. I bent congressional candidate George Bush's ear on busing to the point where, at the time, I believed he understood more than most other Texas politicians about discrimination and the need for education. Above all, kids saw in me not some distant superstar with gifts beyond their imagining, but a little guy who worked hard, an ordinary guy who proved that ordinary people still had a chance to make it in this country.

For all those reasons, I did not want to leave Houston. For a while, I thought I was safe. I had several talks with Spec Richardson, the GM, about Harry and the team. In one talk, I told him that Harry had unfairly sent Bob Watson, a great young hitter, back to the minors because he would not change his swing—as Harry ordered. Soon after, Spec had Watson brought back to the team.

But by season's end, there were rumors, never denied by the front office, that I was on the block. The most persistent of these rumors was that I was headed for Philadelphia. I told my wife, at the time, that if I was going to be sent to Philly, I was simply not going to accept being traded.

"You won't accept a trade. Why?" she asked.

I told her that I wanted no part of a last-place team, that I had invested too much of myself in the Astros and in Houston to be dealt with like a piece of meat. I didn't want to play baseball if it meant constantly playing with losers.

Gloria and I talked over all the misgivings I had. She never tried to talk me out of any of it. She did not try to push me one way or the other, only to understand what I was going through.

"Hey, if you wanna quit, that's your decision. Whatever you do will be all right with me," she said.

I ultimately went to the organization and let them know what was on my mind. I knew enough not to ask if a trade was actually in the works but I made sure they understood that *if* they traded me to the Phillies—which I understood was a possibility—I would retire rather than accept the trade.

I don't know if anyone believed me or not. I'm still not sure I was ever marked for Philadelphia. All I can state with certainty is that on November 29, the Astros announced that they had traded me, along with Denis Menke, Jack Billingham, Ed Armbrister, and Cesar Geronimo, to the Reds for the popular slugger Lee May, along with Tommy Helms and a reserve outfielder named Jimmy Stewart.

Because I was being sent to a good team, I accepted the trade. But my state of mind was such that the idea of leaving Houston seemed like a one-way ticket to Siberia, courtesy of Harry Walker. I was anything but happy.

Part Three

THE BIG RED MACHINE

From the Booth:
Great Teams

The two most overrated stats in all of baseball are batting average and earned run average. I measure a player by his run production. Slugging percentage and on-base percentage actually tell you more about run production than batting average.

Say a guy hits .300. That means he makes out seven out of ten times or 70 percent of the time. If you're making those seven out of ten outs with men on base while getting the three hits with no one on, you're still a .300 hitter but you're not producing runs.

To be a good player you have to either drive in runs or score runs. To be a great player you have to do both. A hitter's place in the order nearly always dictates which side of the divide he's on. Rickey Henderson, a leadoff hitter, scores a lot of runs, but he also can hit home runs and drive in runs—that makes him a great player. Brett Butler, a superb leadoff guy, scores a lot of runs but doesn't drive in a lot. He's a very good player.

Great run producers will score 100 *and* drive in 100 runs in the same season. Very few players do that. Reggie Jackson, for example, drove in over 100 runs six times in his career. In only one of those years did he score 100 runs or more. (Hank Aaron, on the other hand, exceeded the 100–100 mark ten times in his career;

currently, Cecil Fielder, a still surprisingly underrated player, has reached the mark three times in three years.)

With pitchers, the same division occurs with earned run average and wins. It doesn't matter what a guy's ERA is, what counts is how many wins he has.

Say a guy goes through a season with a 2.98 ERA but has a losing record. What that tells you is the guy pitches well enough to lose. A pitcher's job is to bring home the bacon, not to hold down his ERA. Jack Morris is the perfect example of what I'm talking about. Morris finished last season with a 4.00+ ERA—but he won 20 games! True, Morris pitched with a world champion team, but so what. All of those winning games were equal, whether the score was 1–0 or 10–9. The point was Morris did what he had to do to win. He has an interesting career stat: He gives up more runs in the first inning than he does in any other inning of a game. That accounts in some measure for a high overall career ERA but it also suggests what kind of battler he is. He stays at it long enough to make sure his team has a chance to win. (Incidentally, I also believe it's harder to win 10–9 games than 1–0 games. In a high-scoring game, a pitcher has to get out of more jams, face more risks of getting blown out; a guy in a 1–0 game nearly always is sailing along with his best stuff.) The great pitchers, like Sandy Koufax and Roger Clemens, may get themselves into bases-loaded-no-out jams but they will, time and again, come back to strike out the side. Don't look at their ERAs, look at how consistently they won.

The numbers game has always been part of baseball and always will be. In the last decade or so, computer specialists have even made a cottage industry out of the most exotic, sophisticated (and often meaningless) kinds of stats. Nothing wrong with that. But the misuse and misinterpretation of numbers, particularly batting average and ERA, have done real damage. Winning is about teams and the stress on numbers, which emphasize purely individual accomplishments, actually gets in the way of team building.

With payroll costs to management rising, with big money opportunities hanging out there every year for players, owners and players alike pay undue attention to stats to determine the value of contracts and arbitration awards. Management, seeking in every way to hold down costs, demands that star pay go only to stars (players with obvious, individual numbers). Players, wanting to get all they can, consciously or unconsciously do what they can to pad their individual numbers so they can have what they need to bargain with. Bunting has gone the way of the Model T; hitting behind a runner to move him up even though it might cost an at-bat (and a batting average point) is part of yesterday's arsenal. Too many starting pitchers look to go no more than six innings, too many relievers ask to be brought in only at the beginning of innings or to work no more than a single inning. The result is that team play has been badly compromised.

A team is supposed to be set up balancing offensive and defensive needs, getting certain types of high-skill specialists up and down the lineup. Traditionally, the positions on the field calling for top defensive players are catcher, the middle infielder, and center field (count the pitcher, too, because if what he throws can't be hit there is no stronger defense than that). The "offensive" positions are the corners of the outfield and infield.

All of that is now out the window. Playing rosters today have been reduced from 25 to 24 players as a cost-saving device. The player who is a jack-of-all trades but master of none will usually find a place for himself on the payroll. Players who can perform adequately in the field but who cannot hit become acceptable major-leaguers. At the positions, that can add up. Where formerly your first and third basemen were supposed to be run producers, today they frequently are guys who slap the ball around. If your big guy plays center field, like Kirby Puckett, the chances are the guys on his flank are not going to be major offensive threats. Run production, not coming from these traditional spots, therefore will be drawn from other places. Not uncommonly today, you have run producers playing second or short. The defense they give their teams is a bonus when they provide it, but it is no longer essential. There are constant compromises made with talent. Even good teams don't stay together long enough to become great teams.

The New York Mets, for example, made all kinds of moves before last season so that nearly everyone gave them a chance to win, myself included. They signed Bobby Bonilla, Brett Saberhagen, and Eddie Murray, but, somehow, it didn't work out. A look at the team on the field tells you why. For good stretches of the season, they had Howard Johnson, a third baseman, in center field; they had a rookie, Todd Hundley, behind the plate; their middle-infield situation was never straightened out (which was why they dropped their second baseman, Willie Randolph, and traded for another shortstop, Tony Fernandez, at season's end). In that crucial diamond within the diamond, going up the middle of the field, the Mets had simply forgotten about the importance of defense.

If compromises are made on defense they are also made on offense. A team's batting order should work in proper firing sequence. Anyone who has played the game knows you put your slugger in the cleanup spot, and you lead off with a guy who gets on a lot and who can run. Unfortunately, too many teams today seem to have stopped right there. Most teams today have lost the sense of what a batting order is all about.

Your second hitter *should* have the ability to hit behind the runner. On our ballclub in Cincinnati, I often hit second. I had power so I could be dropped to the third slot, but I was a guy you wanted hitting second because I could be counted on to pull the ball in the hole, which meant being able to move a runner from first to third. I had some speed, which you also want in a second-place hitter, so I could stay out of double plays. But speed is not the factor hitting ability is. The good second-slot hitters today—Ryne Sandberg, Billy Hatcher, Jeff McKnight, Roberto Kelly, Jay Bell, Greg Gagne, Jeff Blauser—are none of them (Kelly excepted) noted for their speed. On it goes right down the lineup: Your third-place hitter should do a little of everything, he moves runners along, he's a power guy, he scores runs.

For me, perhaps the surest sign that pure baseball thinking may be brain dead is in the way the eighth-place slot is generally used. Today, team after team sends up the weakest of its regulars to hit eighth. There is just no good reason for that. In the National League, especially, you ought to have a guy hitting eighth who has a good chance of getting on because with the pitcher coming up behind him you want to create a chance, in an otherwise dead at-bat, to bunt someone over into scoring position. You just don't put your two worst hitters back to back. If you do, you create almost four rally-killing passes through the day's batting order. On our ballclub, Cesar Geronimo usually hit eighth; on some of those good Dodger teams of the '60s Willie Davis hit eighth; the big Yankee teams of that era sometimes had Clete Boyer in the eighth slot; the Orioles back then had Paul Blair batting eighth. Today, an eighth-place hitter can be a slow-footed catcher like Joe Oliver of the Reds or a low-average, high-strikeout hitter like Mike Pagliarulo of the Twins.

While money has a way of corrupting what happens on the field, it also affects what happens away from the field as well. There is a whole culture built up around it. Money means TV and media, more interviews, more interviewers, more reporters looking for hot stories. It puts more pressure on players. Living here in Oakland, I've seen up close how much pressure players like Jose Canseco and Will Clark have lived with. It is considerably different from when I played. None of us had 900 numbers or reporters trying to figure out how Madonna fit into our lives. With so much dough on the line, newspapers, TV stations, and magazines all fall over themselves trying to hustle the juiciest, most salable stories they can get their hands on. Never mind that none of it has to do with baseball. Baseball players, in turn, rightly or wrongly, pull back into themselves, increasingly cutting themselves off from the public or, worse, asking that they, too, share in the financial rewards of all public appearances. No one side is to blame in this, but everyone is responsible and everyone loses. Doubt and mistrust are the net result. The game is cheapened even as it prospers.

There are obviously players, organizations, and teams that I like very much today. The two best teams in the game—the Jays and the Braves—got to the World Series last season, and the best team won. The Jays have had good management for years. I saw them come of age in the playoffs against the A's, particularly in Game 5 in Oakland where they rallied from a big deficit to beat Dennis Eckersley. The key was in the way they literally got up off the bench and started yelling at Eckersley when he started showboating after a strikeout. In the past, only Kelly Gruber was willing to stand up against that kind of intimidation. With Joe Carter, Dave Winfield, and Roberto Alomar, the Jays were a different group. The talent was always there; last season they found the character.

The Braves, for years, have been producing the best young talent in the National League and were the natural counterparts for the Jays in the Series. They were the better team when they lost to the Twins (who, without Jack Morris, couldn't repeat) and they were every bit as gutsy under pressure as the Jays. Their manager, Bobby Cox, made sure his ballclub never played scared. In the playoff-winning game against the Pirates, he let an unknown player, Francisco Cabrera, swing at a 2–0 pitch with the game on the line even though a walk would have meant allowing the game's tying run to score. The Braves, all along, had the character to go with their talent.

I believe the Jays, the Braves, and possibly the Twins would have been solid competitive teams a generation ago. But the point is that they did not have to face the day-to-day level of play that was around years ago. And then, again, no matter how good these teams are, how long can they stay together?

In Cincinnati, for almost a decade through the 1970s, we had a team that defined baseball greatness.

The records will show that through the '70s, the Reds won more games and more titles than any other team in the majors. We won two championships, back to back, in 1975 and 1976. But we also wound up winning six Western Division titles and four pennants. But beyond those numbers, inherent in them, was just who we were and what we did.

We were a mix of power and speed, pitching and defense. Johnny Bench, Tony Perez, and George Foster provided awesome home-run power; Pete Rose, Ken Griffey, and Dan Driessen hit for average, high average—which meant not only batting titles but run-scoring opportunities; Dave Concepcion and I both could hit for average and for power, and both of us were base stealers, as was Bobby Tolan. We had solid, if not great, starting pitching along with a bullpen second to none. We had four different guys in the pen who could come into a game and close down the other team. Sparky Anderson, our manager, was called "Captain Hook" because of his tendency to quickly remove starting pitchers in games—but that was only because of the strength of our bullpen.

We probably had the best defensive team in history, especially up the middle. Johnny Bench, Davey Concepcion, Cesar Geronimo, and I were all Gold Glove winners for five consecutive seasons beginning in 1973!

I believe we would have been a powerhouse team in any era, but we were ideally suited to the one we played in. We were perfectly matched to the "new" game that was emerging with Astroturf and more spacious stadiums. The wide reaches of Riverfront and other new National League parks allowed us to take fullest advantage of our talents. In that sense we were not only a team of that time but of the future as well. We were the team, more than any other, that put an end to station-to-station baseball, that slow-as-molasses game where runners advanced a base at a time depending almost exclusively on what the guy at bat did.

For this brief period in the seventies, we were the best—and the brightest. We all knew what we had to do to win, and we did it.

A great player is, before anything, someone who can carry a team. Barry Bonds and Kirby Puckett can get hot and lift everyone else for a while. The truly amazing feature of our team was that we

had four different great players who could step up. If one guy
slumped, another carried the load. On a team with a single star,
other players may or may not take to him, their talents may not
complement his. On our team, because there were four of us, four
very different kinds of individuals, there was literally a leader there
for everyone. But take away one and the whole structure suffered.

8

Three Plus One

I complained all winter about being traded. It didn't matter what Harry Walker or anyone else thought. What did matter was that I had to leave my home (my wife, Gloria, was then pregnant with our second child and could not move with me), community work I had started had to be abandoned, and all the years I had put in in Houston, just when I thought there was going to be a payoff, seemed to have gone for naught.

I spent much time feeling sorry for myself. Gloria continued to be cheerful and supportive. I wish that I had been then as thoughtful of her as she was of me. She listened while I talked . . . and talked . . . and talked.

My father ultimately convinced me that being traded might be the best, not the worst, thing that could have happened. He had real baseball smarts. He reminded me that I had been traded to a winner.

"They've traded you to a team that won the pennant just two years ago," he said. "You've been given a tremendous opportunity. You might be just what they need. I don't see how you can even doubt that."

"I'll give it serious thought, I guarantee you that, Pop," I said.

In the weeks it took for me to cool off, I gradually came around to seeing things a little more positively. When I reported for spring training, I may not have been ready for a new life but I was ready to go to work.

What made the transition a little smoother was coming to understand that I was needed on my new club. The Reds had really wanted me. Bit by bit I pieced together the story:

For the better part of a year, the Reds' advance scout, Ray Shore, had been watching me. He was under orders from Bob Howsam, the team's GM, to ascertain not only what kind of player I was but what kind of presence I might be on the team. The Reds were an extremely conservative organization playing in an extremely conservative area and they had rather set ideas about the kinds of guys they wanted. Short hair was in, short tempers and long opinions were not.

The person behind the move was Sparky Anderson. Sparky had come to the Reds in 1970 and had made an immediate impact on the team. In his very first year, the Reds shocked the baseball world by stampeding the Western Division. The Reds finished first that year by 14½ games over the Dodgers, posting the second-best record in the game. The stampede continued in the playoffs with a three-game sweep of the Pirates—but then the team foundered in the World Series, dropping away in five games to the Orioles.

The following year, the Reds slipped back to fourth place and, in Sparky's mind, changes needed to be made. There was not much to do, he reasoned, but there was a missing piece to the puzzle. In his mind, I was that missing piece.

Sparky said, in response to the questions that were raised about my being a possible troublemaker, that all he really cared about was whether or not I could help the team. He knew the Reds, playing on Astroturf, needed to add speed to their attack. I did not have to be a big hitter, there were plenty of those on the team already, he said—all he wanted to know was whether my speed, my defense, my sense of the game would help the ballclub. When Ray Shore filed his report, he had answered those key questions in the affirmative. He had also answered, though that never came out, the question of whether or not I was a troublemaker. Ray wasn't sure, but he didn't think so. On that basis, Sparky and the Reds went ahead. When the deal was finally concluded at the winter meetings that year, Sparky told Bob Howsam that the Reds had just secured the pennant.

For Sparky and the Reds, the deal was anything but easy. To get me, the Reds gave up two extremely popular players, Lee May and Tommy Helms. May, in addition to being an authentic home-run hitter, was a hometown hero; Tommy Helms was then seen as the second coming of Pete Rose. Even though the Astros threw in a few extras like Jack Billingham and Cesar Geronimo in the deal, there were quite a few opinions expressed in Cincinnati that the Reds had given up too much for too little.

For my part, I didn't care what the press or anyone else said. When I turned up in Tampa for spring training that year, I was there just to play ball, to do what I could to help my new team win. I couldn't have cared less that there was a cloud hanging over me about what kind of person I was.

Fitting into an established team was something else, but that also turned out to be a lot easier than it could have been. There were guys on the team I knew pretty well anyway, guys like Pete Rose, who had been something of a friend even before we were teammates.

Pete and I had become friendly because we basically played the same kind of game, hard and smart. Over the years we had both developed a kind of mutual admiration society. We played a game against the Reds in the Astrodome once when Pete went from first to third on a sharp hit to right. Normally, on Astroturf, because the ball gets to the outfielder so quickly, a runner advances only a single base. But Pete, on this play, took an extra base. I realized then that there was something more than hustle and even speed in what he did. He was either foolish or smart as a fox and I suspected the latter. I asked him the next day, standing around the batting cage, about taking the extra base.

"I saw it all the way," he said.

"Whaddaya mean?" I replied.

"You make up your mind in the first step," he said. "There are plenty of faster guys who get caught because they don't make up their mind to go till they get near second base. I never do that."

The more I watched, the more I came to see that Pete went from first to third as good as anyone in the league.

Sometime during the first season that I wore my small glove, Pete asked me about it. He couldn't believe I wore something that small on my hand. He was a second baseman then (another reason we were drawn to each other) and he couldn't see what I got out of a mitt that tiny. He knew about Mazeroski, of course, but prior to a game at Crosley Field, he came up to me as I was warming up on the sidelines and he started needling me.

"I wouldn't want a tiny glove like that on my hand with some of the left-handed batters they've got in this league," he said.

"Yeah, well, I'm doin' all right," I told him.

Pete smiled. "I'll tell ya something I've learned. Willie McCovey? Man, he's after you. He said he took one look at that little glove and then your little body and that was it, he was gonna burn you every time he had the chance."

"Yeah, that's good to know, thanks for telling me."

The next time I saw McCovey, I told him I knew all about his little game, and then, with a laugh, I let him know that he was in greater danger than I was because he played first base, in closer to the batter, and when I hit, I was gonna rip him twice as hard. And I did. I scorched a couple of balls at him during that series. After one especially hard single that went right through him, he just kept laughing as he went about the business of holding me close to the base. The first-base ump, our base coach, their pitcher, all thought we were both nuts.

Horseplay (and horse sense) made things considerably easier for me.

The pressure I was under was more than I cared to acknowledge. I had to establish myself in a place that was new and strange. I came and went with little more than the ballpark and the hotel in my field of view. I lived in a downtown hotel, had my meals there, watched TV, went to bed, got up, went to the ballpark. I was even a little afraid to go out and enjoy myself for an hour or two. Jimmy Wynn, my old Houston roommate and friend, came from Cincinnati and knew the Kentucky side of the Ohio River, where many players dined after games. Jimmy told me the other side of the river was no place for anyone who was black.

"Room, that's Klan country over there and it don't make no difference if you're a big-league ballplayer. Over there, if they don't like your face, you've had it," he said.

One thing I could count on was that Sparky Anderson would see me as a person, not a color. Early in that first season, Sparky Anderson bumped into me in the lobby of a hotel we were staying in. I was wearing a sportsjacket over a T-shirt with a comic zodiac design featuring different sexually suggestive images for each of the twelve signs. Sparky got all over me for carrying myself unprofessionally. After that, I made sure that I was literally the best-dressed guy on the team. Some time after I retired, Sparky told a sportswriter that he never saw me in the same suit of clothes twice. True. That was my conscious choice.

I also, clearly, had this problem of a "bad reputation" on my hands. During that first spring with the Reds, Harry Walker continued to fire away at me—going public with his complaints that I was a troublemaker, a player not likely to take orders from a manager. With no one on our ballclub or in the organization who knew Harry or the situation at Houston well enough to contradict him, I didn't have to be a mindreader to know that it would be up to me to prove him wrong. Harry's intent was both to justify the trade he made and also to do what he could to poison the atmosphere for me on my new team.

Because the Reds were really a solid team already, and because the players there had been through winning campaigns before, I never felt that they looked at me in any way other than as someone who might be able to add to their ballclub. One of the first days of spring training, a group of us were standing by the batting cage, and Pete came over and asked if my accommodations were okay and to let him know if I needed anything at all. I told him everything was fine and he told me to let him know if I had any trouble along the way finding a place in Cincinnati, with anyone in the organization, anything. I reiterated that I was fine, but, once again, that little touch of his helped.

On the other hand, I realized that for all Sparky's words to the contrary, he didn't know that much about me. He had to be worried, even when he was telling the world he wasn't.

The first thing he did, for me and the team, was to have me locker next to Pete Rose. The locker room at Riverfront has long sides of stalls with three lockers at the far end next to a lounge area. Pete and I had two of the three lockers near the lounge. The one between us was always kept empty for our mail, clothes, and bats.

I eventually discovered that this was Sparky's way of making sure that the right kind of baseball atmosphere would be present for me everyday. Because Pete was such a baseball junkie, because his style of play was so aggressive and street smart, because he was so outgoing and talkative, Sparky figured that we would soon be partners, friends and rivals both, totally dedicated to the Reds and to winning.

From the start, our "partnership" became an almost ongoing show where everyone, the media included, was invited. "Pete and Joe's Corner" became a regular feature of pre- and post-game press coverage.

Pete and I spent hours sitting side by side at our lockers talking baseball, going over the fine points of games.

"Joe," Pete asked, with reporters standing around, "how come you take so many pitches?"

"Because I only swing at strikes, Pete."

"What about you, Pete," a reporter jumped in.

"I swing at everything."

"How can you be a bad-ball hitter and a good hitter at the same time?"

Throwing

. . . and working out with the Houston Astros

Finding the right glove with Nellie Fox

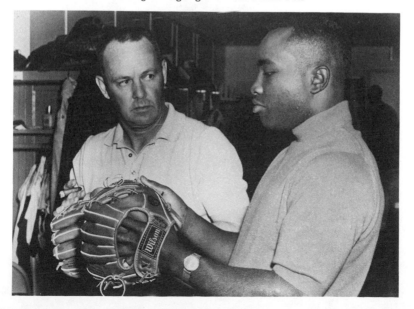

At All-Star Games with Willie Mays

. . . Hank Aaron

. . . Dave Concepcion and
Jimmy Wynn

. . . and Reggie Jackson

It's out of there.

The throw won't make it.

Terry Puhl came in hard, but the play is made. CREDIT: W. F.
SCHILDMAN

New uniforms, but teammates again, at spring training with Pete Rose

Home run against the Dodgers on the last day of the 1982 season

Turning the double play on
Gary Gaetti

My last at bat, a double to left
center

With (*left to right*) my first wife, Gloria, and our daughters, Angela and Lisa

With (*left to right*) Roy Eisenhardt, Sparky Anderson, and my father at the opening of one of my Wendy's Restaurants

With Johnny Bench at the Giants–A's
World Series

. . . Tom Reich

. . . Charlie Sifford and Willie
McCovey

Throwing out the first ball at A's Stadium after my Hall of Fame election

At the Hall of Fame ceremony with Jim Palmer and Commissioner Fay Vincent

My parents' introduction at the Hall of Fame

At the Hall of Fame (*left to right*), my sister Linda, her husband, Billy Taylor, and my sister Patricia

At the Hall of Fame with my oldest daughter, Lisa

. . . and Happy Chandler

At Coors's reception for me at the Hall of Fame with Peter Coors and Swede Johnson

. . . Bill Patterson and Willie Stargell

. . . Bob Howsam and my father

(*Left to right*) Lisa, Gloria, and Angela

With Dr. Jo Geiger and AIM for the Handicapped poster-child Kelly Stichter in 1975 CREDIT: AIM FOR THE HANDICAPPED

With Kelly Stichter in 1988 CREDIT: AIM FOR THE HANDICAPPED

With my second wife, Theresa

Our daughters, Ashley and Kelly

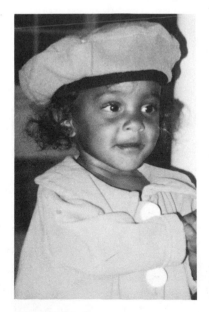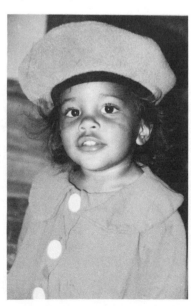

With Stan Musial at the White House for the fiftieth anniversary celebration of Little League

In the Rose Garden with President and Mrs. Bush during the Little League celebration, as Mike Schmidt takes his stance

"Ever heard of Yogi Berra?" Pete said.

"You have to be disciplined to know what pitches you can hit. There are some strikes you shouldn't swing at, and some balls you should," I said.

On the road, Pete and I nearly always went to dinner together. The bond that united us was our fascination with the game.

By the time I learned that Sparky had all the while been behind putting me next to Pete, I already was well aware that the Reds' locker room, like everything else on the team, was carefully designed—to make sure everyone remained focused on baseball. The pitchers all dressed with each other; most of the infielders were side by side, as were the outfielders. But the most obvious pairing were those of Pete and me on one side of the room and Johnny Bench and Tony Perez on the other. As there was a "Pete and Joe's Corner," so there was an Amen pulpit for John and Tony. In most major-league dressing rooms, there is no design whatever in locker assignments. Players will be thrown together by skin color, age, or the inclination of the clubhouse guy. In Sparky's game the team that dressed together played together. And what these assignments told me and everyone else who ventured into the clubhouse was that this was a team built around four leaders—which now included me!

Then Sparky let me know directly that what he wanted from me was special. He called me into his office one day and had me sit down:

"Joe, I want you to understand something," he said. "For as long as you are on this team, until you prove that you're not up to it, I am never going to give you a signal to steal. In fact, I will never give you a sign of any kind. It will be up to you and you alone to determine when and when not to go, when to bunt or not bunt, when to take a pitch or not, you will be the one to put a hit-and-run on. All those years you were in Houston [he was flying by the seat of his pants here], I could see not only how good you were but how smart you were as well. I am turning all that over to you. I will expect you to make the right decisions and I will never question your judgment unless you come to me and tell me you can't handle the pressure."

It was an unheard-of thing. No one else on the ballclub had this freedom. It was such a challenge and such an act of trust. If I had wanted to, I could not have walked away from it. It remained that way throughout my tenure with the Reds, and it worked out well for both the team and me.

Time always creates a haze of romance over eras and teams. That is especially so with memorable teams like the Big Red Machine. It is clear, even to the most skeptical observers, that we fielded a team with all-stars at every position. With Bench, Rose, Perez, and myself, there were four eventual Hall of Fame quality players in our lineup at the same time. But because, in Sparky's words, we put on our pants one leg at a time, same as beggars and presidents, we were always mindful of the problems we had. The Big Red Machine was composed of twenty-five individuals.

There was rivalry and jealousy on our ballclub. And it started right at the top. Shortly after I arrived, it was clear to everyone that Pete and I had become friends. That was no problem. But I didn't feel myself bound to Pete or anyone else. I was finding my way around, wanting to be friendly with anyone who was friendly with me. I was standing around talking to Johnny Bench one day, thinking nothing about it, when, afterwards, another player came up to me and said, "You can't be Pete's and John's friend."

"I can't?" I said. "Why not?"

"You just can't, that's all. On this ballclub you can be friends with one but not with both."

That was stunning to me. I told this player that I treat people the way they treat me; if both of them treat me well, they can both be my friends.

But, as best I could, I kept an eye open after that. I don't think I ever fully appreciated what was involved. At one time, John and Pete had a car dealership together that didn't work. But that was not really the source of friction between them.

The line of division was really a subtle one. John was not a

Cincinnati guy, not a hometown hero. Pete was. He was born and raised in Cincinnati and because he made it all the way to the top, to the big-league Reds, he was the toast of the town, Mr. Cincinnati.

Until John hit town. John was a country boy from Oklahoma, but he had star quality and an easy charm that made people flock to him.

John was a home-run hitter and also one of the game's smartest hitters. He hit under pressure, he had a flair for the dramatic. In the '72 and '76 playoffs, he had big, memorable ninth-inning home runs to help us into the World Series. John commanded a game from his position behind the plate. With his catcher's gear on, he looked like a gladiator. He was just special when he stood behind the plate or at the mound, and everyone in the ballpark knew it. When he came out firing, he didn't look like anybody else. He made the greatest throw I have ever seen a catcher make. It was in the '72 World Series against the A's. Bert Campaneris, a speedster, was on first; our pitcher, Gary Nolan, had a big high leg kick and on this one pitch, threw a slow curveball. Campaneris picked that pitch to run on, got a good jump, and when I went to the bag I held my arms up signaling that there should be no throw. John threw anyway. He put this rifle shot right on the corner of the bag. I went down and caught the ball just as Campaneris's foot hit my glove. Anything John did from anywhere on the field always seemed to have a larger-than-life quality about it.

Then, on top of it all, he had this ease and magnetism about him. John was comfortable in the presence of celebrities and movie stars.

I had a little bit of John's ability to mix with different kinds of people. Before a game at Riverfront one day, I was sitting in the dugout talking to Griffey and Foster. John was sitting down the way. When it was our turn for batting practice, John and I got up to go to the batting cage.

"You're amazing," John said.

"What do you mean?"

"You talk black to the black guys. And you talk white to the white guys."

"Huh?" I was shocked, because I had never noticed this myself.

"Yeah," John said. "Back there with Griffey and Foster it was 'Blood this' and 'Hang with that.' You never talk that way to me."

So I said, "Yo, blood, I'll talk to you like that from now on."

We both laughed. Since then I've thought that there's a serious side to that in sports. Athletes who aren't articulate, who don't talk easily to the press, can quickly be stereotyped as difficult. That happens to black athletes especially, because the stereotype of the black man for many white Americans is "big, black, and hostile." It's frustrating to see a great player and a nice guy like Richie Allen get typecast in just this way, simply because he's quiet and reserved. People who know of Richie Allen, but don't know him, probably bought the press's picture of him as "big, black, and hostile." Those who knew him—his teammates, his manager, Chuck Tanner— knew different.

Pete Rose had none of that ability to talk different ways to different people. Pete was gruffer, funnier, less polished, much more comfortable around everyday kinds of people.

He was a guy who didn't drink or smoke, who went out of his way to be helpful to others, particularly young players. He used his familiarity with Cincinnati to help younger players find apartments, schools for their kids, the whole thing. If you walked down a street with Pete, people would call out to him and he'd not only wave back but the chances are he'd stop and talk. Invariably, they'd have mutual friends, might have gone to the same school together, dated the same girl. When John arrived on the scene in 1968, Pete had been a star for over five years, and he was about to win the first of two consecutive batting titles. Just like that, here came a young guy who could hit home runs with Willie Mays and Hank Aaron, who could drive in runs with anyone, who was also this commanding personality who handled every pitch of a game in a way no other catcher could. From 1968 till I got there in 1972, Pete's popularity had gone from the very heights to somewhere in mid-range. In 1972, he was no longer quite the star he once had been, and for sure it bothered him.

If Pete and John had been the team's twin peaks that would have been one thing, but there was other leadership on the team.

Tony Perez, in every way, was as important a star as we had. I don't know what the Hall of Fame will ever do about him, but no one who has played this game so clearly deserves a place among baseball's best. At the same time, he has remained overlooked.

Tony played for twenty-three years, in six league championships, in five World Series, on two world championship teams. His lifetime average was .279, he hit 379 home runs, drove in 1,652 runs (sixteenth highest to date). In other words, the Big Dog (he got his nickname because when there were men on base he bit the pitcher) was right up there with Joe DiMaggio, Mickey Mantle, Mike Schmidt, Ernie Banks, Rogers Hornsby, and Willie Stargell in producing runs.

But numbers don't begin to tell who this man was and what he meant to our team. Tony came from Cuba. His family still resides there. He had an ability to play ball, and a family that loved him enough to let him go and play even though it meant not seeing him.

When Tony finally came here, he had no guarantee of anything and no money to sustain him. He didn't stick with his first couple of minor-league ballclubs and, on his own, made his way to North Carolina where he was finally able to catch on. He had neither the language abilities nor anything else other than his huge heart and his indestructible belief in himself. Over time, he learned enough English to get along (there was a time when he used to go to a cafeteria and, unable to order in English, just had the same meal put in front of him every day). But along the way, he also happened to pick up enough baseball to get to the major leagues.

Tony was originally a third baseman and actually played a full season at third for the Reds before being switched permanently to first base. (I didn't see too much of him at third that one year, 1967, but he put up some interesting defensive numbers: Tony led the league that year in errors, fielding chances, double plays, and total putouts. In other words, he was quick, got to a lot of balls, had good hands, but was probably not a great thrower—he was, in other words, an ideal first baseman.)

What Doggie did best was win games. I don't know how else to put it. I have never seen a better clutch hitter. There was a tendency among fans to look elsewhere if the tying or winning run was on base. But none of us ever felt cheated if Perez was the guy up there. He was absolutely the one we wanted standing in with two out in the bottom of the ninth. Tony was uncanny in his ability to get that run home. John was more spectacular, Pete was more flamboyant, I was nervier—but Tony was tougher than any of us.

A clutch hitter is a really interesting baseball type. A lot of people tend to look at the numbers, but they are frequently misleading. Clutch hitters may or may not drive in a lot of runs. The most important thing about them is that when it counts, they hit the ball hard more often than other hitters—and there is just no way to statistically measure that.

Tony *always* hit the ball hard when it counted. The reason he was able to do this was because he understood, better than other players, what he had to do in specific situations. How many times do you see sluggers (and Tony was surely one) going up to the plate in a big situation swinging for the fences. It's natural, home runs are expected from these big guys, only that isn't the way a clutch hitter operates. Clutch hitters are perfectly tuned to what must be done to move a runner along—get him home if possible, advance him in any case. I can't emphasize that enough. I've now broadcast hundreds of baseball games, seen any number of bases-loaded situations where guys come up to the plate without having the foggiest idea of what they're supposed to do or how they're supposed to get the runners home.

What a clutch hitter does is make sure he gets a pitch to hit, in every clutch situation. That may or may not result in a hit. But if a hitter is patient enough he will get that pitch and he will then, if he has the talent of a Tony Perez, drive the ball hard almost *every time*.

I loved watching Perez approach the plate in a big situation.

Because I had seen him hit so many times, I could pick up the little bit of difference in the way he stood in when the pressure was on. Coming from the on-deck circle, he had a little spring in his step, something you couldn't quite define that seemed to say to everyone on the field, especially the pitcher, "You can't get me out, I'm gonna hit you hard someplace."

There is a special mentality to hitting in the clutch, it takes a unique type of person—not everyone, not even top hitters, can be one. Remember the '75 World Series? There was Carlton Fisk's home run in Game 6 that is everyone's unforgettable moment. On our ballclub, we tend to also remember the Big Dog's two-run homer off Bill Lee in Game 7 when we were down 3–0 in the sixth inning.

Tony was also a very special person, on the field, in the clubhouse. He was all business, and he was so much fun at the same time. At the beginning of the '72 season, the team got off to a slow start. But Pete and I happened to be hitting well. Before one game, we were, as usual, horsing around, loudly talking about how well we were doing. Suddenly, Tony, in that deep, broken English of his, boomed out:

"You two guys, you think you so great or something?"

I looked up and said, "Yeah, what's your problem?"

"You always talking 'me and you, me and you.'"

"So what? I'm hitting .350, he's hitting .350, what are you hitting?"

"Yeah, okay, the Big Dog's hitting .220, but what place are we in?" (We were in fourth.)

Both Rose and I knew exactly what he was getting at. I tried to wriggle out of it.

"Hey, man, I was just having a private talk."

"Yeah," he said, "it's all private with you two, you don't think about the team. When the Big Dog starts hitting we will go to the top."

Within two weeks we were in first place and, sure enough, Tony came strolling by our lockers.

"Hey," he says, "what place are we in?"

"First place, where we belong."

"Where were we two weeks ago?"

"I can't remember."

"We were in fourth place and you were hitting .350 and Rose was hitting .350."

"Well, I'm still hitting .350," I said.

"Yeah but now the Dog is hitting .280 and look where we are!" He walked off in triumph.

Tony could convert almost any situation to laughter because his heart was so pure, his goals for the team so clear.

We were playing a game in San Diego one night. Rose by then was a left-fielder. On this particular play, there was a hit-and-run on and the Padres' hitter sent a shot to left which Pete somehow caught. Rose didn't have a great arm and he made a high, looping throw back toward first in an effort to double the runner. Perez never saw the ball coming. It was thrown so high, he lost it in the lights! Pete was just steaming. When we got into the dugout he hollered at Tony, "Why the hell didn't you catch the damned ball?"

"Listen, I've been playing first base for twenty years and I never lost a damn ball from no outfielder's throw in the lights before!" he said. Doggie prided himself on his fielding as much as he did his clutch hitting. His explanation was so sincere, so full of genuinely injured feeling, everyone, including Pete, just broke down laughing. Tony stood there, his hands on his hips, looking as though he didn't understand. And then his big sad face slowly melted into a grin no one could resist.

Perez, like Pete, like John, had a single-minded passion for winning. He was a great team player on a team that featured team players. And because he tended to let others get the credit, because he was not as confident in his language skills as native-born speakers, he tended to drop back, asking for neither money nor the recognition that other top stars got. Still, he was a relentless leader who kept things focused even when he was just having fun.

There was one time I came to the ballpark with a fever of 104 degrees. The trainer went to Sparky and told him about it and he immediately scratched me from the lineup even though the game we were about to play was going to be a tough and important one against the Mets, with Jerry Koosman pitching.

After Sparky called me in and told me he was scratching me, I went back to my locker and in front of it were a sleeping bag, all rolled out, a pillow, a glass of water, and two aspirins—with a note which read:

"Take two of these and you'll get over Koosmanitis."

There was only one person in the clubhouse who would have done that and he was doing all he could to keep from laughing. I started yelling at Tony, who only laughed harder. I finally went into Sparky's office and demanded to be put back in the lineup. In fact, it wasn't a demand. I was just crazy.

"I'm playing tonight," I roared at Sparky.

"Oh no you're not," he said.

"Oh yes I am!"

"Oh yes you are!"

It actually went like that, Abbott and Costello or Moe and Curly. Directed by Tony Perez.

I got two hits that night, big hits, and we won a ball game. What the Big Dog knew was not just that I was sick but that I really did want to play. He knew, perhaps even more than Sparky or the staff, a little secret of mine: I hit left-handers better than righties. If I played, Tony thought, we might win. He did what he could, in this situation, as in all others, to help. A temperature of 104? I'd get over it tomorrow.

More than anything, Perez was an intermediary between John and Pete. And when I joined the club so was I. We had a balancing act now. John had Tony, Pete had me. We were a foursome. Sparky not only had us lockering in pairs, he had us hit together. Batting practice on major-league teams is divided into groups of four at the cage. From day one, the unit I hit with included Pete and John and Tony. Whatever rivalry or bad feeling there was on a personal level, the chemistry was there on the baseball side to turn it into something else.

The four of us naturally seemed to take over the clubhouse. It wasn't because we set out to do that but because of who we were. We wanted to be in the center of things, we wanted always to be in the middle of the action just a little more than others.

We used to show up early. Almost invariably, the four of us were the first players in the clubhouse. Sparky, of course, was there ahead of anyone.

By his rule, we had to stop and say hello to him on the way in.

"Hey Sparky, how's it going?"

"Good, Joe. Talked to your father lately?"

"Yeah, he's fine. How's your son, John?"

"Real good, real good."

Pete and I usually beat John and Tony past Sparky's door by a minute or two. In the empty locker room, we slowly settled down near our stalls. There'd be new pieces of fan mail. Pete dealt with his systematically. He turned over the mail to a secretary (he found one for me). He made a point of trying to answer every piece of mail he got (as I eventually did, too).

We cleaned our game bats, which we kept in that middle stall. To anyone peeking in, when we sat there wiping the different bats with alcohol until all the marks were erased, it might have seemed we were into another of those weird baseball superstitions. Not so. Each day we tried to keep our bats clean so that when we hit, we would be able to preserve the telltale marks that let us know where, precisely, we had made contact the day before.

When John and Tony were seated by their lockers, the back-and-forth would eventually get going. It was nearly always friendly—at the outset. Who's pitching tonight? Oh, Don Sutton.

John: "Gotta watch out for him."

Pete: "I hit him pretty good."

John: "Watch the way he takes his glove back. He takes the glove back farther when he throws the curve than he does with the fastball."

Me: "John, better be alive when Grote's running. When the pitcher bunted last time, I circled in behind him and we could have picked him off."

But the banter could warm up pretty quickly—and initially I was surprised by it.

In the very first weeks of the '72 season, we went up against Tom Seaver. Before the game, John came to me and told me the team had trouble hitting him.

"Can you hit a fastball?" he asked.

"I can hit anyone's fastball, Koufax, Seaver, anyone," I replied.

"Yeah? Good luck," John said.

In my first at-bat, I fouled off Seaver's first pitch. He then blew two fastballs right past me. My bat was a yard behind each one. When I went back to the dugout, John yelled at me,

"You said you liked fastballs, what happened?"

"I like ice cream, too, but not a gallon at a time!"

So it began. A couple of years later, there was another Seaver game. Now I was one of the boys, one of the four. In the clubhouse, I started in, loudly, to Pete:

"Well, Pete, I guess we're not going to get anything out of the big fellas down there today, so it's up to you and me."

John: "Who the hell are you talking about?"

Me: "Oh, we weren't talking to you."

Pete: "I guess we'll have to provide the power today."

Me: "For sure we won't get anything from the three and four slots."

Tony: "You check us out after the game, big mouth."

Perez, as usual, was right. John and Tony ripped Seaver that day. Pete and I did nothing, except laugh, certain that we had inspired the big guys to hit that day.

People who came into the Reds' clubhouse for the first time could easily be put off by the way we went at each other. Lew Fonseca, who briefly joined the ballclub at the end of 1974 as an assistant hitting coach, thought we would wind up tearing each other apart. Nothing could have been further from the truth. We were acutely conscious of how to keep our natural, competitive rivalry within bounds. For example, we had two Ping Pong tables in the clubhouse. Because I was an unusually good player (I had won an amateur citywide championship years before in Oakland), Pete, whose temper got the best of him when he lost, never played me. We had player-brackets for Ping Pong, and Pete and I were always in different ones.

We were always there for each other. That could be funny or serious, depending. One day in San Diego, Padres second baseman Tito Fuentes and I seemed to be having a competition in errors. He'd make an error, then I'd make one. According to the record books I'm one of the top fifteen fielders at my position in the history of baseball, but you couldn't tell it that day. I had three errors by the third inning, one in the first and two in the third, and after the bottom half of the inning Tito also had three. I was getting ready to take the field again, and I heard footsteps coming down the dugout behind me. When I turned around, there were Rose and Bench with a big garbage can. They'd put a sign on the can, "Joe Morgan's new glove." They told me, "Take this out there with you, Joe. You can't miss with this." The worst thing about it was that Tito bailed on me and didn't play after the third inning. So I had to take the field with the weight of three errors all by myself. I've been in a lot of big games, in what most people would call pressure situations, but honestly that was as much pressure as I've ever felt on a baseball field.

Another time, we had a July 3rd night game against the Giants which started at 10:30 because of rain and ran till two in the morning. We then had to be back at nine for a special July 4th morning game. I was really bone tired and ill-tempered to be playing at what seemed like the crack of dawn, right on the heels of that long night game. In my first at-bat against John Montefusco, I struck out—and was furious with myself for letting him get the better of me. Montefusco was a guy who was always popping off, always doing things to show up other players.

When I got back to the bench, instead of replacing my bat in the rack and telling myself I would get him next time, I went wild, pulling as many bats from the rack as I could and flinging them out on the field. The guys on the bench, the Giants' players, even the umpires all were looking over at me like I had lost it. No doubt I had. Then Pete came over to me.

"Hey, I know you're pissed and so am I," he said, "but if you go o for 4 today that means you have to get 3 for 4 tomorrow just to make it up, so you better stay focused enough to get your hit today, because it'll make it a hell of a lot easier tomorrow. I don't feel like playing today either, but you can't give in to that."

What Pete said made such perfect sense, it helped me not only then but through the rest of my career, whenever I felt like giving in to aches and pains and temperament on the field. Before anything, all of us had a job to do to help our team win ball games. That was the understanding the four of us mutually shared, the secret strength that was more powerful than horseplay, ego, or personal rivalry.

9

Seasoning

When I joined the Reds in 1972, we were not favored to win the pennant. The year before, the team had finished fourth in the division. The Giants and the Dodgers were the pre-season favorites of most writers.

But there were some remarkable changes about to take place in the National League.

Nineteen games into the season, the Giants traded Willie Mays to the Mets. True, the Giants still had Willie McCovey and Bobby Bonds. Dave Kingman, a very underrated but very productive ball-player, was back. So was Juan Marichal along with a bunch of talented young pitchers including Ron Bryant. Never heard of him? He wound up winning 24 games for the Giants one year and was going great—until he hurt his arm.

But the loss of Mays, even though age had clearly caught up with him, was incalculable because of his leadership. He was the Big Four all rolled into one. In his last years in San Francisco, Willie was actually the unofficial manager of his team no matter who was nominally in charge. He positioned the different players in the field, when he wanted lineup changes they were nearly always made, it was common knowledge in the dugouts around the league that

Giant managers usually consulted Willie before they made moves of any kind.

The Dodgers, too, lost a leader that year, Maury Wills. The record books show that Wills was a great base stealer. He was so much more. He was a pioneer, a guy who almost single-handedly was responsible for the revolution in playing style that came to the game during the 1960s, and that marked the kind of play the Big Red Machine would perfect during the years that followed.

It takes a while for a team to find its level. I knew we were going to be good in spring training because I knew how good the Reds had been till then. But still, in that shaking-out period, I was busier adjusting to my new surroundings, feeling out the different guys I would be playing with, than thinking about what my particular role on the ballclub would be.

My middle infield partner then and for the entire time I was in Cincinnati was Davey Concepcion. Davey was a player I did not take to at first. I actually believed then that he should not have been playing every day. He made too many mistakes, he didn't hit, it was hard to see why Sparky stayed with him. But he did, obviously because he knew what he might eventually get from him.

Around the clubhouse, it was impossible to tell what kind of player Davey might be. He was probably the quietest guy on the team. He lockered across the way from Bench and Perez, next to Denis Menke, the likeable and sure-handed third baseman who came over from Houston with me in the same trade and who Sparky hoped might engage Davey.

But Davey seemed to be attached to no one. If you looked at the team in terms of leadership, no one would have put Davey up there alongside the Big Four. Davey, more than any guy on the club, didn't seem to fit.

Larry Bowa, who was statistically the surest-handed shortstop around then, used to call Davey "Elmer." "Why do you call me that?" Davey asked him one day. "Because I keep seeing 'E Concepcion' in the box score every day. So I figure the 'E' must stand for Elmer."

Pete regularly referred to Davey as Bozo—as in Bozo the Clown—because while Davey was quiet he was also funny and unpredictable. Whenever we hit a losing streak, Davey was sure to do something silly. One time, in the '72 season, we had been going badly and we lost an especially tough game to the Dodgers at home. When we got back to the clubhouse, Davey, instead of undressing and going off to shower, suddenly made this noise—like a cry or a muffled scream—and headed across the locker room to the big commercial laundry dryer located in an equipment area. He opened the door and said, " I cannot stand no losing no more." He climbed in and one of our pitchers, Clay Carroll, walked over and threw the switch. Like a load of soiled clothes, Davey went spinning around and around. He got out looking like he felt happy. Maybe he was. He took other trips in the laundry dryer after that.

What wasn't so funny was that it took a while for Davey to blossom. As he tended to keep to himself in the locker room, he sometimes seemed to be unaware that what he did on the field affected others. There was one game where he just wasn't in position on a relay throw, another where he was late in covering second on a steal, another where he either didn't see or ignored a take sign. He always seemed to do things that irritated Sparky or that got on the nerves of his teammates. His play would get lackadaisical or he'd lose concentration. Whatever it was, it stood in the way of his ability.

But Davey, from the start, wanted to be thought of as a star. Seemingly out of nowhere, he'd stop and actually ask teammates if they thought he was a star. Invariably, his teammates put him down:

"Rose and Bench and Perez and Morgan are stars, you're not!"

Davey sometimes tried to get into the back-and-forth between the four of us and it just wouldn't work. We'd be yelling and screaming about taking a pitcher deep and Davey would suddenly pipe up:

"I hit this guy better than any of you."

We'd look at him. Pete, deadpan, brushed him off.

"Hey, Bozo, can't you see we're talking."

But his lackadaisical play was no laughing matter. In one game, early that year, Davey hit a routine grounder to the infield and jogged down to first. Everyone in the dugout was hollering at him, "Run the ball out! Run the ball out!" On our ballclub, *everyone* ran out ground balls. I went over to Davey and screamed at him when he came back to the bench:

"You're never gonna be a star. You think you're a star, that's why you didn't run, but you're not a star and you never will be!"

"Hey, whaddaya mean I'm no star, I'm a big star like you."

"No you're not, you don't act like a star. You gotta act like a star if you want to be a star."

"How do I act like a star?"

"Run the damn ball out, that's how."

I think Davey thought he was being teased again, but I was angry. And in the silence that followed, I think he finally caught on.

Davey, of course, eventually accepted the notion that he had to put out to become a star—and he did. He became the best defensive shortstop in the game until Ozzie Smith came along, a guy who could hit well and hit for power.

Anyway, we started as middle infield partners in that first spring and our work together, contrary to the popular notion that double-play combos get what they need from each other in just days, improved over time.

Beginning that spring, we established a kind of routine with each other. We spent hours every day taking ground balls, working double-play throws, learning each other's footwork around the bag. There were days we put aside just to work on double plays. No hitting that day, no work on anything else but the double play. When the season came, we always made sure that we took infield together. We learned each other's moves perfectly so that not only were we able to anticipate what the other was going to do, we could also take the kind of liberties that other players could not. For example, during my time in Cincinnati, I was able, largely because I knew Davey's moves as well as I did, to pick up a double-play grounder and flip it sideways toward the bag without having to pivot. So far as I know, I was the first second baseman to do that. I kept working on the move so that after a while I could do it from a considerable distance, as far over as the second-base hole. The fraction of a second saved meant a higher chance of completing a double play.

What made Davey so exceptional was his concentration in the field and his agility. Because of him, I became a better player, my moves became sharper, surer. We had the same rhythm, the same quickness (many double-play combos don't have that—Jose Lind, one of the best of today's second basemen, had all kinds of trouble because his quickness clashed with the relative slowness of his Pirate middle infield partner, Jay Bell). I was able, ultimately, to position myself farther right, toward first base, because I knew exactly how much ground Davey was able to cover. I give him a big assist in the five Gold Gloves I won and in my establishing a record consecutive errorless game streak of 91 in 1977–1978 (broken in 1990 by Ryne Sandberg).

Davey may or may not have been the star he thought he was, but when I think of someone like George Foster, then a young player who had just joined the club the year before, I am reinforced in the sense of just how tenuous and difficult the term "star" is.

George, for a while, was the game's premier home-run hitter. During the season (1977) when he hit 52 homers, he didn't hit them all in bunches, the way many sluggers seem to. He hit them day after day, with a kind of monotony that simply had to be terrifying to the opposition. There seemed to be no limit to what he could do with his power, and yet the key to what he did was being able to lose himself in the team he was playing for.

George was a very quiet guy—quiet and funny. There was one time George was accused of corking his bat. He had had a particularly good game against the Phillies and afterwards, Danny Ozark, the Phils' manager, told one of the writers that the reason Foster was hitting for such power was because he cheated. The writer, hot to pursue a lead, quickly came over to our dressing room and confronted George. I happened to be standing next to him at the time.

"Danny Ozark just told me that you cork your bat, George. Do you have any comment?" the writer asked.

"I don't cork my bat, I cork my arm," George said, softly. The writer, scribbling furiously, did a double-take. He looked up from his pad and broke out laughing.

Because George had the freedom to stay back and let others on the team lead, because he had the room to just do his job, he became a simply awesome hitter in his time with the Reds.

He was a major disappointment when he moved on to New York in a 1982 trade. The Mets and all of New York looked to George to be *the* big man on the ballclub. They had confused his ability with an ability to lead, which he really did not have.

It takes a very special type of personality to be a team leader. Most people outside the locker room (including people in the front office) don't fully appreciate that.

The most common misconception is that a leader has to be loud and aggressive, willing to put himself forward. This is not so. All the noise and self-promotion in the world will not induce others to follow someone else's lead. No one followed Pete, John, Tony, or me because we carried on a loud vaudeville routine in the locker room. The only criterion for team leadership is the sense of absolute trust others have in a teammate that he will *always* put the team before himself, that everything he does on the field will clearly have the objective of winning in mind.

When all of us left and George stayed on in Cincinnati, he was a star in his own right and could do his own thing anyway, but when he went to New York and he suddenly had pressure on him to be the second coming of Babe Ruth he just couldn't handle it.

George wasn't a great base runner, he wasn't especially good defensively, but he could hit. He could hit for average (which surprised some people) and, most of all, he could hit that long ball the way few players in the game could.

But George's personality just didn't fit the role of superstar. He was a nice guy wanting to do nice things—hit home runs. And New York wouldn't let him. I think of a player like Reggie Jackson alongside George, and there was a guy who wanted the stage that New York provided, who thrived on the glitz and the controversy, who used it to vault himself into the Hall of Fame. I believe if George had stayed in Cincinnati he might have put up the sort of numbers that would have led him to the Hall of Fame, too.

The other side of the coin on our ballclub was probably Bobby Tolan, a guy I became close to in that first year. If anyone was a rebel on our ballclub it was Bobby. He grew a beard once, in open defiance of a standing rule against facial hair of any kind. He didn't care about fines, threats of trades, any of that. When the team suspended him, he went to the Players Association and filed a grievance, which he won because there were no league rules that said anything about mustaches and beards.

Early in the year, Sparky asked me to room with Bobby on the road. Players then commonly got out of rooming with one another by personally making up the difference between a single and a double in hotels. (Today, singles, at no extra charge, are the rule.) I reluctantly agreed to Sparky's request. He wanted to see if I could help straighten Bobby out.

I liked Bobby a lot, didn't find him to be particularly "difficult." I found it easy to socialize with him (in Houston, I introduced him to his future wife). But it was clear to me that Bobby was ill at ease with almost every aspect of life on the Reds, from the squeaky clean conservatism of the front office to what he felt was favoritism among fans and the media.

In one game, Bobby got a key two-out hit to tie the score. The winning hit was subsequently delivered by John. The papers the next day were full of Bench's heroics, barely mentioning Bobby. He carped about it.

"Just look at that shit," Bobby said, holding up a Cincinnati newspaper with headlines about Bench's game-winner.

"Yeah," I said, trying to make light of it, "he makes better copy than you."

"That's bullshit, they should report what any player on this ball-club does."

"Listen," I finally said, "he's your teammate, why don't you think about it that way?"

That ended it—for then.

We did not immediately jell as a team. Long before the Big Dog started doing his thing, we lost something like 14 of our first 18 games. On opening day in Cincinnati, I remember (all too well) there was a snowstorm. I woke up that morning, looked out the window, saw the snow coming down, told myself, "Well, no ball game today," and promptly went back to sleep. Around noon the phone rang and a team official asked where I was. I looked at the winter wonderland outside and said that I was in bed. What did I know about weather forecasts—or Zamboni machines.

"Get down here right now—we start in one hour!"

Needless to say, I flew from that point on—but it was no way for a championship season to begin.

When a team gets off to a start like ours did in 1972, it can knock things out of synch for a long time. The person I credit most for getting us turned around is Sparky.

There were managers in the game, before and afterwards, who were better strategists. Gene Mauch and Earl Weaver, between them, could produce multi-volumed encyclopedias on the "inside" game. Although Sparky knew what buttons to press, his great ability was to keep twenty-five players focused on the single goal of winning.

At the bottom of a losing streak—I don't remember the precise count in the standings but we had been dragging for a month and were in last place—Sparky came through the clubhouse after a losing game and told us we would win a pennant that year. Simple. The way he said it made it seem like fact, not opinion.

Sparky had a unique and wonderful ability to take the pressure off while at the same time keeping us at it. There was discipline, there were rules that Sparky cared about and enforced, but in such a way that life became easier, not harder.

"I don't care what you guys do behind closed doors," he said once, "so long as what you do does not embarrass the Reds." That was his yardstick: everything for the team and everything for the player, provided that it did not get in the way. In all the time I was in Cincinnati, I saw Sparky blow up only once: when a player anonymously badmouthed another player in the press. He did not launch a witch hunt to find out who the loose-lipped player was but instead came to all of us, in a rage:

"I want to tell ya something," he said, shaking a newspaper in the air. "Anytime I catch a player criticizing another player on this team, that player is gonna be going someplace else. And one more thing: If you ever go out and say something to the press, at least have the guts to put your name on it."

Sparky came down, when he had to, on big-name and no-name players alike. When one reserve player complained that the stars on the team got preferential treatment, Sparky shot back:

"You're damn right they do and don't expect me to treat you the same. When you contribute to the team what they do then you'll get the same kind of consideration."

On the other hand, Sparky never was afraid to let one of his stars know what he thought. I had a tendency to be moody, to sometimes pull back into myself. He jumped all over me if he saw that I was in a funk around the ballpark. He got on Pete for womanizing because it was out in the open and an embarrassment to the club and to the players' wives. He got on Johnny Bench because John was reluctant to sign autographs: "You sign autographs because the fans are the lifeblood of this game and don't you ever forget it," he said. That struck home with John. Not only did he sign autographs graciously, he took the time to do it right. A lot of players will just scrawl an initial and a blur. John made his autograph legible.

I was a scrawler myself at first, until John stopped me after I had just signed an autograph that was more a scratch on the ball than a name.

"Why do you do that?" he asked. "You have good handwriting. I've seen you sign letters and checks as clear as anything."

"I'm in a hurry," I said defensively.

"You shouldn't be in a hurry. Someone wants that to read it."

I knew he was right, and ever since I've signed autographs in my best handwriting. It just goes to show you what an effect Sparky had on us as people, not just players. The Reds liked Sparky, although sometimes we showed it in odd ways.

A few years before I joined the Reds, the team was on a road trip flying from Los Angeles to Houston, where the Astros' pitching regularly took it out of the Reds' lineup. Lee May got into his attaché case on the plane ride and as they approached Houston he said, "We ought to phone these fucking games in and go on home to Cincinnati." When Sparky took exception to that as unprofessional, Lee piped up, "Aw, what do you know? You're just a minor-league motherfucker." And that became Sparky's nickname.

Sparky had played ten years in the minors, before making it to the big leagues for just a single season. So "Minor-League Motherfucker" might seem a cruel nickname. But we used it affectionately (and unofficially, without ever telling the media), because to us it said that Sparky would challenge anyone any time he felt he was in the right.

Incidentally, the nickname "Sparky" stems from the same source. During one of the years he played in double-A, Sparky—"George" then—regularly got into fights with umpires and opposing players. The fights roused his mates, who got around to the nickname "Sparky" because he was the spark that got the team going.

Sparky was able to chew players out, to speak his mind, because he came on like everybody's Uncle Charlie. When Sparky asked about your family or just said "How ya doin'?" to someone, you knew he meant it. He was just that way.

For me, personally, the most impressive thing about Sparky was that he was one of the only people I've ever met who was truly color-blind. He was born and raised in a small town in South Dakota. Maybe because of his humble origins or because his own playing career was so modest, he always dealt with people by what they were inside. He used to tell me that if I walked into a room and there were twenty-five white people and twenty-five black people there I'd only see fifty people. The same was true with him. He never had to make a show of his friendship with black people or white people, because friendship came naturally to him. Sparky really was living proof that it was possible to judge a man not by the color of his skin but by the content of his character.

There's a part of me that believes Sparky was too decent a man, had too much class, to be a manager. On our first road trip to San Diego that year, we were in a scoreless game in the eighth inning when we suddenly exploded, batting all the way around. When I came up for the second time, the pitcher promptly drilled me. Clay Carroll, our pitcher, came over to me before the next half inning started and said, "Joe, don't worry, I'll get him for ya."

Well, Sparky overheard the remark and jumped in: "Hey, Hawk, you don't do that on this club, you understand, you just leave it alone." Now I was upset. I understood Sparky's desire to play by the rules but there were these unwritten rules, too.

After the game, Pete told me a story about a game we had the year before against Steve Carlton. Johnny Bench, that day, hit three homers off Carlton, and after the third, Carlton drilled Lee May, who was hitting just behind Bench. Wayne Simpson was pitching for the Reds and Sparky immediately came over to him on the bench and told him he wanted to make sure he understood there was to be no retaliation. "If you hit him," Sparky was supposed to have said, "I'm gonna fine you $500. I don't do that, I don't throw at people. Because they don't have any class doesn't mean we're gonna play that way."

Well, Simpson went out and as soon as Carlton came up he promptly nailed him. He came in to the bench and Sparky was screaming and yelling at him. Wayne had his answer all ready for Sparky: "Hey, Skip, the ball got away. You know I'm wild." And that part of it was true. Wayne Simpson was a pitcher who had big problems finding the plate. Sparky had no choice but to go along.

But not this time. When we got back to Cincinnati the next day,

I immediately went to Sparky's office and told him that I did not believe in playing under the kinds of restraints he imposed the day before and that I thought it was wrong.

"That's my way of playing, Joe."

"I don't care if that's your way of playing," I said, as sharply as I could, "you can't do that. The guys don't like it and won't go along with it."

"I understand they don't like it but I can't play the game differently." I think Sparky understood that we were going to do what we felt we had to do out on the field. I could see his expression grow kind of sad but there was nothing I could do about that.

"You can't be a good team and let people intimidate you," I said. "We're the ones who are supposed to intimidate the other guys. We're the Big Red Machine, not the other teams."

After that, we did what we had to do. Our pitchers took the liberties they knew they had to take, and Sparky, although his feelings over time, and not very happily, did change, kept silent. I wish it could have been different—but how could it?

We caught on soon enough, not because our pitchers drilled batters, but because we came together as a team. We came together under, not above, Sparky's leadership. He kept us pointed in the same direction by letting us play, by letting us have fun winning.

We lost a tough game one day. We were all feeling down, glum and silent. Sparky, Uncle Charlie, just waved it off.

"Look, you guys don't have anything to worry about. When you lose it's my fault, and I will always know that when we win it's because of what you guys did," he said to no one in particular but to everyone within earshot.

Sparky *always* was able to take the pressure off because he instinctively knew how to do it.

And so, well before the All-Star break that year, we were on our way, headed to what we all believed was going to be a world championship. It was strange seeing the way we just got stronger and stronger. It wasn't about finding talent that we didn't know was there. It was more about seasoning, different elements and personalities coming together.

There is an attitude that a powerhouse team gets (and we surely had it) that can be mistaken for cockiness. It is not that. When we walked out on the field, we *expected* to win. Most teams go out *hoping* to win. There is a difference. There were many times, I know, we won *before* the first pitch was ever thrown because other teams were that intimidated.

Alone among all the teams we faced, only one—the Pittsburgh Pirates—gave us anything like pause. They were loaded with big-time, big-game hitters, Clemente, Stargell, Al Oliver, Richie Hebner, Manny Sanguillen. They had a pitching staff that could give any team trouble. They took the N.L. East by 11 games in '72, while we won the West by 10½. Playing them for the pennant was what baseball was all about.

In my first playoff at-bat ever, I homered off Steve Blass to give us a 1–0 lead, which we promptly lost in the bottom of the first. The Pirates rallied for three runs then, and got two more on an Al Oliver homer in the fifth as they went on to win, 5–1. This opening game loss was doubly tough because we had used up our best pitcher, Don Gullett. With the league championship series in those days limited to five games, the Pirates were well on their way.

We took the second game, though, coming out strong in the first inning with four runs and then holding on to win 5–3. Just like that, we had accomplished what we wanted, a split in Pittsburgh. The best two out of three for the pennant would now take place in our park.

But the Pirates quickly regained the edge, winning Game 3 3–2, on an eighth-inning single by Manny Sanguillen. We tied the series with a 7–1 blowout. But in this game there was a real price to pay. Running out a ground ball in the seventh inning, I hit the first-base bag and severely injured my heel. Initially, I didn't know quite how badly I had hurt it because I was able to walk on it for a while. But by the time I got back to the clubhouse, even with immediate icing, it was clear that I no longer had the use of that foot. It was all I could do to leave the park unassisted.

I iced the injury all night. The pain was such that nothing quieted it and that meant I couldn't sleep. The following morning, early, I returned to the park, the fifth and final game ahead of us, the likelihood of my playing all but nil.

The team doctor, examining my foot, told me not to play, not to risk further damage. But I could not accept that. I told him I had to play, I was needed, I had to go out there if only for a couple of innings. So we decided then to inject my heel with novocaine, an extremely tricky thing to do because deadening pain is really a way of losing the only reliable monitor one has with an injury.

The doctor injected the area, then taped the entire ankle so that I was able, if I stayed up on my toes, to move around on both feet. Around ten in the morning, long before the Pirates showed up, I went out and tried all those little things I would need to do in order to play. I found that I could just barely get by—but that was enough.

I stayed in the clubhouse and in the dugout. I did not take batting practice or fielding practice. At the same time that I was shielding my injury I was masking it from the Pirates. In a final game, a crucial game of any kind, each side looks for any advantage it can get. The loss of a single player can certainly mean a lift to the other side— not necessarily because that player, for one game, is irreplacable, but because the psychological edge given to the other side can be just enough to change things.

About thirty minutes before game time, I had the foot injected again and I went out to play. Fortunately for me, no balls came my way, and I did not have any hits to run out. We were 3–1 down in the eighth inning, when Geronimo hit a homer to close the gap to 3–2.

Going into the last of the ninth inning the Pirates had gotten a superb game out of Steve Blass. He had pitched into the eighth inning when he was replaced by Ramon Hernandez, who in turn was replaced, at the start of the ninth, by Dave Giusti, the Pirate closer.

Giusti was a former teammate of mine at Houston and was one of the top relievers in baseball at the time. His best pitch was a palmball. He had a great change off his fastball so it was really hard to hit him. He was the perfect pitcher to use on power hitters who were all too likely to surrender any advantage they had by trying to pull the ball.

Johnny Bench was the leadoff hitter for us in the inning. In this situation, down by a run, needing a long one to tie, it would have been not only natural but expected for John to try and jerk one out. Before he went to the plate, he told me what he was going to do or, rather, what he was not going to do. He had no thought of trying to pull Giusti, he said, he was going to take him to right field. By doing that, he was going to give himself the chance to wait on the pitch, to not overcommit himself.

Bench then, incredibly, homered to right center field—tying the game. The fans saw the heroics; we saw that, but also the smarts that allowed him to hit the ball out. Johnny Bench could have hit 30, 40 home runs every year if he had wanted to, if he had played strictly for his own numbers.

With that homer, we all knew what was coming. We were going to win the pennant, just as Sparky had promised.

The Big Dog followed with a single, Denis Menke followed with another hit. Giusti was out of the game, Bob Moose was in. Moose uncorked a wild pitch, and we were in. To date, it was the biggest thrill I had had on a baseball field.

The work of that first season, however, was not yet done. There was a world championship still to win, and when we sat around that evening and through the following day, we still did not know who we were going to play.

The Detroit Tigers and the Oakland A's were locked in a five-game series of their own, the last game coming up, the day following our final game, in Detroit. The extra day gave my foot more time to heal and I welcomed that but there was more going on.

Professional ballplayers all make a show of saying they don't care who they face in the World Series. I was pulling for the A's because I wanted to play in my hometown. When the A's won the next day, 2–1, I couldn't have been more pleased. In retrospect, I could have done without the distraction of so many excited friends and family members all wanting time, and tickets, when what I needed most was to heal and to stay focused.

We ran into trouble immediately in this Series. We lost the opening game in Cincinnati when Gene Tenace, a reserve catcher who had hit five home runs all year, homered in his first two times up, to lead the A's to a 3–2 win.

We dropped the the next game, too, this time 2–1. The A's were playing without Reggie Jackson, who had injured a leg in the league championship series, so these wins had to have given them a tremendous boost. They were halfway home—and now they were going home. Two wins in three games was not too much for them to expect.

On the other hand, we still expected to win. If we had been down by three games, we would have felt the same. We were the Big Red Machine. So long as there were games to play, we thought of ourselves as favorites.

On the plane to Oakland there was a new wrinkle. The media, always starved for good stories, discovered that the reason I hadn't yet gotten a hit in the Series had nothing to do with my heel (still sore but functional) but because the pressure was getting to me. A story out of Cincinnati, picked up nationally, quoted Bobby Tolan as saying that the reason I wasn't doing well was that I had never been in a World Series before and just couldn't take the heat.

Three writers accompanying us on the flight to Oakland came back and asked me about it. That was the first I had heard of the story. I shrugged it off. Actually, Bobby and I were sitting there together playing cards and his response must have been even more puzzling than mine: He didn't know what story these writers were referring to.

When the reporters left, we pieced together what had actually happened. Yes, there had been an interview. But Bobby had never said anything about pressure, only that I happened to be playing in my first World Series. All the rest, analyzing the state of my psyche, had been supplied by the writer.

It was a media tempest in a teapot but because it raised the question of Bobby Tolan once again undermining unity on our ballclub, we worked out a way of demonstrating for public consumption that there was absolutely no trouble between us.

We decided that we'd have a special greeting for each other when we were introduced in pre-game ceremonies, one that our teammates as well as people in the stands could see. He was hitting third that day, I was hitting second. So when he was introduced he came running out and I met him about two feet in front of the foul line and I gave him a hug, my way of saying Bobby was my friend and the Reds were okay.

In fact we were okay, but we needed a spectacular game from Jack Billingham to prove it. In front of a full house of screaming A's partisans, we won 1–0, eking out that lone run in the seventh inning. The Big Dog singled to open the inning, was sacrificed to second, and scored on a single.

The following day, though, everything fell apart. There are key games in any Series. For us, it was clearly Game 4. We led it 2–1 in the ninth inning when the A's put together four consecutive singles, including three straight pinch hits, for two runs, the ball game, and a seemingly insurmountable Series lead.

The odd part was that even though we lost and were now down 3–1 with yet another game to play in Oakland, the mood on the club was anything but despondent. We still knew we were the better team and that, therefore, no matter what anyone else said, the odds were really with us. It certainly did not require anyone to lecture us about the penalties of losing another game. What we understood was that if we played as we were capable, we would win. All we had to do was stay focused.

The A's started Catfish Hunter in what they hoped was the last game. We got a run in the first off him but then, in the bottom of the second, Gene Tenace hit one out with two men on. The A's had a 3–1 lead which became a 4–2 lead going into the fifth inning. In my second time at bat, I drew a walk. I still had not gotten a hit in the Series but there was a difference for me now. My foot was much better. In this situation, I was determined to steal and get myself into scoring position.

The pitch I broke on was one Bobby Tolan decided to go after. He lined a hit to right field. I had gotten such a good jump that I was almost at second base when the ball was hit. Because there would have been no chance for me to get back to first if a catch was made I just kept going. When I got to third, Alex Grammas was waving me home. I wound up scoring on a routine single to right!

I heard the play rebroadcast sometime later and it was funny listening to Curt Gowdey's call:

"Morgan's going . . . and there's a base hit to right field, he's going to third, and the throw comes back in . . . and he scored!"

A play like that gave me as much satisfaction, maybe more, than if I had homered or driven in a run with a hit. The result was the same, a run scored, but the lift that came was different. Everyone in the dugout got excited. It was like we had come alive and sensed that we were going to come back and win.

We tied the game in the eighth on a similar play. I walked, broke for second on a steal, Bobby Tolan lined a long single to right center field, and I scored. The hit this time was not a routine single so the play was less spectacular, but it was the tying run, late in the ball game.

We went ahead with a single run in the top of the ninth and then the A's came back, once again, in the bottom half of the inning. Tenace led the inning with a walk, was replaced by a pinch runner, Blue Moon Odom, who, with one out, went to third on a single. The A's had the tying and winning runs on with Bert Campaneris, a good, solid contact hitter, coming up.

Campy lifted a high twisting foul down the right-field line behind first base. Perez and I converged on the ball and I didn't like the way Tony was positioning himself so I called him off, knowing that that would most likely induce the runner on third to try and score. The scouting report on me was that I had a weak arm which should be tested whenever possible.

I caught the ball in good position, I thought. But because it had been raining in the area for the past couple of days, the ground in foul territory was especially slippery—and my feet went out from under me. I put my hands out immediately so that I would be able to bounce up from the turf as quickly as possible. I then jumped up and threw a strike home. John, who had totally blocked the plate, caught the ball, swept down with the tag in one motion, and Blue Moon and the A's were out of Game 5!

I have had many thrills in my career but this one ranks among the very best just because I was able to help win a game without ever having gotten a hit. We were all excited because winning also meant we were going home for the last two games and we knew we could take two games in a row from anyone.

In Game 6, I finally got my hits, a double in the first and a run-scoring single in the seventh when we erupted for five runs, putting the game out of reach. We tied the Series at three games apiece with a lopsided 8–1 victory and now it all came down to just one game, the season in a single game.

Oakland started Blue Moon Odom in this last game. With Vida Blue, Catfish Hunter, Ken Holtzman, and Rollie Fingers all on the same staff, Blue Moon never got the respect he deserved, but in the Series against us, at any rate, he had better stuff than any of them.

Blue Moon pitched into the fifth inning and left with a 1–0 lead after we had gotten a couple of base runners. I don't know what would have happened had they left him in but he was replaced by Catfish Hunter, who was tough enough. We tied the game then but the A's went back out in front in the following inning, scoring twice, putting us deep in the hole. We were doing nothing against Hunter. We went to the bottom of the eighth still down 3–1.

The half inning that followed was decisive for us, and, personally, for me. I realized then, not intellectually but in my gut, that I had been seasoned as a leader over these many months, that I was actually a different player than when I had first arrived. I wasn't any noisier, bossier, more active in the dugout. I had no need to show anyone that I had rah-rah spirit. I played with great players, was protected by them as much as anyone, but now I felt this desire, this passion to go out and get it. The pressure of that moment actually lifted rather than hindered me.

"This is the inning, now is the time to do it," I called out on the bench—and I meant it. And I knew it was going to happen.

Sure enough, Pete Rose led off with a single. When I then got into the batter's box, I felt both calm and alert. Nothing was going to stop me from getting done what I had to do.

Because I had not hit well in the Series, I saw that I was not being played to pull—even though I was a pull hitter. They were playing me off to the left side.

I also noticed that they were not holding Pete at first—perhaps because he was no real threat to steal but also because his run was unimportant. Then the pitches that came at me from Ken Holtzman, a left-hander, seemed to slow down, I saw them perfectly. I pulled a 1–1 fastball inside the first-base line down into the right-field corner.

From the second I hit it, I was thinking triple. I saw the right-fielder shifted far over into right center, I saw the open space between him and the ball, and the ball kicking around far from him down the line. I was the tying run and I was going to make sure I was at third with none out when the play ended.

All of that was great except that Alex Grammas, the third-base coach, and Pete were not thinking along with me. What bothers me to this day is that I *know* the A's were not worrying about Pete Rose—he wasn't the tying run. *I* was. So Pete should have been able to score easily. Instead, when I rounded second and was halfway to third, I looked up and saw Pete standing there and Alex waving at me to stop and go back.

This could have been the most embarrassing moment in my career, but it wasn't. The A's, because they were worried about me and not Pete, let the outfield throw go all the way through to third base, thereby giving me a chance, ten feet from third, to safely retreat to second.

I was very upset. I looked over to Pete and Alex and they were saying that with no one out they didn't want to take the chance of having had Pete thrown out at the plate. That was logical, except for the fact that the defense had made clear that they were not going for Pete.

With that, even though we now had runners on second and third with no one out, we lost the World Series. Tony followed with a sacrifice fly, but I couldn't move up. So we were still a run down and now there was one out and it would take a hit to score me. The hit never came. Two fly balls later we were out of the inning and out of the game. The A's took it, 3–2, though we fought to the last out. The game ended with the tying run on first and Hal McRae sending a line shot that was taken up against the wall in left center field.

There were no recriminations afterwards, no need for anyone to remind anyone else of anything. The season was over and in the course of seasons, those plays—in midsummer weekday games or in the Series—happen. And you go on. But I still get sick thinking about what might have been. I don't know how many games, how many pennant races I've been through, but none promised more joy and delivered more pain than this one.

10

Almost

The reason there was such joy and pain for me in that Series, in that season, was because it was really the last year of my innocence as a ballplayer.

When I got to the Reds I had passed through two distinct phases as a player. The first was merely to survive, to get to the major leagues. The second was to stick, to have a career. Next I learned what it was to be a vital part of a great team. But sometime after the season ended, reality in the form of a contract proposal came crashing through the mails.

The previous season, I had made around $60,000; the new offer was for $75,000.

Now I was never a babe in the woods, not in Houston, not here. When I was with the Astros, I became interested not just in what went on out in the field but also in the front office. I knew I was in a business, and business interested me. I periodically visited the Astros' offices and sat down with different officials, asking questions, discovering what I could about different phases of the operation I really knew little about. I wound up socializing with a few front office guys, Pat Gillick, Lynwood Stallings, Tal Smith, Spec Richardson. So I knew that a ballclub's front office has to make deals with individual ballplayers that are good for the team.

After 1972, the Reds had four stars to deal with. It was well and good to have lots of ink about the Big Four, it was something else to pay them. But the Reds had done well. Home attendance in Cincinnati was over 1.6 million, the second highest total in club history. I knew they were not short of cash. I also was well aware of what I had done. There were a number of people, sportswriters, other players, who thought I should have been the MVP that year. I wasn't; Johnny Bench was and Billy Williams of the Cubs could have been.

It didn't bother me to lose out on the MVP vote, John and Billy were both logical choices. But, coming down the stretch in '72, I knew it was a sensitive topic on the ballclub. With just a few ball games left in the regular season, I was nowhere near 100 RBIs (important to get if I was going to win MVP). Pete, Tony, John, and I were taking our turns in the cage one evening and I started to rib Pete because the night before when I hit a long double and he was on first he did not score.

"You know, I can see how you get 100 RBIs," I said loudly to John, "you've got guys on base in front of you. Now take me. I hit one up the alley last night and Rose stops at third instead of bringing my run in, what am I gonna do?"

Though what I said really was in fun, Pete couldn't stand it. He knew, as each of the three of us did, what 100 RBIs meant. He exploded. It was one of the only times I saw him get really mad when he was being teased.

He took his bat and tossed it.

"Go ahead and hit! Fuck it!" he shouted, and stomped off.

I wound up with 73 RBIs that season—and I believe the Reds' front office was as sensitive to that, in a cynical way, as Pete had been in a purely emotional, thin-skinned way.

The offer I got that winter, though it represented a raise, was well below what I thought I should have gotten. Because I made it my business to keep tabs on things like player salaries, I knew what players like John and Pete got. Their well-publicized salaries were at or slightly above $100,000. I expected to be paid the same. I mailed back the contract the Reds sent and went about my business.

The guy who did contracts for the club then was Chief Bender (an executive, not the old ballplayer) and he called me soon after I sent back the contract unsigned. He seemed surprised. Let's get it done, he said, what was I looking for?

"One hundred thousand—same as John and Pete," I said.

"Impossible," he said.

"Why?" I asked. "I contribute as much to the ballclub, I finished third in the MVP balloting, I've been doing pretty well in the league for a number of years now."

Bender went on for a while about how the team couldn't pay this and couldn't pay that, that it wasn't a question of talent but of only having so much money for the payroll.

"Why do I have to answer for that?"

"Well," Bender said, after a lot of hemming and hawing, "you didn't have the best World Series last year."

It was all I could do to keep from hanging up on him. He knew about my heel injury, he knew what I had done throughout the season, he knew as well as anyone that when the time came I played hurt.

"Look," I said, "Bench and Rose made $100,000, my numbers are every bit as good and better, I want what they make!"

"Seventy-five thousand is as high as we can go," he said.

"I tell you what, Chief, don't call me again. As far as I'm concerned I'll play out the year at whatever you want and then when my option is up, I'm gone." With that, I hung up on him.

I soon heard from Bob Howsam. Howsam was the president and top guy on the ballclub then and when he called I was just as put off by the tack he took.

"Hi, Joe, what's the problem on the contract?" he asked—as though he knew nothing about the conversation I had had with Chief Bender. If I had a problem, it was not being able to take it when someone treated me like a fool or assumed that just because I was a ballplayer I needed to be addressed as a person of limited intelligence.

"The problem is money, Bob," I said, with anger in my voice.

So we went round and round. I finally managed to explain to Howsam that money meant respect to me—not wealth but respect. I brought up Tony Perez. Why was Perez, who deserved every bit as much as John and Pete, only making $75,000? (And, P.S., he hit .435 in the Series.) Did he realize what kind of impression that created?

"I'm not sure we're even talking about baseball, here," I said. I was angry enough to believe that I had not left Harry Walker behind in Houston.

I asked Howsam outright if he thought my contribution to the ballclub was less than John's and Pete's. We went back and forth over that for a while. He had chapter and verse laid out before him on my season. In one series, I went 2 for 10, in another 0 for 12, he said. Ultimately, he agreed that my contribution was as solid as anyone's—but still they couldn't pay me $100,000.

"Then leave it," I said. "I'm not happy with this offer and as far as I'm concerned there's nothing more to talk about."

"Well, let's make it $97,500—will that do it?"

I told Howsam that was something else and I would have to think about it. I'd get back to him, I said. It took a while. First, I vowed to myself, that no matter what I signed for, I would never again talk to an executive about salary without having my own book, chapter and verse, on what I did and did not do during a season. From then on, I always kept a little notebook on my day-to-day performance to make sure no one ever again could put me at a disadvantage in playing the numbers game. In the end, because I loved playing for the Reds and because I liked Bob Howsam—he was no Chief Bender—I agreed to $97,500.

Still, I had a bad taste in my mouth and it took a while to realize why. The real question had been *equal* pay, not pay that was almost equal. One hundred thousand was a symbolic figure even more than an actual one—and I had let myself back away from it.

My anger extended beyond myself as well. As determined I was to never go through that again, I also wanted to make sure Tony didn't get taken again, either. I knew he had been taken advantage of because he was a really nice person, because he had trouble with the language, because he was only too grateful just to be playing. I had Tony contact Tom Reich (the agent who was my friend though he had done no agent work for me), to make sure that in the future he had someone to represent him whenever the subject of money came up.

However sore the question of contracts, what I had been through as a player was another matter entirely. I looked forward to playing in '73 with the passion of an also-ran determined to get to the top. Same as everyone else on the ballclub.

During that winter, I worked out every day, harder than I ever had before, to make sure I would be in the best shape of my life when I reported for spring training. Beginning in December, I began swinging a leaded bat in my garage. In February I began hitting off a tee at a local field. I wanted my wrists and arms strong, my batting stroke precise from the start.

I spent a lot of time figuring out what I could do to personally improve my game. During that first year with the Reds, I realized one aspect I had not taken fullest advantage of was power hitting. I had always had power, I was always a pull hitter. But I had never really been a home-run hitter. Beginning with spring training, '73, I began working with the team's hitting instructor, Ted Kluszewski, on that single goal of being able to put more balls into the seats.

Klu was one of those guys who made the game better simply by his being there. Like Nellie Fox, he was the epitome of an old-time ballplayer. Everything was for the game and for the people who played it. He loved baseball, its secrets, its stories, its details.

When he was a player, Klu, of course, was a power hitter. He led the National League in home runs one year with 49 and hit 40 or more homers in a few other seasons. Klu also *looked* like a home-run hitter. He was big and brawny and he wore his uniform shirt cut off at the shoulders so that his huge muscles had room to breathe—and to scare the opposition.

But Klu was also a real hitter. He hit close to .300 through seventeen big-league seasons and the really remarkable thing about him was that he rarely struck out. There were any number of seasons where he hit more home runs than he had strikeouts. This meant that he not only had a great eye and superb bat control but that he also thought about hitting.

Klu was the first guy I knew who used video to study hitting. Nowadays, every team uses video to study every aspect of the game. Klu was a pioneer in the use of video. In those days, it was no easy task. He did his own editing. Camera technique was also a problem. Whereas today camera angles and locations are sophisticated, there was only a single position then—and the camera guy Klu had was a schoolteacher friend of his who came to the ballpark every day, setting up shop directly behind home plate.

Klu divided his footage into sections which showed a player what he was doing when he was hitting well and what he was doing when he wasn't. Klu usually spent the better part of a winter getting his reels ready for the different players he worked with.

There was no more eager pupil than I was.

Klu got me thinking about hitting under the ball more. By swinging with a slight uppercut I had a better chance of getting the ball in the air. Long fly balls in Riverfront with its shorter fences and helpful outdoor winds meant more home runs.

We also worked on extending my arms. Arms extended meant more body going into the swing. More body, more power. In Houston, at Nellie Fox's suggestion, I had developed a "chicken flap" with my left elbow as I stood waiting for a pitch. This was mistaken by many writers as a timing device. It was not. It was just a way of reminding myself to keep my elbow out away from my body. Klu reinforced the wisdom of this peculiar habit because it so clearly was a way to help make sure that my arms were extended when I swung.

The payoff for me was that I wound up hitting 26 home runs in '73 (my high in the majors to that point had been 16, which I had in '72). Thereafter, the home run, and just the threat of one, was an integral part of my game.

It seems odd to think of the Big Red Machine as a team needing to gain maturity, but we did. And we all knew it. We didn't think of it in terms of wine or chemistry but only of getting back to the World Series and winning.

When I was in Houston, I often went to the ballpark early to do extra work, hitting practice, fielding practice. It seemed like everyone turned up for early extra work on our club in '73. John, Tony, Pete, and I took the lead, others joined in. Pete and I often took batting practice after we played a day game at home. Klu and George Scherger, another coach, would go back and work with us.

The Reds had a kind of team intelligence I have never seen anywhere else. We were always looking for ways to gain that little extra, to help each other out.

Bench was absolutely the best I have ever seen at being able to sit in the dugout, look at a pitcher, and figure out what he was going to throw. It had nothing to do with sign stealing. John could read a pitcher's motion in terms of what he was throwing the same way I could in terms of stealing. We'd sit in the dugout and he'd say, "Curve." The pitcher would then throw a curveball. "Fastball"; he'd throw a fastball. Off-speed, same thing. John could have hit .800 if he had been able to have the same vantage point in the batter's box. As it was, he picked up enough to intimidate almost every pitcher in the league.

On the other hand, I did not do as well if I knew what was coming. I was a better "reaction" hitter. John had a good eye for mechanics. He would help me by noting when my hands were moving forward too soon before the swing. "Keep your hands back," he'd remind me.

Tony could always tell when John started to pull off a slider. It wasn't something obvious, John didn't bail out so much as he moved his weight slightly away from the pitch as he strode into it.

Tony was the best knuckleball hitter I have ever seen. In fact, he beat up on both of the Niekros. He hit Phil as well as he did Joe.

When I was a base runner, I was able to pick off a catcher's sign from *first* base. Usually, runners at second, who have a direct line of sight to the catcher, can do that, but the danger is that the signals then will be changed to deceive the runner. Signals aren't changed with a runner at first because the catcher is secure that his signaling hand can be hidden. But because I had learned pitchers' moves so well, I could take a longer lead and peek in.

I disguised my sign-stealing. I never tried to do anything out of the ordinary with my hands, my uniform, my belt-buckle, etc. The other guys, John in particular, only wanted to know whether a pitch was going to be fast or off-speed. On a breaking or off-speed pitch, I moved an arm, a leg, a shoulder. On fastballs, I took my lead and remained motionless.

During one series in Los Angeles I picked off every sign Dodger catcher Joe Ferguson put down. I got on base a lot in those games and John was hitting behind me. He got ten hits in three games and then we went on to San Diego, where no matter what I did, I couldn't pick off a single sign. I told John, "Man, you're on your own." He didn't do as well there.

Cesar Geronimo, another Houston player who came with me to the Reds, was perhaps the most underrated ballplayer on the team. He was a quiet guy, totally professional, dedicated as much as anyone to doing for his club. He was a great defensive center fielder.

Though I maintain to this day we were the smartest team ever assembled, we had our share of troubles trying to hold together as we made it through the season. There was always a thin line between the absolute togetherness we had developed on the field and the potential for bad feeling behind the scenes.

During that time, we had a reserve infielder on the ballclub, Darrel Chaney. Chaney was not having a particularly good season and a local newspaper put out by fans called *Red Alert* lit into him. When the paper later came to Johnny Bench for an interview he told them to get lost, because he thought they'd gone too far against Chaney.

None of that would have mattered except that *Red Alert* was heavily underwritten by Pete. To most of us, it was Pete's paper—and so John and Pete got into it over John's refusal to grant an interview.

The argument started at the batting cage when the four of us were there to hit. Pete asked John to cooperate with *Red Alert*. John replied that he wasn't about to cooperate with any group that blasted Darrel Chaney.

"That's pretty chickenshit, ya know!" Pete said.

"Why?" John snapped. "Darrel Chaney's just trying to make a living like everyone else."

"And so fuck the fans, huh? They don't have a right to say what's on their mind, huh?"

"That's okay for you to say but Darrel Chaney isn't making your kind of money!"

When we walked back to the dugout, everyone within earshot knew something was wrong, everyone except Tony, who somehow thought Pete and John were just kidding around.

"Hey, you know what," Perez chimed in, "fuck the *Red Alert!*" Rose turned livid.

"Fuck you, you're just like Bench, he's selfish and so are you."

Tony now caught on, saw that Pete was furious, and that save for his body interposed between John and Pete, there was an actual chance of physical confrontation between them.

"You know what," Tony said, "I'm gonna do the interview."

John and Pete both looked at Tony with exasperation, but, once again, the Dog had done just enough to take the edge off. We returned to the dugout without a fight breaking out.

There was a mid-season flare-up with Bobby Tolan. Bobby had been sent up to pinch-hit in one game and afterwards went back up into the clubhouse only to find Chief Bender there, waiting for him. The beard again. The front office wanted Bobby to shave it, the Chief was on his case about it, even though the game downstairs was still in progress. Bobby and Bender nearly came to blows. Fortunately, a couple of pitchers were in the clubhouse at the time and broke it up. I was alerted in the dugout and got back there as quickly as I could.

Bender had just left when I got to the clubhouse and found out what happened. The room was charged. The players standing there were clearly jumpy and on guard.

The next day I got a call from Dick Wagner, the general manager and new front office powerhouse.

"Joe," he tells me, "I wanna have a meeting with Bobby and you and Chief, I wanna make sure that Bobby apologizes to Chief for what happened."

"Well, you can have the meeting without me," I said. "As far as I'm concerned Bobby had every right to react as he did and, furthermore, you guys should know the clubhouse during games is for players only."

The meeting never came off. But the bad feelings surely lingered. Bobby was traded to San Diego at the end of the year.

We had a close race, closer than anyone had anticipated, with the Dodgers. The new, young Dodgers chased us down the stretch and though we maintained the best winning record in all of baseball that year, they kept after us till the very end.

Pete took a batting title that season, a real return to form for him. But his troubles seemed to grow. He was booed everywhere he went. His hustling style of play had too much of the hot-dog in it for a lot of fans. And it was true. As good as he was, Pete always made sure fans knew that Pete was Pete. John pointed out to me just how Pete managed to lose his helmet when he went tearing off on a base hit.

"See the way his left hand comes back like that after he drops the bat?" John laughed.

Sure enough. Pete had a nearly unnoticeable way of flicking off his helmet with a trailing hand after he set out from the batter's box. It was beautiful. And every time he walked, he ran, all out, to first base. Everyone assumed that was hot-dogging. It was, though it also was smart because it rattled the opposition and left open the possibility of capitalizing on an unforeseen mistake, a ball thrown away, a player being inattentive.

In Los Angeles, a game was actually halted when a fan, enraged at the sight of Pete, tossed a wine bottle out of the left-field stands at him. The bottle sailed within a few feet of his head and then Sparky pulled us from the field. We sat in the dugout for a long while unsure that the game was going to continue. All of us, but especially Pete, insisted that it go on. Pete went tearing out to his position when play resumed, letting everyone know that he and his team were not about to be intimidated even by threats of violence.

We pushed and battled all the way in '73. We won games by bludgeoning teams, we won by outsmarting and outhustling them. There was one game that exemplified the kind of effort all of us were making that year.

It was against the Phillies in Cincinnati. The game was tight, we were down by a run in the sixth and we had two runners on with none out. I was the runner on second, John was the runner on first. We put on a double steal. I got such a terrific jump on the pitch that I not only knew I had third stolen easily, I also knew that any throw on the play would go through to second base. When I got to third I didn't slide, I didn't even slow down. I just kept going, all out, to the plate.

Dave Cash, the Phillies' second baseman, caught off guard, hesitated, and then threw late. I beat the throw home—I had stolen two bases on one pitch!

This play actually turned the league on its ear for a while. Because there seemed to be no provision in the scoring rules to allow more than a single steal at a time, one of the stolen bases had been ruled a fielder's choice. Of course, the ruling by the official scorer made no sense, but the league then devised a "Morgan Rule" which stands to this day. A player cannot be credited with more than a single stolen base on any one play. Who cared. We took a ball game with it. That was all that mattered.

We wound up winning 99 games that season and taking the West by three lengths. Pushed as we had been, we had achieved that first of three big steps we were determined to take.

The playoffs against the Mets put us up against a team whose top-flight pitching gave us all kinds of problems. The Mets of '73, like the Pirates of '72, were a team we could not scare merely by walking on the field. We knew each time we went out there we would have to scratch and claw for everything we got. We could hope Tom Seaver would be off but even that would not mean much. We had him on the ropes in a game earlier in the season, sending shots all over Riverfront. We had five runs off him in two innings. The Mets stayed with him, though, and he got stronger inning by inning until he was throwing invisible fastballs past us in the late innings. The lefties on the team, Koosman and Matlack, always seemed at their best against us.

Seaver opened for them at Riverfront and he was on from the start. He pitched a complete game, struck out 13, but threw two mistakes—both of which cost him. With the Mets carrying a 1–0 lead into the bottom of the eighth, Pete homered to tie the score. In the bottom of the ninth, John homered to win it.

The next day, Jon Matlack pitched an even better game. The Mets carried a 1–0 lead into the ninth inning and then got four more. 5–0 might as well have been 50–0. The series was even as we headed to New York.

When we got there, no one needed to tell us we had a job to do. The series was now a best two of three, all to be played at Shea Stadium, a place none of us enjoyed. The stadium, with its raucous, highly partisan fans and the constant noise of jet planes taking off from nearby LaGuardia Airport, should have been closed down as a health hazard.

At breakfast that morning, Pete and I were sitting reading the New York papers, which were full of glowing accounts about what the underdog Mets had done to us in the last game. Suddenly, I saw something.

"Shit, look at this," I said, jabbing my finger at a column of newsprint. In the story, Bud Harrelson, the Mets shortstop, was quoted at length as saying how he felt the Reds had choked, had been intimidated out of their game by the Mets' superior pitching.

"Damn, where does he get off saying that," I said. "That pisses me off."

It bothered Pete, too, because trash talking is always cheap and always meant to get that one extra inch of advantage, which should not be yielded. Pete and I decided we were going to have a few words with Buddy when we got to the ballpark.

When we suited up and went out to the field, however, Harrelson was nowhere to be found. I asked Rusty Staub, my old friend, where he was and he didn't seem to know.

"Well, tell Buddy I want to see him, okay?"

Rusty laughed. He knew the game as well as anyone.

Pete and I then made a little pact between us that whoever had the first opportunity during the game would send a little message to Buddy—a hard slide into second, a tag when he came into the base, something.

The Mets put the game out of reach in the first two innings, taking a 6–0 lead. By the fifth, they led 9–2 but that was when we had our chance. It happened that it was Pete who was the guy rather than me. On a double play, Pete roared into second from first and hit Buddy like a semi out of control. Buddy got up and called Pete "a no-good motherfucker," so then Pete went after him.

Of course, both benches cleared. It was crazy out on the field. Pedro Borbon, one of our relief pitchers, went down on the bottom of a pile and came up wearing a Mets' hat. Debris rained down from the stands, and coaches from the Mets had to walk out to the outfield to quiet people down so the game wouldn't be forfeited. Pete, who had been booed all season long, was now vilified as never before. He was suddenly the dirtiest player in all of baseball, a disgrace to the uniform, to the game. It got worse.

After the game, because Pete was so visible, people shouted at him leaving the ballpark, out on the sidewalk, in the hotel lobby. He went up to his room and there were telephoned death threats. It was so bad that guys on the team, wanting a little peace and quiet before the next day's game, tried to steer clear of him and the little black cloud that seemed to follow him wherever he went.

I was supposed to go out to dinner that night with Joel Lupkin and Jerry Deutsch, friends I always looked forward to seeing in New York. But it was obvious that Pete, who normally was ebullient and outgoing, was feeling down and confused. In fact, though we had been constant companions over the past two seasons, I had never seen him like that before. Pete was a guy who lived on what others thought of him. Later on, when troubles of a far deeper kind gathered around him, I would understand that better, but I was struck at this point by how much he was hurting. I know the booing and even the bottle-throwing in the recent past had gotten to him but it was nothing like this. New York was normally Pete's town, a place where he could enjoy being a celebrity to the hilt. But now he was like a person on the run, a guy with a price on his head.

We went to the Cattleman's that night. Normally we'd go to places Pete more regularly frequented—places like the Four Seasons or Marty's Bum Steer. Pete loved steak. I think he ate steak every day, it was part of his routine, part of what made him Pete. But he wasn't hungry that night. He poked at his food, he was dejected to the point of silence. I don't think I ever spent a more miserable few hours in his company than I did that night. The baseball talk that normally filled our time together was completely absent.

He was no better the next morning. He was quiet and withdrawn. We had breakfast together in the hotel. It was like being at a funeral or a wake.

But the Reds, and Pete, bounced back that afternoon, in one of those games you always remember. The reason I remember it was not just because the game was so close, 2–1 in 12 innings, or because we had to fight back in the late innings, first to tie and then win the game, but because of Pete. Whatever he was going through off the field, he somehow managed to put it aside once the action began. Pete went 5 for 5 that day, and we won the game in the 12th inning on Pete's home run. The New York fans were silent as he circled the bases.

The fifth and final game was no contest. The Mets had Tom Seaver at his best going for them—and gave him some offensive support as well. The combination was too much. The line score shows the Mets won 7–2 but that wasn't the story. The most drama-filled part of the day was how we managed to escape the field after the final out. The Mets fan who had been silenced the day before erupted in full fury as their team headed for the champagne. Perhaps it was lucky for us that the game was so lopsided because we knew well in advance of the final out that trouble was brewing. From the seventh inning on, the mood of the crowd grew uglier and uglier as the moment of celebration approached. We became worried enough so that we moved the player wives who had accompanied the team into the dugout before the top of the last inning.

With the last out, all we saw was a surging sea of fans, engulfing the field. If there was police protection of any kind it was swept aside. Fans began ripping up the turf, grabbing huge hunks of it, small fistfuls, anything that gave way. They mobbed the Mets players, tore their uniforms from their bodies. In the grandstands, seats were broken into splinters. In front of us, the surge grew and came forward, to do what, no one knew. John, Pete, Tony, and I took bats in our hands and stood guard on the steps as wives, girlfriends, and relatives exited through the tunnel to the clubhouse under the grandstand. Other players joined us. For a time, the fans' rage seemed to be heading toward the point where they would rush us, whether we had weapons in our hands or not. But when the last of our people cleared the dugout, we peeled off, too, and retreated safely to the tunnel leading off to the clubhouse. It was a couple of hours, at least, before the area outside was secure enough for us to board the team bus and leave for the airport.

There were no recriminations among us, no outbursts of finger-pointing and excuses. We had been beaten, that was all. Everything we had fought for from the first day of spring training had come up short. But no one was blamed. There were guys who had been outstanding—like Pete—but they were as down as anyone. All of us knew that we had lost as a team, just as all of us knew that come the following season, our task remained the same.

Statistically I had a great year, my 26 homers and 67 steals were personal highs, I had 82 RBIs and an overall batting average of .290 to go along with that. All this while batting second. I also won my first Gold Glove, an award that meant more to me than any other individual achievement.

We were just as dedicated and just as strong in '74 as we were in

'73. Once again, we were in a race with the Dodgers. The Dodgers, now a year older, a year stronger, were great rivals. Our games, invariably sold out in both Cincinnati and Los Angeles, seemed like playoff games rather than part of the regular schedule. The Dodgers passed us in the standings in early summer and we wound up chasing them right through July and August.

With a month left to the season, we made our move and closed to within a few games of them. When they came to Cincinnati for their final trip of the season, we had moved to within a single game of the lead.

In the game for first place, we dropped behind early but then rallied to pull within a single run. In the seventh inning, I led off with a walk. John, hitting behind me, singled sharply to right center field. I had third base on my mind and in my sights. Nearing second, I took a quick look over my shoulder to see where the ball and the outfielders were. I saw Alex Grammas, the third-base coach, waving me on. But as I rounded second, I caught my foot in a seam on the Astroturf. I could feel my ankle give way under me. I made it into third but I knew I was injured. The only question was how seriously.

Because the full extent of an ankle sprain doesn't register for a while, I assumed the best, not the worst. I wanted to stay in the game. But as soon as I cooled down, even before the beginning of the next inning, I found that I could barely walk. Sparky wanted me to come out of the game. The game was so close, so much was on the line, I told him I wanted to stay in for at least one more at-bat.

"Let me hit one more time and then I'll come out," I told him. He let me stay.

We had tied the game in the seventh and the tie held into extra innings. The Dodgers went out in their half of the tenth inning and we came to bat. I got that additional chance—against Mike Marshall, the league's top reliever.

There was no one on, no one out, when I limped to the plate. The pain in my ankle was almost all I could think about. Yet just because of it, I forced myself to concentrate even more. I stood in,

thinking only that the inside of the plate was mine, making sure
that my hands felt comfortable, that my elbow was out from my
body, that my head was still. I got the pitch I wanted, down and in.
I saw it perfectly and hit it just right. From the second the ball left
the bat, I knew it was gone. I could barely get myself around the
bases. I hobbled and rabbit-jumped all the way to the plate where
my teammates mobbed me. What a finish! As good as *The Natural*.
For me, Kirk Gibson was *déjà vu* all over again.

Except that my season was over.

Following the game, I did nothing for two or three days but by
then it was clear that the sprain I incurred was so severe there was
no way it would heal in the few weeks that were left. Sparky asked
me if I could play at all. I said I would try. He explained to the
media, who wondered whether a utility guy shouldn't be playing,
that half of Joe Morgan was better than all of someone else. So I
played. I couldn't move in the field, I wasn't able to steal bases, my
hitting was way off. Still, when we went to the coast for our final
six games, we were three games out—and we had three games left
with the Dodgers.

We took the first two games at Dodger Stadium to pull within
one. One more and we would be in a flat-footed tie with three
games left. We reached the ninth inning of that final game, same as
the month before, all tied up. We got two runners on, moved them
up, and, with two out, I came up to hit. Behind me was Johnny
Bench.

The Dodgers walked me intentionally to load the bases. John, in
this situation, gave us the advantage we could only hope to have.
John, like Tony, was a great clutch hitter. The Dodger pitcher was
Don Sutton.

Sutton worked John to a full count. So there it was. The game,
the division, everything on the line, everything down to a single
pitch. John fouled that pitch off. And the next one. And the next
one. Bench fouled at least four more pitches away, looking for the
one he was going to drive. But each pitch was the one Sutton
wanted to throw. Who was going to give? Here was the game at its

very best, what all competitors, what all fans live for.

Don Sutton then threw the greatest pressure pitch I have ever seen: a perfect breaking ball on the outside corner for called strike three. It was the kind of curveball that paralyzed the hitter, left him helpless, and then was impossible to hit under any circumstances. Never mind that the game remained tied, it was over. The Dodgers went on to score in the bottom of the ninth—but it was that single pitch that was the game-winner. And the season-ender for us.

There were other rewards in that losing year for me. My numbers were solid again, I won another Gold Glove. But most memorable was being there when Hank Aaron hit the home run that tied Babe Ruth's record. It was opening day before a full house in Cincinnati. I didn't know Hank well but I had followed his run for the record keenly.

The fact that he was a black player was highlighted only because of what he had to go through to get to that moment. Hank had had to endure not only an increasing load of hate mail and death threats, but his team had literally been taken away from him. Wherever the Braves went, Hank was separated in the hotels they stayed in for fear that a bomb attack or some other act of violence might get to the other players as well. Hank lived with security guards in those final months—and with his own thoughts. He did not talk much to anyone though it was clear all the joy, all the pride he should have been able to claim for himself, was poisoned by this zone of unreasoning hate he had to walk through.

For me, being in the game as I was, I had a chance to see more than the hate. It was obvious to me, standing on the same field with Hank, for example, that the overwhelming number of fans at the ballpark were pulling for him. There were always fans who turned out to vent their private feelings about everything other than baseball. But it was hard to hear them then; the real fans were there, cheering, even when Hank first popped his head out of the dugout that day . . .

Baseball commissioner Bowie Kuhn had made a ruling before our season-opener. There had been some talk about Hank sitting out the first games of the year so he could hit the tying and record-breaking home runs when the Braves were at home. The ruling was that Hank had to play—in at least two of the first three games in Cincinnati.

He hit home-run number 714 on his very first at-bat. The roar of the crowd, the people rising to their feet in tribute, was some small answer to the hate mongers, and I hope there was some measure of reward for Hank in taking that in.

I happened to be at second base at that moment. Like everyone else, I watched the ball disappear over the left center-field wall. But then I was just one of a few players in the field—in the infield—who would, for that second in his passing, be shoulder-to-shoulder with him as he made that trip into history. I think I felt as proud as he did.

When he passed second base, we briefly made eye contact. I moved up on the basepath to be closer to him when he passed. I wanted to say something to him—but what could I have said that would have been up to that moment? Instead there was eye contact. Did he see in my face what I was feeling? I don't know. I couldn't tell, either, what he was feeling. He had no expression, neither pride nor joy nor relief. His eyes were alert and alive. And for that briefest moment he seemed to take me in as he jogged by.

"Nice going!" I blurted out.

Such moments—I was there in Houston for Willie Mays's 600th home run, the scoreboard went crazy, the fireworks went off—were as much a part of what I cherished in my years in the game as any individual or even team honors. They made the game better, they made the standard by which all of us played that much higher.

At the end of 1974, I was thirty-one. The Reds and I were both a little older, both scarred a little more, both as hungry as ever. It had been two full seasons since we had been to the World Series. If we were a Big Red Machine, we were becoming something of a used model. If we were the best team in the game, we had yet to prove it.

11

──

The Big Red Machine

Over the winter, changes were made. They were not the kind that immediately catch the eye but they were ones that were necessary and helpful. Our bullpen, which had become a problem in the last two years as Clay Carroll and Pedro Borbon became less effective, was considerably strengthened with the addition of two new guys, Will McEnaney and Rawly Eastwick. McEnaney was a left-hander, Eastwick a rightie, and between the two of them, we suddenly had two closers who threw hard, could keep the ball down, and who came at you from different sides of the plate.

In '74 we had had a real problem at third. For much of the season, Sparky played Danny Driessen there. But Danny was really a first baseman and so a key link in our inner defense was missing. The first step in the solution was Pete Rose's adaptability, and his willingness to move to third from left field, where he'd won Gold Gloves. He gave up the strong possibility of more Gold Gloves, and even of making the All-Star team, to help the Reds. At the beginning of '75, Pete moved back to third, and Danny became our top pinch hitter and a backup to Tony at first, his natural position. This move also allowed us to add George Foster's powerful bat to the lineup full time.

These moves were all possible because we had a new addition to the ballclub, Ken Griffey. Griffey played for us briefly at the end of the '73 and '74 seasons and came aboard full time in '75. Five or six years younger at twenty-four than the rest of us, he was the best fastball hitter I had seen. It did not matter where you pitched him, in, out, up, or down, he was always able to handle heat. He had speed, he could throw, he was smart in the outfield and never missed a cutoff man. That in itself was a tremendous boost, not only because it enabled Sparky to move Pete to third but because it also permitted us to realign the other outfield slots as well. For a year, Sparky had had to use Cesar Geronimo in right because he needed his arm strength there. George Foster had been shifted to center. Now with Griffey able to cover right, Foster could be moved to left and Cesar back to center, where he was king.

There wasn't much of a race in the West that season. We got off to a big lead early and coasted the rest of the way. The Dodgers, with basically the same team they had the year before, started slowly and never were able to put any pressure on us—largely because we had been through enough to not let down even when our lead became comfortable.

We won the National League West that year by 20 games. We all had outstanding years together. Tony hit .282, had 20 homers, knocked in 109 runs; John hit about the same, had 28 homers and 110 runs knocked in; Pete, Ken Griffey, George Foster, and I all hit .300 or better. I had my best year so far. A month into the season I moved to third in the batting order, which was a turning point in my career because it let me drive in more runs. I led all second basemen in fielding percentage, won another Gold Glove, and was the league's MVP.

The Pirates won the East that year and, though they had a tougher time of it than we did, they clearly were the most formidable opponent we could have had, the Lumber Company of old: Willie Stargell, Dave Parker, Richie Zisk, Richie Hebner, Al Oliver, with Manny Sanguillen and Rennie Stennett as well.

Even though we had better pitching and a stronger defense, the

Pirates offense always made them a threat. We could go into their park and rattle the walls and they could come into our place and do the same. There were times they put on batting displays against us that left very much in doubt who would be standing at the end of any playoff series between us. Some of our games that year were classics.

There was one game I remember vividly—because I wasn't playing. In the first game of a doubleheader in Cincinnati, the Pirates simply slaughtered us. The final must have been something like 12–2 but the memorable part was the way they hit. They had eighteen or twenty hits that game, all of them rocket shots, along with another ten or so line drives that were caught.

Danny Driessen, who was also sitting out this first game, went down to a corner of the dugout with me while the carnage unfolded—and we just laughed. We infuriated our teammates who had to go out there and endure the assault, but it was one of those perfect hitting games you see every once in a while. When a team full of hitters erupts collectively like that there is nothing anyone can do except get out of the way—and enjoy it. Our guys on the field couldn't do that. Danny and I could.

Perhaps because so much firepower was brought to bear in our games, we also used to get into a lot of fights with the Pirates.

In one game in 1977, Chuck Tanner, who was then managing the Pirates, had been working on a strategy to keep me from stealing. Because the Pirates were a favorite team of mine and because I loved to play in their ballpark (the hitting background was excellent, the ball carried well, the turf was fast), I usually was at my best against them.

What Tanner worked out was to have Willie Stargell position himself at first base a little bit differently when I was the runner. Instead of having him stand at the bag to receive throws from the pitcher, he was told to move out with me so he could receive any pickoff throw and then get the tag down more quickly as I scrambled back to the base. The idea was not to catch me off base so much as to get me to shorten my lead.

The other part of this maneuver was having Stargell edge himself in front of me so I couldn't see the pitcher. He'd stand there blocking my view, then, as I moved, he'd move with me, all the while trying to keep himself in front of me.

The first time Willie got in the way, I complained to the first-base umpire, Doug Harvey. I told him Willie was blocking my path, he couldn't do that. Harvey told me he had a right to set his position.

"Fine," I said, "let him set his position and then I'll move outside of him or inside."

Doug said he agreed with that and then Tanner came running out of the dugout, screaming, "Hey, you can't tell my guy where to play!"

Harvey was now totally confused. Technically, Tanner was right—but so was I. What could he do? He didn't know.

I said, "I know what to do, I'll just knock Stargell on his big ass."

And then I just pushed him, gave him a big, operatic shove. Willie turned around and with this look of fake outrage on his face, raised a fist over his head. Meanwhile, the fans, who had no idea that Willie and I were close friends, started howling and screaming. When we saw what we had touched off, we started laughing, throwing our arms around each other, till the fans caught on and they joined in the laughter, too. When the game finally resumed, I told Willie, "You can't stop me. If you do things like that I'm going to have to go ahead and steal the base so don't you try it again or go get others around the league to try it either."

"But we gotcha now," he said.

"Yeah," I said, "just watch." I stole second on the next pitch.

But some of our fights with the Pirates had a different tone.

In another game, the Pirates were again beating our brains in. It was also the first game of a doubleheader—this time in Cincinnati. With the game out of reach, in the middle innings, Frank Taveras, their shortstop, got on base and then stole second.

Now you don't have to be a sophisticate to know that with a 6 or 7 to nothing lead you don't gratuitously go stealing bases. It's not only bad form but it's stupid. The other team *has* to respond. And so we did. We got all over Sparky to make sure our pitcher—I forget who he was then—sent a message to Taveras the next time he hit.

Sparky, who by then had finally come to accept that brushback pitches, even hitting batters, were sometimes necessary to protect players on his own team, ordered our pitcher to get Taveras's attention on his very next at-bat. He did—but it was one of the weakest knockdown pitches you ever saw. Our guy obviously didn't feel comfortable throwing tight.

Sparky jumped to his feet.

"Time out!" he bellowed. He ordered veteran reliever Joe Hoerner, who was sitting on the bench, down to the bullpen to begin warming up. Then he went to the mound and talked and talked and talked until finally the ump came out and broke it up. Sparky went back to the bench but then before the next pitch was thrown he popped out of the dugout again, to remove the pitcher and bring in Hoerner. It was the only time in my life I have seen a pitcher brought into a game for the sole purpose of drilling a guy.

Joe nailed Taveras in the middle of the back—and all hell broke loose. Taveras threw his bat at Hoerner and charged the mound. Both teams came pouring onto the field. But because it was late in the game and another was still to be played, half the guys on either side were up in the clubhouses cooling off. When word of the fight came, it was like battle stations being called in the middle of the night. Pirate and Red players, half-dressed, some in their underwear, pulling on their pants as they ran, came stumbling out onto the field. It was an unbelievable sight and it is hard for me to this day to imagine what people in the stands made of the spectacle.

When we got down to the playoffs that year, however, we were as lean and mean and as confident as we could be.

The first two games were in Cincinnati and we won them handily. The third game, in Pittsburgh, was a great game, because rookie John Candelaria showed the poise of a veteran in striking out fourteen batters in fewer than eight innings. Manager Danny Murtagh showed a lot of guts starting a rookie in the third game, at home. In

1980 Tommy Lasorda chose not to start rookie Fernando Valenzuela against Houston, although he was clearly the Dodger's best
pitcher at the time. L.A. lost.

The game seesawed right to the end. We took a 1–0 lead into the
sixth, they scored twice to lead into the eighth, when we scored
twice to take the lead back again only to have the Pirates tie in the
bottom of the ninth. We won it with two runs in the tenth, completing the sweep of the series.

On the same day that we won the National League pennant, the
Red Sox and the A's were finishing their series in Oakland. The Red
Sox, like us, had won their first two playoff games at home and
were going for the sweep.

Because most of us still remembered 1972, and because we believed they were the best team out there for us to beat, most of us
were pulling for the A's.

The Red Sox, of course, couldn't have cared less about what we
thought. They wanted to finish their season with their own World
Series victory. Boston won the game.

Going into Boston was a mixed blessing. As a black person, I had
heard plenty about the town and about how tough it was for non-
white players there. Bill Russell had told me how, during his great
championship seasons with the Celtics, the fans had complained
because these were three black starters. Years later, showing how
little had changed, Kevin McHale spoke about how great it was to
be a white Irish kid playing for the Celtics.

Still, I knew little about the town when I got there. I had never
played a game in Fenway Park, had never seen the place. And
because rain played a factor in this Series, leaving us a lot of free
time, I had a chance to take in the city in ways that I would not
have been able to in the normal hurry of games and travel. Two
friends, Sheldon and Sandy Bass, gave Gloria and me a great tour of
the city's historic sights.

It did not take me long to get over any sense of disappointment I
had that Oakland was not our rival. The big point was that whom-
ever we were playing, *we* were in the World Series.

Because I had never seen it before, the first view of Fenway was a shock and a delight. The exterior of the building and then the underground passageways, through the stadium to the locker room, were dingy and grimy. But then, almost because of the age and decrepitude of the place, you became aware of those who made this trip before you. Legends and shadows follow you everywhere. This was a place I knew even without knowing it—so many great ones had been here, had stood on this or that part of the field: There was Babe Ruth and Jimmie Foxx and Tris Speaker and Bobby Doerr and, most of all, Ted Williams.

One of the first things I noticed about the playing field was not the Green Monster or the hand-operated scoreboard, but the infield. Before I did anything else, I walked out, felt the ground under my feet, let the texture of the dirt become familiar to me. I was struck by how smooth the infield was. It was perfect. I had played on hundreds of infields in my life, and this was the very best. It was almost magical. How was it possible to build such a space, such a small corner of the land in this way?

Then I looked at the Wall. From top to bottom it was 37 feet with a 23-foot-high screen above that. The base of the Wall was concrete. Just above the concrete there was padding and then above the padding there were different kinds of metallic slats, and above the slats, who knows what. There were live spots and dead spots all over the Wall. In batting practice, the sounds of the ball off the Wall—one time it was *thunk*, another time *boiiinngg*, or *crack*, or *splat*, or *clink*—advertised its treacherousness. Indeed it was a Monster.

The Wall was a notorious trap for right-handed hitters who too often wind up altering their swing in order to pull the ball. But left-handed hitters also try to change their swing to go the other way and reach the Wall. That did not interest me, nor did it interest Ted Williams who, with the Wall and the Shift begging him to go the other way, just kept hitting the ball harder and harder the way he knew best.

Right field was more interesting to me than left. Because of the peculiar dimensions of the park, there was room to hit the ball out in right center and then the line around the foul pole. I felt not only this current of history go through me but also the sense that I was going to have a very good Series here. I thought, after what we had done in the regular season and then the playoffs, we would wind up having an easy time against the Red Sox. But after underestimating the A's, we weren't going to make the same mistake with the Red Sox.

In the opening game of the Series, we went up against Luis Tiant. This great and very popular pitcher was at his best against us. I was mesmerized watching him. He had us eating out of his palm all day, and yet I just loved watching him.

People talk about Luis's motion—it was surely something to behold. It was said that if you were in the stands, regardless of where you were sitting, Luis Tiant would make eye contact with you sometime in the course of a game he pitched. His head movements made Fernando Valenzuela's look stiff-necked by comparison.

I had to make up my mind to look away from all the herky-jerky moves and to just pick up the spot where Tiant released the ball if I was going to have any chance of hitting him. I got a hit off him the second time I came up, but it didn't mean anything. He shut us down completely. The Red Sox took the opener, 6–0.

The next day I went out on the field to compliment Tiant and comment on the fans' reaction.

"It must be great to be so popular," I said.

"When I'm in the ballpark, I'm a hero, I'm El Tiante," he said. "A block away from the ballpark if I try to get a cab, I'm just another black man nobody will stop for."

After losing the opener, the second game loomed as the key game in the whole Series. We remembered the Oakland Series all too well when we put too much pressure on ourselves, having to battle back from a 2–0 deficit.

The Sox started their top left-hander, the "Spaceman," Bill Lee, in Game 2. Lee was one of these guys who threw slow, slower, and slowest. Even knowing that and waiting on him, we didn't do much with him anyway.

Down a run in the fourth inning, we tied the score when I walked, Pete singled—for the first hit we had off Lee—sending me to third, and then Tony, who once again did what was called for, hit a grounder to the right side, wide enough to keep us out of a double play, placed well enough for me to score.

The Red Sox, though, got a run home in the sixth and there matters stood till the ninth. With the score 2–1 and with Boston needing only three outs to win, John got things started for us by doubling to right. He didn't try to go at the Green Monster. The Red Sox then did us a favor by going to the bullpen. That was just the fifth hit we had had off Lee but, with a couple of right-handed hitters coming up, the decision was made to go to the pen. Tony moved John to third with a ground-ball out. But then George Foster flied out to short left and John had to hold. We got the tying run home on a hard infield single by Davey Concepcion, who then stole second and came home when Ken Griffey lined a double off the Monster. We snatched a game most people thought we had lost. We were elated, obviously, but we played to win games like that. We were an older, wiser, more mature team than we were in 1972.

When we got back to Cincinnati, we were bubbling with confidence, almost overconfidence. To a man, we said among ourselves that we were not going back to Boston. We knew we were the better team and we had just accomplished a split on the road. All that was missing in our calculations was the grit and determination of the Red Sox. They were playing for themselves and probably for every other Red Sox team that hadn't made it since 1917. The ghost of history helped as well as hindered them.

The third game was an all-out barnburner, with a lot of the big guys weighing in and doing dramatic things. The Sox took an early lead in the game when Carlton Fisk homered. We came back with Bench, Davey, and Cesar Geronimo hitting homers, and Pete hitting a triple and coming home on my sac fly. We carried a two-run lead into the ninth when Dwight Evans tied the game with a one-out homer with one on. The Red Sox nearly won the game then when they got another runner into scoring position before the inning ended. But then this almost perfect game was marred by one of those plays that will be forever controversial in World Series history.

In the tenth, we got our leadoff guy, Cesar Geronimo, on and then, with the pitcher's spot coming up, Sparky sent up Ed Armbrister to pinch-hit. He was obviously up to sacrifice and that's just what he did—he tapped the ball out in front of the plate. Fisk brushed past Armbrister, fielded the ball, and threw wildly into center field. He then went wild, arguing that Armbrister interfered with him, thereby causing his throw to go wild, putting the Red Sox into a hopeless situation.

No one will settle the argument but to me there really was no argument. If you run that play back on video, you will see that Ed clearly tried to get out of the way. He bunted the ball and then actually backed up a step to avoid being called out for interference. Fisk fielded the ball and threw *before* Armbrister moved past him—and that's what the ump, Larry Barnett, saw. He made the right call: no interference.

It wasn't funny to Fisk or the Red Sox then but every time Pudge and I run across each other now on the dinner circuit, we go into our routines over what happened. He'll argue with me all over again, I won't listen to any of it. Instead, I'll start waving my hands against that sixth-game home run he hit—just the way he had. Only I'll be gesturing toward foul territory.

Many people say that that World Series was the best ever. Who can say. But I do know that six of the seven games we wound up playing were memorable, all that anyone could ask for in World Series competition.

Some people compare the 1991 Atlanta–Minnesota World Series to the Cincinnati–Boston Series. But while the games in 1991 were close and the Series went the limit, that was because both teams kept making mistakes that helped the opponent.

In the fourth game, the Red Sox, unwilling to take a knockout blow, came back. We had a 2–0 lead on them, they scored five runs in the fourth, we came back with two to narrow the lead to 5–4 and then Luis Tiant, pitching all the way, and clearly not at the top of his form, held us off. Luis threw around 150 pitches and every pitch to the very last out in the ninth inning seemed to have the game hanging in the balance.

We took the fifth game easily, the only one-sided game in the Series, and then headed back to New England. It wasn't bedlam but rain that awaited us. Three days of it. Three important days for Luis Tiant's arm to grow strong again while we could do nothing more than take in the sights.

When we finally did get down to it, it looked as though those rain gods had done their work. The Red Sox jumped off to a first-inning 3–0 lead on a homer by Fred Lynn and then went into cruise control with Tiant doing his thing. But, once again, he did not have his best stuff. The ball was coming up to the plate the way it did in the fourth game rather than the first. We rallied to tie the game in the fifth, went ahead by two runs in the seventh, added another in the eighth; it looked almost certain that we were going to be the world champions.

When Bernie Carbo came up in the bottom of the eighth with two men on and two out, I still thought we were going to make it. Rawly Eastwick had come into the game two batters earlier and had gotten them. He was pitching outstanding relief for us—and he clearly was in control in the situation. Eastwick got two strikes on Carbo, and made him look bad in doing it. Then he threw him a pitch that, from where I stood, looked unhittable. It was a sharp-breaking slider, down and in, and Carbo swung at it awkwardly. It was a funny swing, the kind a batter makes when he is completely fooled. Carbo barely touched the ball—it was just a tick—but he fouled it off. When Eastwick came back with a fastball, Carbo hit it into the center-field bleachers—and we were tied.

I remember everything then went blank for me. I knew the second the ball was hit that it was out. I don't think I heard the crowd or even saw Carbo circling the bases. I came to thinking only that we were tied, that the rug had been pulled out from under us just at the point where we were going to be world champs. I thought of that Oakland Series in '72 and that maybe we were snakebit.

The game continued, more like a war of attrition than a baseball game. Somewhere in here we tied a World Series record when an eighth pitcher from our team entered the game. There were maybe twelve pitchers in all for both teams, also a record or near-record. It figured to happen with Captain Hook, Sparky Anderson, managing one team. In any case, it became clear to players on either team, to the fans, to everyone watching, that this game could only end on some kind of dramatic, spectacular note.

In the eleventh inning, we got a man on and with one out I had a chance to hit. I got the pitch I wanted from the Red Sox reliever, Dick Drago, and I hit the ball hard to right. I got a little bit on top of it, I had too much top hand in my swing, but the ball was going to carry out of the park anyway. But because of the topspin on the ball, I kept watching Dwight Evans: and he didn't seem to be giving up. I said to myself, Whoa, where does he think he's going, he can't get to that. But he kept going back, back, and then he leaped—and caught the ball. I couldn't believe it: and neither, apparently, did anyone else watching the game. It was one of the great catches ever—and what was more, because Evans was a supremely intelligent player, he remained in the game all the while. As soon as he made the catch, he wheeled away from the grandstand, remembering that was only the second out in the inning, and threw to first base—knowing that the runner, like everyone else, had thought the ball was out. This great catch was now turned into an even more impressive inning-ending double play.

There was even a spooky side to this play. Sometime later, I learned that Evans, just before I hit that ball, had a picture pop into his head where he saw himself going into the stands to take a home run away from me! That's hard for me to believe, but in this particular game, anything was possible.

When Fisk hit his game-winning homer in the bottom of the twelfth, my reaction, standing at second base, was a bit strange. The first thing I did was to wait to see if the ball was going to be fair or foul—like Fisk, like everyone else. The angle I had made it especially hard to tell.

But then, when I saw that the ball was fair, I had no sense of disappointment or dejection. I still had a job to do. With the crowd screaming and the Red Sox players leaping from the dugout, I stayed in place waiting to make sure that Fisk actually touched the bases as he made his way around the diamond. Imagine what would have happened if he had missed one.

Our clubhouse was like a morgue. But there were some guys, especially Pete, talking about what an honor it was to play in such a game. That's not what I felt, though.

When the writers came to me wanting to know how I felt, I said, "Hey, it was a good game." They wanted more. They wanted to to know what the effect of losing a game we had just about won would have on us in the seventh game the next day. I said what I honestly felt, that it would have no effect whatsoever. "When you come out here tomorrow," I said, "you'll see the best team in baseball go at 'em again. And we will win. Hey, I'll take these guys every day of the week in the seventh game of the World Series."

One of my very favorite pictures is a photograph which John gave to me sometime later of us lined up along the third-base line the next day during the player introductions. The shot was of the nine starters in the game, that is, eight guys and Sparky. The looks on our faces are worth a million bucks. Not one of us is smiling, not one of us has the same expression. We were nine different people each lost in his own private world. The picture says it all: This is the battle, this is the Seventh Game.

We fell behind early, 3–0, against Bill Lee, who had been so tough against us before. We were actually lucky to be down only 3–0 in that game because in the inning when the Sox scored their three runs, they could have really blown the game open, but didn't. Don Gullet, in a bases-loaded and one-out situation, struck out Fred Lynn. It was the kind of great, clutch strikeout you need to win games, and it gave us a terrific lift even though we saw ourselves falling behind.

The game kept going along, though, and we didn't come back.

Bill Lee was as tough late as he was early. We reached the sixth inning with the score still at 3–0.

The bench on a major-league team is not a place where a lot of rah-rah stuff goes on. Ours was almost silent. Each of us was all too aware of what we had to do. As the Red Sox took their inning warm-ups, Sparky suddenly got up and walked from one end of the dugout to the other. This was completely out of character for him, but he was talking to us:

"Look, fellas," he said, "we've got some outs left, I don't want anybody to panic, don't go up there looking to hit the ball out— somebody get on base and Bench, Morgan, or Perez will hit a home run and we'll be back in it."

Talk about eerie and spooky moments!

Pete opened the sixth with a single and then, after I flied out, John forced Pete at second on what should have been an inning-ending double play, but the relay throw to first was wild and we had life—with Tony coming up.

Perez homered on one of Bill Lee's famous slow curves—just as Sparky said—and we were back in it! Their scouting report should have told them that slow curves were the Big Dog's meat.

We tied the game, and almost won it in the seventh. With one out, Ken Griffey walked and the Red Sox did us a huge favor by replacing their starter Bill Lee, who was the kind of off-speed pitcher who gave us fits. With two out, Griffey stole second and Pete then singled him home. The inning ended when John fouled out with the bases loaded.

Ninth inning. I can still feel the chill of that New England night on my skin. The sound of 35,000 fans, waiting, expectant, abuzz, still runs like a current through my body. I can feel the time and place as though it were yesterday, not eighteen years ago.

At the top of the inning, the Red Sox brought in a rookie left-handed pitcher, Jim Burton, to try to hold the tie. The choice of a rookie was risky because no one could know how he would respond under such enormous pressure. But we had left-handed hitters coming up. The risk had to be taken.

Burton walked Ken Griffey opening the inning. Cesar then sacrificed Kenny to second. Danny Driessen grounded to second and Kenny moved on to third. At that point, with Pete, a switch-hitter, coming up, the Sox called time, and the manager, Darrell Johnson, went to the mound. Good, I thought, they're going to walk him. Because I wanted to be the guy who hit in that situation. The move was so obvious—walk Pete, who was a switch-hitter, to pitch to me, left-hander against a left-handed batter.

But, no, they went after Pete! When I saw Fisk get down in his crouch, I couldn't believe it. I yelled at him, "Hey, what's going on!" That was nothing new either. There were two or three times during the years where Pete had been walked to get to me—and I used to yell then, too, but at Pete: "They're gonna walk a judy to get at *me*!"

Everybody thinks they pitched around Pete, but they didn't. Pete took two strikes then went to 3 and 2 before he walked. I was the happiest guy in the place.

Call it cockiness, ego, whatever, this was what I lived for. When I was a little kid, I used to play a game with myself in the backyard at my house: "Seventh game of the World Series, I'm at bat, winning run is on." Boom, I get the base hit every time. I was going to do that right here. I knew it.

But this kid Burton was ready. If he was a rookie, he never showed it. His best pitch was a hard, late-breaking slider which was really difficult to pick up. Fortunately for me, I had been working with Lew Fonseca on keeping my weight back as long as possible to avoid overcommitting on breaking pitches—and our work now paid off. With the count 2 and 1 I lined a breaking ball inches foul down the left-field line. Then with the count 2 and 2, Burton threw me a really tough, late-breaking slider which I went for and got up into the air.

I knew I did not get good wood on the ball. I could feel the dead heaviness of the ball against the bat. I saw a blur of white heading toward center field, and as I ran I watched it hit the ground. The Red Sox fans fell silent, and a cheer burst out from our side of the field.

Standing on second with the run home, I tried to suppress a grin.
I looked into the dugout. The guys were ecstatic. Normally, when
one of us got a broken-bat hit, the dugout would carry on, yelling
out to the hitter that he had just embarrassed the Reds. I couldn't
have gotten a bigger reaction from them if I had sent one over the
scoreboard on top of the bleachers in dead center field.

Of course, none of us really knew we had it made then because
this team we had so badly underrated had yet another at-bat, another chance for the sort of heroics they had been pulling off almost routinely throughout the Series.

We brought in Will McEnaney to pitch the bottom of the ninth
and he put down the Sox in order, finishing by getting Carl Yastrzemski on a harmless fly ball.

The celebration in our clubhouse went on for hours. After everyone was doused with champagne, they were doused all over
again by buckets of water. The bedlam was so great, I actually didn't
know what I was feeling till I went out to the reception room for
family members and friends and saw Gloria's face, beaming with
pride and happiness.

It had been four full seasons since Sparky had said I was the
missing piece of the puzzle, four years since we had gotten to a
World Series only to lose it. At long last, we were the Big Red
Machine everyone said we were, world champions, the greatest
sound in team sports.

12

Things Fall Apart

I won my first MVP award in '75. That was the fitting end to the best season I had had in baseball. I've since told friends that I had statistically better seasons than '75, but I never had a better year. I hit .327 that year, a career high, but I had fewer homers (17) than I had had in recent seasons, fewer runs scored, fewer doubles. But it was as though every hit, every run batted in, every stolen base counted.

There was a big downside to my season, however. In the middle of our run for a championship, I learned that Nellie Fox was seriously ill with cancer in a hospital in Maryland. I hadn't seen much of him since we were teammates but we had kept in touch by phone since then. When I heard he was ill, I called him immediately.

"Naa, I'm gonna beat this thing, nothing to worry about," he said. "Even though I'm an old American Leaguer, I'm pulling for you in the Series, Joe."

When it was announced that I won the MVP, Nellie called to congratulate me.

"You shoulda won it the two past years also," he said, weakly.

Weeks later, he was dead at the age of forty-eight.

The business of baseball, as opposed to simply playing it, was another, very different kind of sobering reminder to me that the world I lived in was contradictory and unpredictable.

With the kind of year I had, I was, professionally speaking, in the kind of bargaining position a player dreams of. My contract the previous season was for around $125,000, so I clearly was in line for a raise. In addition, there had been a recent arbitrator's decision declaring that two players, Dave McNally of the Expos and Andy Messersmith of the Dodgers, had the right to play out their contract options and become free agents. That meant that all players subsequently would have the same right. Free agency, between the '75 and '76 seasons, had become a reality.

I had no thought of playing the free agent market then, but I was surely aware of it. The Reds, even before the season ended, had wanted me to sign a multiyear pact (three years at around $200,000 per). I was tempted but I did not want to bind myself to a long-term deal of any kind because I reasoned I still had not reached my full potential. And then I wasn't sure of what Dick Wagner's strategy was. On the one hand, he told me I was the best player in the game; on the other, when it came to dollar figures, he seemed to be a little concerned that perhaps I had let up a bit when the pennant was won.

This time I had my tiny spiral notebook ready:

"Down the stretch, Dick? How 'bout St. Louis against Ron Reed. Only got one hit but I had four walks. Eric Rasmussen the next day, 2 for 4 and a steal; sat out the next two because I got a shot for a hand injury. But now how 'bout two walks, a double, a run scored against Andy Messersmith opening the Dodger series?"

I did not want any distractions going into the playoffs and Series so we decided to leave all negotiations till after the season, and then the decision I made was to sign just for a single year at $235,000, enough as far as I was concerned.

Because of the season we had in '75, we were heavily favored to win it all again in '76. For me, for all of us, that meant hard work over the winter. John and Pete, who had been MVPs before, said the key to coming back strong was to forget all the successes and start from scratch. That was perfect, as far as I was concerned.

The reason it is tough to repeat is exactly that you have to start from zero, as if you hadn't won the year before. Most teams can't make that adjustment.

The Dodgers were stronger that season with the acquisition of Reggie Smith, the Astros had good young players, the Phils in the East were powerful, more so than anyone thought they might be.

The Dodgers pressed us a little more than they did the previous season, but once again we had things in hand by midsummer. We won 108 games in '75; in '76 we won 102—and the division by 10 full games. The narrower distance between us and the Dodgers was not significant. We were simply a powerhouse.

Our hold on the Dodgers actually stretched back to '72, when we caught them from behind for the first of two years in a row. In '74 at the All-Star Game in Pittsburgh I was talking to Reggie Jackson and Ron Cey at the batting cage. Reggie told Ron, "If the Reds catch you from behind again this year, you should move your team to the Philippines and call yourselves the Manila Folders."

Coming down the stretch that year, Ken Griffey got the fans, and his teammates, excited by making a determined run for a batting title. We got involved in Kenny's quest because he was so quiet and so hard working he never complained that his closest competitor, Bill Madlock of the Cubs, regularly took days off when he faced pitchers he didn't like. In the final week of the season, Kenny led Madlock by several points but had 190 hits to Madlock's 140. Each day, the box scores told the same story: Griffey played against everyone, Madlock only against those he chose. The race tightened.

Down to a handful of games, Kenny went 0 for 4 one afternoon; Madlock sat out. Only a few points separated them now. I went to Kenny and told him to do some sitting himself.

"There's no disgrace in it, Madlock is trying to win any way he can, its not fair. You're closing in on 200 hits, he's nowhere close."

"I'd sit out if I could," Kenny said. By that he meant it was not his choice. So Pete, Tony, John, and I went to Sparky and had a talk with him. Sparky listened. I laid out the case for Kenny sitting. John thought he shouldn't play. So did Tony. Pete argued that he should be in there.

"When I won my batting titles, I won by playing," Pete said.

"Madlock doesn't play every day," I said.

"That's a different situation, Pete," John said.

Tony nodded in agreement.

Sparky, who had only been listening to that point, said, "You know, for me it's a question of the kid standing up and being a man."

"What! Sparky, that's horseshit," I said, "this has nothing to do with manhood, it has to do with Bill Madlock sitting on his ass so he can steal a batting title!"

The end result was that Sparky left it up to Kenny. But not before he brought him into the office and gave him the same speech about manhood. Kenny decided to play. He went o for 4, Madlock played and went 2 for 4, bringing the race down to the last day with only two points separating them.

On the final day, Sparky said that maybe Kenny really shouldn't play. Madlock would have to go 4 for 4 to beat him out. Again, the choice was left to Kenny and this time, with no one pressuring him to go out there, he sat.

During the game, we got updates from the Cubs' game. It didn't seem likely that Madlock could go 4 for 4 but the reports we got indicated that he got a hit his first time up, then a bunt single in his second at-bat, and another hit his third time up. At that point, even though we had a six- or seven-run lead, Kenny was sent out on deck as a pinch hitter.

As soon as Griffey stepped out of the dugout, however, Dave Bristol, the Braves' manager, ordered a lefty to start warming in the bullpen. We all thought that was inexcusable, why would he go out of his way to use a pitcher just to stop one player when it had nothing to do with the outcome of the game? You played to win, not to ruin an individual player's season. Kenny never came to bat in the inning, though. Meanwhile, it was announced that Madlock had gotten his fourth hit and now led Kenny by one one-thousandth of one percentage point.

Kenny was announced the following inning, and immediately, Dave Bristol brought in his lefty. Kenny failed to get a hit, the title belonged to Madlock.

As disappointed as Kenny was, as all of us were, we had other business to take care of. We had a second season ahead of us and we were eager to get on with it.

When we got to Philadelphia to open the playoffs against the Phillies, the huge national contingent of media that had assembled was almost exclusively concerned with whether or not we'd be able to repeat. I told a large group of reporters the day before the first game that we were playing better now than at any time since I had been in Cincinnati.

"You're going to see something special this week," I said. I wasn't sure what that was going to mean, but I knew we were at the top of our game.

I felt good. Statistically, I had had a stronger year than I had the previous season. I had hit .320, drove in 111 runs, stole 60 bases, and was being widely touted to win another MVP.

The Phils did not pitch to me in the playoffs. Their strategy was to walk me any time they could. In the opening game, which we won 6–3, I was walked three times; in Game 2, we again won easily, 6–2. I was walked a couple of times more. On one walk, I trotted down to first base and Richie Allen, who had a habit of writing messages in the dirt with his spikes, wrote one for me: "Hi Joe."

We got pushed in Game 3 in Cincinnati. Trailing 6–4 in the ninth inning, George hit a bases-empty home run. It pulled us within a run.

As George rounded the bases, I noticed that he made a clenched-fist gesture of frustration. I understood it perfectly. The inning before he was in the on-deck circle with a runner aboard when the inning ended. If he had hit his homer then, we'd be tied.

The following batter was Johnny Bench. On the first pitch, he put one over the left-field wall to tie it! Technically, John hit a one-run homer; in reality it was the game-winner because, immediately following, we put together successive singles to win it. Every hitter who went to the plate knew he was going to hit. The Reds were in a collective hitting trance, and Bench, with his heroics, had been the hypnotist.

It was winter cold for the Series which opened in Cincinnati against the Yankees. In my first at-bat, hitting against Doyle Alexander, I got my first World Series homer. I came as close to hot-dogging it as I ever have on the field. Circling the bases, I saw my mother and father sitting next to Gloria in the stands, and I waved to them.

I had another hit in the game as Don Gullet completely closed down the Yanks, 5–1.

The second game was a little different. We jumped out to a 3–0 lead but then saw the Yankees catch us. We went to the ninth tied at 3. The Yanks went down in their half of the inning, the first two hitters in our half were retired. On a slow chopper to short by Ken Griffey, the Yank shortstop, Fred Stanley, hurried his throw and put the ball in our dugout. Suddenly we had the winning run in scoring position—and I had a chance to bring it home.

The Yankees walked me intentionally. I was angry, frustrated, but also pleased. Tony Perez hit behind me.

"Big mistake!" I said to Thurman Munson, the Yanks' catcher, as he stood to the side of the plate with his mitt extended.

I trotted off to first and the Big Dog promptly laced a single to left to win it.

While we now had a 2–0 Series lead and while we clearly believed we were the better team, we were not inflated with ourselves. We were, before anything else, prepared for the Yankees. Even though we played in different leagues, we knew their personnel very well. We had that whole team down on videotape and all of us had studied the tapes. We knew their pitchers cold, their moves, their habits, their tricks, everything. I had studied the pitchers as well to read what they did with men on base. I got our base stealers together and worked with them till all of us knew the

Yankee staff as well as that of any team in the National League. By
the time of the first game, each of our guys knew that Catfish
Hunter made a little movement with his shoulder before he came
to the plate, a movement he didn't make when he went to a base.
Dock Ellis? Kenny Holtzman? Hey, we wore them out in our
league, why couldn't we do it again?

There was talk, too, about Billy Martin, the Yanks' manager; he
was the kind of aggressive manager who did the unexpected, who
was able to steal signs, do things to unravel another team. Well, he
could steal all the signs he wanted from the Reds, but we had so
few signs that knowing them meant nothing.

Moving on to New York, to Yankee Stadium in particular, was
special. When I first got there, I walked out to the monuments like
any little kid to look at all those bronze plaques. I gawked at the
familiar shape of the place, the triple-decked grandstand, the
bleachers with the elevated train, and the courthouse looming
beyond.

But then, when I finished gawking, I coldly analyzed the place.
What a great park to hit home runs in. Right field was so close. The
first time I stepped in during batting practice, I hit routine fly balls
that landed in the third deck! The outfield space in left center was
huge, so if a good left-handed hitter was consistently pitched away
he had yet another advantage. The place was so tantalizing, I briefly
recalled the time when, as a youngster, I had heard a rumor that the
Yankees had been interested in me. If I had played the same number of years in Yankee Stadium . . . ah well.

We took Game 3, 6–2, meaning that we had now won six consecutive post-season games without a loss. No team had (or has)
ever swept all its games in both the playoffs and Series in one
season, and we were on the verge of it. The papers were brimming
with talk of a sweep and a championship repeat. Yet, for us, there
was only unfinished business.

The Yanks took an early 1–0 lead in Game 4 behind Ed Figueroa,
a good, tough right-hander who had won 19 games that season and
was not afraid to pitch inside.

In the fourth inning, we got to him. I walked, stole second, came home on a single, and then watched as John unloaded a two-run homer into the left-field seats to give us a 3–1 lead. The Yanks countered with another run and there the score held into the ninth. When Figueroa walked the first two hitters in the inning, he was replaced by reliever Dick Tidrow. Tidrow got George to fly to center but it was deep enough for the Big Dog, our lead runner, to advance to third.

With two on and one out, John came to the plate and belted his second home run of the game. The blow was like the long-awaited eruption of a threatening storm, clearing the air for us. More hits followed, another run. Bench, who had, for him, a mediocre season, was simply memorable in post-season play. The blowout final was 7–2, we had done it! There never had been a team like ours and, as far as we were concerned, whooping it up in the dressing room, there never would be.

By almost unanimous consent, we stood atop the baseball world not just as the year's best team but as one of the best ever.

For a while, the euphoria of our accomplishment carried us all. The civic celebrations back in Cincinnati, the awards, the dinners, all reinforced the sense of what we had done. John was named the Series MVP, Sparky was the Manager of the Year, I was named league MVP for the second consecutive season.

But over the winter, another kind of reality began to assert itself. Baseball was into its second year of free agency and already its revolutionary ramifications were beginning to be felt. Don Gullett, a top young pitcher for us, decided to leave Cincinnati and seek fame and fortune elsewhere; he wound up signing with the Yankees. Bigger names—like Reggie Jackson—were on the move.

The Reds' front office undoubtedly had a problem. With a team of many stars, they reasoned they could not enter a bidding war to keep all of them. Whether true or not, it forced certain kinds of economic decisions they probably were reluctant to make.

That winter, I signed a three-year deal worth around $1.9 million. But as financially rewarding as the negotiation was, it was diffi-

cult on all sides. I wasn't thrilled at the idea of signing a long-
term contract. I no longer concerned myself with how much
more I could discover about myself as a player, but I just didn't believe in multiyear pacts. If I had a year that surpassed all expec-
tation, I should be paid for that; if I had a sub-par year that should
be part of the picture, too. I liked the challenge and the incentive
of playing one year at a time. On the other hand, with that kind
of money out there, I wasn't about to cut off my nose to spite my
face.

But far more troubling to me was the announcement made on
December 16 that the Reds had traded Tony Perez along with Will
McEnaney to Montreal for pitchers Dale Murray and Woodie Fry-
man. Tony was thirty-four at the time but still, clearly, as great as
ever. He had come off a year where his RBI total had dropped to 91,
his home-run output to 19. But he had missed some games with
injury and so the decline in numbers meant nothing.

There were two things at work. One was Dick Wagner. Clearly,
he wanted to put his own stamp on a team that had been built by
others. He thought he knew best how to keep the Reds strong. The
other, more practical problem, had to do with the prospect of
keeping four stars signed at new salary highs driven by free agency.
John had a so-so regular season but he was the World Series MVP,
so any trade talk involving him was impossible; Pete was considered
an untouchable and, with my two MVP seasons on the board, so
was I. The Big Dog was odd man out.

At the time Tony was traded, I publicly criticized the Reds'
management for what they did. Never mind business needs, never
mind age or anything else, didn't anyone stop to think that much of
the success we had and hoped to have in the future depended on
Tony Perez? Didn't the people who ran things understand that
teams, even great ones, depended on the sort of leadership he gave
us? The very first time I visited the Reds' front office years before, I
noticed that from the reception desk to the rear offices there was a
single black face. Brooks Lawrence, an ex-player, held down a
make-work job in "community relations."

"Hey, Dick, even the telephone operators are white," I cracked to Dick Wagner at the time.

"Huh? What do you mean?" He seemed flustered by what I'd said.

"Just observing the scenery," I said.

The front office came down on me hard. I was a ballplayer, not an executive, what did I know about the needs of the front office or even the long-range needs of the team?

Gloria, as always, helped me through these tough places, where anger or hurt got in the way of my being able to see straight.

"Is it more important for you to be mad at them or for the ballclub to get going?" she asked. Obviously, the problem of another season would soon be upon us and what mattered, bottom line, was how we played. The cruelty of the game in the end was beside the point. I by no means felt relieved of my concerns but my sense of proportion returned. I was still a member of the Big Red Machine.

It's strange. I've spent so much time talking about where I've been and what I've done that I've scarcely mentioned my wife and family.

When we got married, my desire was to have a family, a real family. And, for me, Gloria was the perfect baseball wife. By that I mean, she understood what my life would be like, she knew about the traveling, the absences, the constant pressure, and about my need for a family. I say she was the perfect baseball wife because she was able to be a mother and half a father to our children. There was never the sense, in all of the years I played, that I was somehow shirking my role as a parent. The most important thing both of us understood about families was that their strength was not in any particular kind of lifestyle but in the love, understanding, and interest shared among family members. We had that always.

But there was a price to pay. I never fully saw that Gloria, all the while, needed to develop her own strong interests and ambitions. She was such a devoted mother and wife that her support seemed simple and uncomplicated. I didn't quite see, till much later, till after I was out of the game, that she wanted more.

We got off to a slow start in '77. For the first month of the season, we seemed to be no better than a second-division team. We lost more than we won, we were slow to seize on opportunities when they presented themselves, we were anything but a Big Red Machine.

The ghost of Tony Perez was everywhere. In the field, I'd look over to first base and be surprised at seeing Danny Driessen there. When I hit, I'd often make a point of looking over my shoulder to the on-deck circle.

In the clubhouse, around the cage, it was just not the same without Tony. No one said anything but no one had to. His presence and his give-and-take with John, Pete, and me were so much a part of everyday life on the Reds that his absence was like a death in the family.

When we all got around to acknowledging—about six weeks into the season—how much we missed him, we began to play better.

Just before the trading deadline in June, the Reds traded for Tom Seaver and, in one stroke, the entire character of the team changed. For the first time, we had a top star who was a pitcher, a guy who went out there every four days, rather than every day. The difference in having a Tom Seaver—or a Roger Clemens—at the top is that a team will unconsciously look for that fourth-day boost. Pitchers on the ballclub seeing overpowering shutout performances from the guy at the top wind up trying to do more than they can when they pitch. Hitters tend to let the top pitcher carry them instead of the other way around.

Seaver was a very different kind of presence in the clubhouse. I enjoyed him because he was so cerebral, but was also a little mystified by him because he was so much an East Coast person. He couldn't get through a day unless he had his copy of the *New York Times*. He always talked about New York, about the theaters, the restaurants, the big names.

Before Seaver came to us, I used to wonder whether New York

itself wasn't one of the reasons why he did so well. Because New York was a place where everything seemed oversized and magnified, it was the kind of environment where certain kinds of players outdid themselves. Reggie Jackson needed a stage that large and found it in New York. So did Sparky Lyle, who wasn't the same player when he went elsewhere.

Seaver surprised me because he was every bit as good in Cincinnati as he was in New York. The only difference was that, playing behind him, I could see what I didn't in facing him.

Tom slowed a game down the way few other pitchers did. He was such a perfectionist that everything from wind conditions to his jersey sleeves had to be just so before he let a pitch go. Sometimes, Tom got too slow. He'd walk around, fidget, kick the dirt, back off. When he did that, I'd go to the mound.

"You wanna throw it or you want me to throw it?" I told him one time.

"Thanks, man," he said, as though he needed that.

But we did not repeat in '77. Though we picked up the pace in May, we wound up chasing the Dodgers through the summer, finishing 10 games behind them at the end. Even with the addition of Tom, we were still a team that had not lived up to the expectations.

I had a good but not great year. I hit .288, had 22 home runs, 78 RBIs, and 49 stolen bases. I won another Gold Glove and began an errorless game streak at second of 91 games that would continue into the following season. Other guys had strong seasons, too. Pete hit .311; John had 31 homers, hit .275; Kenny had another .300-plus season; and George had his monster year with 52 home runs and 149 RBI.

But because we had not won, because our invincibility had been cracked, the future suddenly was unceratin. The team that was about to establish a dynasty a year ago was now one that would have to establish itself all over again. And no one was quite sure how that would happen.

I had probably my poorest year in the majors in '78. I pulled a muscle in my stomach early in the year and I never went on the disabled list. I had played through pain before and because I had always been durable and quick-healing, I thought I would be able to do it this time. It was a foolish choice. Because the injury got worse with playing, I knew by midsummer there would be no real improvement until the season ended.

I kept playing for the ballclub and, most specifically, because I was worried about Sparky. I didn't need a pundit to tell me that his job was now clearly on the line and the only thing that would save it would be another pennant.

I also realized during this season that Pete was probably going to leave. We talked about it a little. I understood from him that the Red were making no moves to induce him to stay once his contract was up—which meant they were inviting him to become a free agent.

The reasons for this have been debated. A lot of people in Cincinnati never forgave the front office for letting Pete go; there was still another group of people that blamed Pete for becoming a free agent, saying it was his own selfishness and greed that drove him away.

While it took a while to figure it all out, I am now almost certain that the real reason the Reds let Pete go was because they had, by then, become concerned about his gambling. When precisely this happened I do not know but I do remember when I first became aware that more might be going on than I knew.

I had a friend in Cincinnati, a guy named Bob Connelly (who passed away in September 1992), who was friendly with a bookie who had told him that the word was out that Pete was going to get his legs broken if he didn't pay his gambling debts. I thought I knew the extent of Pete's gambling and so I was surprised. I went to him and told him what my friend had said.

"Hey, man, you can't be messing with these guys and not pay them," I said.

"Hey, don't worry about it," Pete answered, "nothing's going to happen, I don't owe any money—and besides they're not going to do anything. They'll get themselves in trouble if they try."

He was actually confirming what my friend had warned me about, by saying that because he was Pete Rose no one could touch him.

I really didn't think too much about it after that because Pete was still Pete to me, he played as hard, he was as much into the game, playing it, talking about it, living it as ever.

But at the end of the year, the Reds did not try to re-sign him and he moved on. At the time, I did not make the connection between his gambling and the decision to let him go. I felt only that the Reds had made yet another colossal personnel blunder, as they had with Tony. But, during the time the commissioner's office was investigating Pete, according to a *Cincinnati Post* story, they indeed had been worried all the while about his developing problem with gambling. According to the story, Dick Wagner had learned there were guys out there ready to break Pete's legs over his gambling debts.

And then there was Sparky.

To be fair to the Reds, Sparky was Bob Howsam's man, not Dick Wagner's, and every GM wants to build a team in his own image. That much, I suppose, is understandable. But Sparky was such a special man and manager. He was not replaceable to me and, as far I was concerned, he was not replaceable to the ballclub.

Sparky was the sort of man who could naturally be a close friend and a professional at the same time. During contract squabbles, run-ins with the front office, Sparky was an ally and a friend in ways managers rarely were.

During my '76 contract negotiation, for example, Sparky at one point wanted to know how things were going. At the time I was at the depth of my anger and disillusionment.

"Joe, lemme ask you something," Sparky said. "What can't you buy with $650,000 that you can buy with $700,000?"

"It's not about money, Sparky," I said.

"No," he said. "Okay, then, I'll give you the difference between what you want and what they're offering, what do you say?" He was laughing—and then so was I.

When Sparky was finally fired after the '78 season, I could not take it. The most difficult part for me was that Sparky, well in advance of it, at the end of '77, had come to me and said that if anything should ever happen to him, no matter how unjust I thought it was, he wanted me to keep silent, to not make waves, to just accept that being fired was part of the game for a manager. He was concerned, he said, because there would be a new manager after him and he would need all the help he could get from his ballplayers. It would embarrass him, and the new man, if key players like me went public with any criticism. I thought he was being foolish but I promised him that I would do as he asked anyway.

One day I got a call from Dick Wagner at 5 A.M. California time. Because it was barely dawn and because it was so strange to hear his voice at that hour, it was hard for me to concentrate.

"Joe, I'm calling you because I know how close you are to Sparky . . ."

"Yeah?"

"We're having a press conference later this morning to announce that we are making a managerial change."

"You're firing him?"

"We wanted you to know before you picked it up on TV or read about it in the paper . . ."

"Thanks."

I called Sparky immediately afterwards. I was in tears by then. I told him about Wagner's call.

"They can't do this," I said.

"You just forget it, little man, I just want you to remember that you promised me you wouldn't say a word."

I kept that promise for fifteen years. That's a long enough time. Circumstances have changed. The record then, and now, has been waiting to be put straight.

With Tony, Pete, and now Sparky gone, the heart of the Big Red Machine had all but ceased. John, nearing the end of his playing time, and I were the last of the "Big Five" (count Sparky in any look at the Rose–Bench–Perez–Morgan era in Cincinnati). And it was then, before the '79 season was even under way, that I decided to play out my contract and move on.

We happened to win the Western Division in '79 under John McNamara but that changed nothing. We lost in the playoffs to the Pirates, I went 0 for 9 as we were swept, and I hated leaving on that kind of note—but it was over.

I know that my feelings about very particular people whom I cared very much about were bound up in my decision to leave, but there was also the sense of just not wanting to stay behind to see something that had been great turn mediocre. For two years, there had been no team like ours. We sat alone on top of the baseball world taking in all those media comparisons with the great teams of the past. Because I had been part of something that was so exceptional I could not stand the idea of seeing it run down.

When we won the division, the Reds called, wanting to offer me another contract. Tom Reich, who handled contracts for me now, let me know that the Reds were offering two years, the money was fine, the terms were fair.

But I just could not do it. That fall, I became a free agent.

I was first drafted by the Dodgers, my team of choice. Because they had been our archrivals over the years, they were almost part of my own makeup as a player. I liked the organization, liked the team's chances, and believed I could help them win. In addition, playing on the West Coast meant that I would be closer to home, something I needed in my life.

I had a meeting with Tommy Lasorda. At the time, Davey Lopes was the Dodger second baseman and, Lasorda said, the plan was to move him to center field. That would have been a perfect situation for all of us because the Dodgers needed a center fielder at that time and Davey would have been a better center fielder than he was a second baseman. Only Davey wouldn't go along. Or, that is, he attached some sort of condition to it, the forgiveness of a loan or something, and management refused.

Instead, I was asked to come in as a second baseman anyway and, later on, to let things get sorted out. I would not do this. It was very tough for me to say no, too, because the draft was over, I could no longer shop. But I could not put myself in a situation where I would be the center of dissension on a ballclub trying to win a pennant.

Half the guys would have been pissed off at Davey for not switching to center field, half the guys would have been on his side, and I would have been in the middle. So I said no—and for a while I was out in the cold.

At that point, I announced that I wouldn't sign with anyone and went back into what they then called the secondary phase of the draft.

Two teams then drafted me. One of them was the New York Yankees. George Steinbrenner called Tom Reich and told him that I had a home in New York anytime I wanted.

I didn't know much about the situation in New York, had no idea how the Yankees might have resolved the question of having Willie Randolph and me doubled up at second base. Steinbrenner was an owner I had mixed feelings about. The usual thing is to hate him and poke fun at his heavy-handedness. But I knew he was a guy who wanted to win and who would always shake things up to get it done. That part was fine. But I also didn't like the idea of his bullying people and firing them at the drop of a hat. In the end, even though the American League had the designated hitter and the Yankees the stadium with its short porch in right, the Yankees were not for me. I was at that stage in my career where I just wasn't willing to put up with all the back-page craziness that would go with playing there. I told Tom to just say no.

The only other team that had bid for me then was the Houston Astros, the team I had grown up with.

In retrospect, it is entirely possible that if it had been any other team, I might have sat out the year—much against my will. Fortunately that decision did not have to be made. I had very specfific things I was looking for in playing. I was an older player; the end of my career, I knew, was not so far off. At thirty-six, I already had the kind of career where I could think about the way I wanted to go out of the game when the time came.

The Astros, during the past season, had had an 11-game lead over us and we caught them at the end. I knew the team was a good one and that an adjustment or two might get them to the top. One of those adjustments would be the presence of a veteran player, like myself, able to provide maturity and leadership down the stretch.

I went down to Houston to meet with Tal Smith, the team's GM, and with the manager, Bill Virdon. What they were looking for and what I felt I could give were the same.

"We're not looking for you to hit .300 or to drive in 100 runs, what we want from you is the kind of leadership that will help us avoid repeating what we went through last season," Tal said.

Perfect. I liked Tal Smith and Bill Virdon—and I liked the idea of returning to Houston.

Part Four

THE LONG WAY HOME

FROM THE BOOTH:
The More Things Change

When I entered the game, I had no idea that my career would take place right at the time baseball itself was about to change.

Because I came up in the "old school," much of what I know and still value in the game harkens back to ideas and practices that had been around almost from the time baseball began.

The ideas I cherish about team play, playing to win rather than to simply amass numbers, are not unique. The skills of the game, what gives baseball its special and mysterious beauty, are really only the collective experience of generations of ballplayers who managed to pass on what they acquired to those who came after them. If these skills are not passed on, the game suffers.

I recently broadcast a game in Chicago between the White Sox and the Yankees. A number of interesting things caught my eye in this game. And they were typical.

On one play, the White Sox shortstop, Dale Sveum, came over from his position to take a throw from the catcher on an attempted steal. He took his position behind the base, bent over to apply the tag, but the runner was in ahead of him. A seemingly routine play—only it was not. Sveum should have covered the base standing in front of it, not behind it. If he had caught the ball in front, he would have cut time and distance on the catcher's throw, the angle he needed to make the tag on the runner coming in would have been better, the distance to cover between his hand and the sliding runner would have been less.

Sveum should have picked up that small but subtle piece of positioning long ago. But apparently there was no one around to teach him. He's been in the majors for several years.

Tim Raines has been around longer than that. One of the great leadoff hitters ever, he looked sluggish and tentative to me at the plate. On a 3–1 count, I noticed that he guided his bat at the ball rather than attacking it. He should have had someone around to remind him that especially on a 3–0 or 3–1 count, that's the time to take a rip at the ball. These are things easily overlooked—but not to people who have seen all of it before.

For the longest while, the game was actually structured in such a way that skills and traditions could be passed on. Teams were much tighter, closer units than they are today. Travel took time. Long hours on trains or hanging around hotel lobbies were part of a summer's routine. There was time to talk, to swap stories, to teach, to listen and learn.

That has all changed since the age of air travel, stereo headsets, and easy movement by players between teams. Most of all, money has done much to sever this critical lifeline between the generations.

I look around today and see that very few of the great old stars of the game are still in it. Joe DiMaggio, Stan Musial, Willie Mays, Ted Williams, Maury Wills, Lou Brock, and legions of other stars are not out there in any capacity—and why? For the simple reason that with the advent of skyrocketing costs coming from free agency and from running the game like big business, salaries for certain baseball employees—like coaches and scouts—are insultingly low. It is a crime for these great stars of the past, with all that they still might contribute, to wind up, in effect, banished from everything except occasional dinners and old-timer games.

I can't imagine what kind of career I would have had without the presence of someone like Nellie Fox. The value to any team of having guys like Nellie, or Willie Mays or Maury Wills, is so obvious it should not require explanation. But today, there are precious few people around who can pass on to young players skills like base-stealing, fine points like sign-stealing or bunting or learning what it is to think like a winner.

"Thinking like a winner" doesn't happen automatically but it should. Take the matter of base-stealing. Not long ago, I broadcast an A's–Red Sox game in Oakland. The game was tied 1–1 in the eighth inning and Rickey Henderson, who will probably retire with more stolen bases than anyone in history, reached first to open the inning. He never stole second. When he was moved there on a bunt, he never stole third. There was nothing physically wrong with him, he just didn't want to risk being thrown out.

If Rickey had been "thinking like a winner," he might have tried to steal. Henderson and others like Vince Coleman, like a lot of speedy guys today, know how to steal bases but they are not base stealers—as Maury Wills and Lou Brock were. Wills and Brock would have been embarrassed to be bunted over in a crucial situation, costing the team a valuable out. So would I. When I learned to steal bases, I had also had drummed into my head by Nellie Fox and others that you stole bases only to help your team win. Eighth inning, game on the line? That was exactly the time to go.

The obvious way to keep some of the teaching power of the old stars in the game is to let them manage. The pay, while not on a par with player salaries, is more than that offered to coaches and scouts. The problem with ex-stars as managers, of course, is that it can be hard to bridge the gap between their own performing careers and what they see in front of them. That is one reason why guys who did not have great playing careers, like Sparky or Earl Weaver, could make good managers. Stars, very often, become impatient with the lesser players who are out there playing for them.

Another way to assure that the skills of the game get passed on is to pay far more attention to player development. At present, neither the minor leagues nor college baseball programs assure that players coming up will have anything close to the experience they need.

Years ago, the minors did provide enough talent for the major leagues. Not so today. After World War II, there were approximately 500 minor-league teams in the country. Today, the number is a little more than a third of that. And the fewer teams do not necessarily produce better players. There is neither the money nor the personnel at the minor-league level to guarantee a coherent development of talent. All too often, managers and coaches at the lowest levels of the minors are ill-prepared to train young players.

More than ever, colleges are left to develop talent today but there is no money or working agreement to assist them. Young college players are brought along using aluminum bats, which completely distort hitting. The wooden bat, used exclusively in professional baseball, has a live power area of about 5 inches. There are almost 25 inches of juice in an aluminum bat, meaning that all too many college hitters learn habits that are hard, if not impossible, to break later on. Several years ago, Jeff Ledbetter, an NCAA home-run champion from Florida State, was signed as a first-round draft choice by the Boston Red Sox. Ledbetter stopped hitting home runs as soon as he picked up a wooden bat. He never made it past double-A before he was out of baseball entirely.

With fewer players playing fewer years before they reach the majors, talent continues to be diluted. Expansion means more jobs at the major-league level but who will fill those jobs? I have always maintained that a star is someone a fan will be genuinely eager to pay money to see play. How many of those are in the game now? At the end of last season, I broadcast a game featuring a pitching matchup between Nolan Ryan and Roger Clemens. The game was tense and exciting, even though both teams were out of the pennant race. In the eighth inning, Ryan was replaced by a pitcher named Matt Whiteside; in the ninth, the Red Sox replaced Clemens with Tony Fossas. The air went out of the game like a balloon with a bad leak.

In the end, the passing on of tradition doesn't have to do so much with fan interest as with participation, getting out and playing the game, in the streets, the lots, the yards, the makeshift fields all over the country. For the better part of a century, the enthusiasm of amateurs, of kids, guaranteed that there would always be a large pool of talent to draw from.

Major-league baseball once had the look and feel of a genuine nationalpastime. Whenitwasplayedintheday, whenkidseverywhere followed it, baseball was popular in ways that went far beyond profits. Professional baseball once took pains to bring the game to the fans. Prices were reduced, special days were held, barnstorming tours were arranged so that even in the farthest reaches of the country, big-time baseball was close enough to touch. There were doubleheaders on Sundays for fans to look forward to.

Today, television has replaced barnstorming, urban life has closed off all too many fields of dreams. Baseball, sadly, seems hardly to have noticed. There is little or no support for those ama- teur programs—Little League, Babe Ruth, Pony League—that have been around for years. There is also little concern that those pro- grams tend to be too structured, too organized for kids to actually get the hours of free playing time that are so necessary in learning.

On the other hand, there is some activity out there. One of the really interesting new ideas floating around is the development of baseball schools, particularly in the inner cities, where baseball is losing athletes and fans to basketball and football. A group called "R.B.I.," Revitalizing Baseball in Inner Cities, headed by John Young with an assist by an old Houston teammate of mine, Bob Watson, has been steadfastly trying to get major-league baseball involved. The idea, which makes good sense beyond baseball but that also offers a vital new connection between the game and its future, is that these schools or academies, in major urban centers all across the country, will teach and promote the skills of the game, provide the equipment, the know-how, the personnel to organize leagues and associations, to enable kids to learn the game while at the same time coming to respect the demands of discipline, sacrifice, and commitment necessary to succeed. The fact that this idea is still in the developmental stage, even with major-league baseball's support, indicates all too well where we are right now. What a boost it would be if the game's great old stars could somehow find their way to programs like these.

For a variety of reasons, our game, even as it counts its profits, is in steady decline. No reason gives more concern for alarm, however, than baseball's almost mindless disregard of its own roots.

13

Exile's Return

When I left the Reds, I really did hope to play for one more team and then step down. It was not to be the case. Between 1980 and 1984, when I finally retired, I played for four teams. It's funny. With each of those teams, I was looking for the same thing. A chance to be with a winner, which meant being in a situation where everyone was pulling together—like the Reds. I wanted to go home again.

I came back to a very different town and very different team. There were a lot of guys there I hadn't played with originally but whom I knew well from having played against and whom I liked. Enos Cabell, Art Howe, Terry Puhl, Jose Cruz (one of the best and most underrated players I have ever seen), Alan Ashby, Craig Reynolds, Joaquin Andujar, J. R. Richard, and Nolan Ryan were all members of the Astros in 1980. Cesar Cedeño, enormously gifted, was a holdover from my time. It was no wonder they came so close the year before. I was just one of many people who expected them to win it all in the very immediate future.

I had a wonderful and, in the end, painfully disappointing season in Houston.

I could not have asked for more in terms of teammates. We were a group that was both hungry and easygoing. There were kids and, with Art Howe and me, veterans, there were guys who were all business, guys who didn't know from business, guys who were outright characters.

Nolan Ryan was one of my all-time favorite teammates. Here was a guy who was a superstar and future Hall of Famer who just worked his tail off every day, every week, every month, all year round. Yeah, I liked his work ethic, but it was the attitude behind it that counted.

Nolan is not a guy who brags or throws his weight around or tries to play macho man. He just goes out and does his job. But his job includes being aggressive as a pitcher. He knows what he has to do—and he's got a heart as big as Texas, all full of a competitor's emotions.

We were sitting on the bench one day in Houston. Dave Winfield, in his prime, and a youthful Ozzie Smith were then both members of the Padres. Something had obviously happened during the game that I had missed because when Nolan took a seat next to me during this half inning, he was fuming and talking to himself.

"I'm gonna get that little s.o.b.," he was saying. "I'm gonna get that little s.o.b."

I didn't know who he was talking about and as I thought I fit that description myself, I asked him.

"Who are you going to get, Nolan?"

"Ozzie Smith, I'm gonna get him and you better believe it."

Who was I to argue? If my teammate is worked up about something, he's still my teammate. My teammate right or wrong.

So we go back out in the field and when Ozzie comes to bat, the predictable (almost) happened. Ryan throws one of his 105-mph fastballs and knocks Ozzie down. What Ryan may have overlooked (although to overlook the guy was sort of like overlooking Mt. Rushmore) was Dave Winfield, on deck.

Winfield immediately started screaming at Ryan. I mean there was a shower of abuse that was probably picked up in the last rows of the bleachers. In any case, Ozzie, one way or another, got to first base (I am not sure how, it makes no difference). Well, when

Winfield stepped in next, Ryan, sure enough, went after him. First pitch, ZZZZZIP, right under the peak of his helmet. Dave went down and, I swear, before he hit the ground he was charging the mound. And when I use the word *charging* that doesn't begin to describe the look of this very berserk giant flying out toward the middle of the field. He had death and destruction written all over his face.

Now, as a teammate, I could do only one thing—charge right toward the center of the field (hoping that somehow I would never get there!). The huge, surging mixup (thank God) cut off my path to big Dave, but I could see him diving over the top of the pile, throwing punches at Nolan, who absolutely held his ground. In fact, Nolan ducked under everything Dave threw, all the while refusing to back off an inch. It was an amazing and almost unbelievable sight.

After Winfield was finally subdued and the players separated and the inning finished, I took a seat over toward the corner of the dugout and Nolan again came down and sat next to me. It was like he was in another world.

"You know, Joe," he says, "I'm six-five, I'm a big guy, right? And I'm standing on the mound and that gives me another six to ten inches on top of that, but I swear when Dave Winfield was charging me I was looking up at him. You know if one of those right hands would have hit me, I'd be dead. You realize that?"

"Yeah," I said, "I realize that." And we both laughed.

Another great teammate was J. R. Richard. J. R. inevitably brings to mind the image of a great personal tragedy. The tragedy was all too real—and, in a baseball sense, I believe it probably cost us a world championship. None of us who played there that year can forget what happened.

At that point in his career, J. R. was still getting better. To me, he was another Sandy Koufax. He had the greatest stuff I have ever seen and it still gives me goosebumps to think of what he might have become.

All through the first part of the season, he went out there and simply destroyed the opposition. He was 10–1 and each of those wins represented an overpowering star performance. He'd pitch a two-hitter then come back with a one-hitter. He'd strike out ten guys in one game, come back with thirteen in the next and fourteen after that.

J. R. stayed behind on one of our road trips because he had developed pain in his shoulder and was going to have tests run to see if they could find out if anything was wrong. The tests indicated he was okay. Nothing wrong, he was told. He went to the ballpark to work out before rejoining us and it was then that he collapsed.

The news that he had a blood clot was devastating. The first concern all of us had was for J. R. the person, never mind what he meant to the team. I think one of the reasons we were really such a good team was because when a blow of that magnitude hit we really did redouble our efforts on the field. J. R.'s misfortune became a motivation for us to play harder.

After we understood that J. R. was not going to die, the most difficult thing for all of us to accept was that this great, great talent was really to be no more. When any athlete is cut down there is always a special sadness because the glory of athletes is what they have been able to do with their bodies. When an athlete with the abilities of a J. R. Richard is lost, you start asking questions. Why should such a person have been singled out? If he was old or he led a dissolute life it would be one thing, but he was young and strong . . . and very fun-loving. He was a kind of innocent. Among the guys I think of as "characters" on that Houston ballclub, J. R. ranks right up there. He just wasn't a candidate for tragedy.

He was a big, easygoing guy from Louisiana. He had a down-home, folksy quality about him, you couldn't get him mad or get him down. He didn't know what was going on in the rest of the world—and he didn't care. He learned the secrets of a good life right down there in Cajun country and he was like a manchild in the promised land without an ounce of ego or confusion. He went after what he wanted, whether it was pitching or cooking, because he enjoyed it.

That spring, J. R. and Enos Cabell had a house together. Cesar Cedeño and I each had separate houses. But the four of us used to take turns cooking for each other. We worked in rotation—and everyone just waited on J. R. because he was a second-to-none New Orleans chef, the likes of which you don't find in French Quarter restaurants.

I remember, though, the first time I went over to J. R.'s for dinner. I had heard about his cooking exploits so I went out of my way to make the occasion really festive. I brought a bottle of Dom Pérignon with me.

When I got there and offered this champagne to the guys, they turned me down.

"No, no," J. R. said, "we got champagne opened already."

I looked at the table and saw a bottle of Cold Duck.

"Man, you've got to be kidding. Throw that away. *This* is champagne."

J. R. didn't know what I was talking about, but he did after he took a sip of Dom Pérignon. He was just like a little kid. But then he served a four-star meal that just knocked us all off the table. From then on, everyone was a champagne connoisseur.

I hit only .243 that year, but I contributed in other ways. I hit 11 homers, led the league in walks, stole 24 bases. Even though all those numbers suggested to me that my best days were behind me, that season in Houston was one of the best I had. I was needed on that team.

I was signed because the team needed veteran help. That was just what I could give. Younger players sought me out and I, in turn, could tell them things I had picked up through my years in the game. I never talked to anyone like I was a big shot and I never pushed anything. My goal, always, was to get people thinking in the same direction—winning, and doing things that were smart. I also had very much come to appreciate the difference between playing at ease and playing uptight over the long haul, something I had learned particularly with the Reds.

With our guys, just because they had tightened up in the clutch the year before, I knew that laughter and having a good time could count just as much as swinging the bat or catching the ball.

Joe Niekro and I were sitting around one day talking about how often guys went to their crotch in the course of a game. Next to spitting, players pawing at their cups is baseball's most noticeable nervous tick. We decided to watch Enos Cabell, our third baseman, through the course of one game when I wasn't in the lineup. We made an actual count: The guy pawed himself 520 times! On the bench, everyone but Enos, who didn't know what was going on, was in stitches. After the game, we told Cabell the results of our research. He didn't believe it—but there were all kinds of witnesses to back us up.

Cabell, thereafter, made an acutely conscious attempt to keep his hands off his crotch. That was even funnier than when he wasn't thinking about it. You'd see him out there, particularly at bat, start to go for his cup and then stop himself in mid-swipe. He couldn't laugh, couldn't indicate that he was thinking about that, so it just got to be like a hopeless comedy routine which everyone loved.

Joe and I, with assistance, counted Enos's crotch grabs in a second game, well after he had been working on restraining himself: 311 attempts. Not bad, we told him, you've lowered your batting average by 40 percent.

We should have but didn't pull away from the rest of the division. I thought I could see why. When you play for a winning team over a long period of time, as I had with the Reds, you pick up habits that become ingrained and that help you win—just as habits are acquired on losing teams that have the opposite effect. We had great talent but we didn't play like that. It was as though each of the guys individually knew they were good but hadn't yet picked up the habit of pushing and thinking together as a team.

When the Dodgers had pulled within one game, we were in San Diego. I called a team meeting and asked Bill Virdon, the manager, and the coaches to leave. This was just to be a players' meeting. I had some specific things I wanted to get off my chest to my team-

mates and to no one else. I did not clear the meeting beforehand
with Bill but, then again, there was no need to. Players regularly call
players-only meetings in the course of a season when things need to
be aired out.

I told the guys that whether they knew it or not they were
playing for their salaries, not for the pennant. If you play for
bonuses and salary hikes, you play one way; if you sacrifice and
forget about all that, you play another way. To win, you *had* to
sacrifice. There was no choice. Everybody's got to think, I said,
about what can be done, specifically, to win a game. You don't
think that once and let it go, but five or ten times during a game:
every time you come to the plate, every time you're on base, every
time you're in the field. That's why the Reds caught you last year.

"You're all thinking about your statistics because they're so good.
Now me, I don't have to think about mine because they're so bad."

Everybody laughed—which was just what I wanted. I asked one
player why he didn't bunt the night before in a game we lost. I
asked another player why he didn't try to hit the ball to the right
side in an at-bat where he needed to. After I finished, I asked the
guys if they had anything to say. I waited, not at all sure now how
they would react.

Joe Niekro finally said:

"Joe, I think you're right." And then Enos Cabell chimed in and
then some of the others. I was pleased but I wasn't really looking to
feel good.

"Okay, then what are we gonna do about it?" I said, and then
answered my own question. "From now on we gotta play smart.
We've gotta hit behind guys to move them along, lay down bunts
when they're called for, help each other out. We've gotta get the
numbers game out of our heads and think only about winning every
game we're in. Just that. Every guy is as responsible as every other
guy."

After that meeting, we won nine games in a row. The only
problem I had came not from any teammate but from the manager,
Bill Virdon, who resented my stepping into an area that was really

his. I tried the best I could to defuse the situation. The media soon caught on to what had happened and they came to me asking for details about the meeting. I told them that I had only tried to pass on the experience I had, that I hadn't done anything, the players themselves had come to the simple decision that they were going to win—that was all. If they weren't into that from the start, they wouldn't have listened to a word I said. But there was nothing I could do to get off the hook. From that day forward my relationship with Bill changed.

After every victory the players gave me more and more credit, kept widening the gap between Bill and me. In a week's time I became the bad guy for good.

Bill was a guy who had a long playing career, just as I had. He had played all those years on some great Pittsburgh teams. He was the center fielder alongside Roberto Clemente. He had an ego. Particularly when it came to being the leader of a team. As the manager he was the leader. It was that simple. He needed to let guys know he was the boss.

Some of the players were really funny in the way they responded to him. Jose Cruz, for example, was amazing. His nickname was Cheo and he referred to himself in the third person—like Jesus Alou (did these guys talk to each other?). He was, as well as being the best player on the club and a truly outstanding clutch performer, just the most good-natured person in the world.

Virdon would come after him and Cheo would laugh in his face, not scornfully, but good-naturedly. That would infuriate Bill, who would then get on his case with other players around, just to show who was boss. Cruz used to laugh, as though he were enjoying every minute of it, and then say to everyone within earshot, "Hey, no problem, Cheo just keep on hitting and driving in runs, hey, no sweat, you got the Cheo Cruz, you gonna win some ball games."

I noticed the change with Bill immediately. From the first meeting I had had with him in Houston that previous winter to the present we had always talked to each other. We shared insights and ideas, swapped stories, found time to just sit and shoot the breeze.

He was at ease enough to ask me for suggestions from time to time and I never felt awkward in answering him. We were a pair of old professionals.

But that stopped right away. Within days of that team meeting, Bill and I stopped talking. He would barely nod to me when we passed each other in the clubhouse or out on the field.

Then a whole bunch of little things began happening. Bill started pinch hitting for me—when he hadn't done that before. Or he'd actually pull me from games when we had a lead. A lot of times I'd find myself getting two at-bats in a game and then going to the bench. Sometimes I'd get on base and he'd send a guy out to run for me. I understood what was going on but there wasn't anything I could do about it.

The odd thing was that because the players saw this so clearly and because they sensed how unfair Bill's actions were to them, they rallied around me and pulled closer together. In a few short months, this team matured and became battle-tested. Watching these guys find themselves as a unit was really beautiful but, in the end, was too painful to take. This team deserved to win a pennant, should have won a pennant—and it did not. The main reason, as far as I was concerned, was Bill's stupid hang-up about being the Leader.

The team chasing us down to the wire that year was the Dodgers. The schedule makers must have known something because we were going to finish the season with three games in Los Angeles.

During the week leading up to that final series, we were on top by a couple of games, matching each other's wins as we approached our showdown. Our final home game was against the Braves. I got the winning hit in the ninth inning of a 3–2 game that put us three games up with three to go—because the Dodgers lost that same day.

A three-game lead with three to go seemed almost like a lock. We were supremely confident going in, even though we were going to be playing in their building, before all their fans.

We went right at them. This first game was hard and close but we took a 3–2 lead to the ninth inning. Our pitcher that day was Ken Forsch and he had pitched well, if a little shakily, till the ninth. But we had the best relief pitcher in baseball that year in the bullpen, Dave Smith. Bring in Smith and the game was over.

Bill stayed with Forsch. The Dodgers got a one-out hit—and Bill still stayed with Kenny. There was a fly-ball out and then another hit—runners on first and second with Ron Cey, a hard-nosed clutch hitter, coming up—the game, the season, the pennant on the line: still Bill stayed with Forsch.

Cey lined a single to left scoring the tying run and moving the winning run into scoring position. Bill once more refused to bring in Dave Smith! This was incredible. Everyone on the ballclub knew that Bill and Kenny were close personal friends but here with the pennant on the line, Bill was letting his own personal thing get in the way.

Forsch got the third out—a bullet to left center field that was taken on the run—and we went to extra innings. Believe it or not, Virdon still would not make a change. And then, of course, the inevitable: Joe Ferguson, the first Dodger batter in the bottom of the tenth, homered, and the champagne we had almost tasted turned to vinegar.

The next day, the Dodgers killed us—no contest. And then, in the finale, they beat us again.

Meanwhile, thanks to one of those coin flips done weeks earlier, we were now set for a one-game playoff with the Dodgers—right there in Chavez Ravine. Fortunately, we had a hot pitcher in Joe Neikro—who should have been the guy opening for us in the championship series—ready for the Dodgers. We won, becoming the first Houston team to get to the playoffs, but it had cost us.

Still, we were ready for post-season, stronger again because we had refused to quit. Despite what we had been through, we had never lost belief in ourselves and we did have the personnel now to carry us in the playoffs against the Phillies.

We lost to Steve Carlton in the playoff opener in Philadelphia. Nothing to be done there because Steve was on, and he was just the best, particularly when it counted. He had great stuff, obviously. His slider was unhittable, he had a great fastball and pinpoint control. All of that added up to a lot of wins but the most impressive thing about him was his mental toughness. He *never* gave in. He pitched for a losing team for years, which surely toughened him, and then he undertook a daily martial arts training program that was as much about strengthening his mind as his body. He beat us that game.

But we came back, winning a thriller the next day, earning a split. Steve Carlton or no Steve Carlton, that was all we had come to Philadelphia for. We took the series back to Houston in great shape for the final three games.

We won Game 3 1–0 in eleven innings. Joe Niekro pitched ten scoreless innings, Dave Smith came on for the win. In the eleventh inning, I led off with a triple—and Bill immediately pulled me for a pinch runner. I had hurt my knees a week earlier, so it was the right move. The next two runners were intentionally walked, then Denny Walling hit a fly ball, the opposite way, to win the ball game.

We were up two games to one now, needing a single victory to get to the World Series. We should have gotten it the next day but didn't. We took a 2–0 lead into the eighth only to have the Phillies come back to win in extra innings.

In the fifth and deciding game, we thought we were in the driver's seat because we had Nolan going for us, at home, in front of our fans.

The game, in fact, was tight, too tight, for six innings. The Phils led 2–1, but then in the sixth, Greg Luzinski, the Phils' left fielder, misplayed a ball into a two-base error and we tied the game on a subsequent single to right by Alan Ashby. In the seventh, we exploded for three runs, capped by a two-run triple by Art Howe. We had what seemed like an insurmountable lead.

As soon as we took the lead, Bill sent one of his coaches, Deacon Jones, down to where Art Howe and I were sitting on the bench to tell us that we were out of the game. He said it just like that, too:

"Art, you're out of the game. Joe, you're out of the game."

Art, who was everybody's hero at that moment, didn't say any-thing, but I did. Virdon may not have been able to acknowledge it but he needed us for the last innings—he needed us just because we were veteran players who had been through it before. I told Deacon to tell Bill that if he took me out of the game now he was going to need another second baseman in the World Series because I'd never play another game for him. I was in a rage and I couldn't contain it. The game was not over. This was the fifth and final game, anything could happen. I tried to calm myself.

"Look," I said to Deacon, "we need to win. Tell him not to take us out of the game."

So he went back down to the other end of the bench to talk to Virdon. I don't know what he told Bill but he came back and said, "You're out of the game."

Art and I together then left the dugout and went upstairs to the clubhouse to watch the rest of the game on TV.

We both knew what had happened and why—and we both understood just how much risk the team had been placed in by Bill. What's certain in baseball is that nothing is certain, all of that stuff about the game not being over till the last man was out came from experience, not wishful thinking. And, sure enough, as we sat there, we saw the whole season start to go, all the while knowing that if we had been out there in the field we might have made a differ-ence.

In the eighth inning, the Phils got a leadoff man on against Nolan. Then there was a bunt—and Nolan fumbled it. Now they had runners on first and second and none out—and no one went to the mound to talk to Ryan. Art and I, both infielders, were guys who as a matter of course would have done that. All that was needed in that moment was for somebody to go in and let Nolan know that, hey, no one was hurt, we were up by three runs, just take a breath and get the next three guys. What most people don't understand is that, especially in big, big games like the playoffs and Series, pitch-ing is the toughest and loneliest job on the team. All of the pressure that position players feel is double that for the guy on the hill. You're standing out there in front of 50,000 people and some-times—even if you're Nolan Ryan—you need someone to go out there and pat you on the back, let you know you really aren't alone, that the magic circle you're in is protected by the guys behind you.

So, in that situation, which needed only someone to make sure an extra breath was taken, nothing was done—and then Nolan walked the next couple of guys, and they wound up tying the score. I remember Howard Cosell was broadcasting and he said, when the tying runs came in, that Houston was in a fix now because the team's two best hitters had been taken out of the game. Cosell, on the air, as only he could, said that Virdon's move was just plain dumb—and he was right.

If I was angry before, I was beside myself now. I was watching a whole season go down the drain because one man couldn't separate his damned ego from the job he was hired to do. Right there, in the clubhouse, I got Tal Smith on the phone and I started telling him the same thing I had told Deacon Jones—no matter how this game came out, I was finished playing for Bill Virdon.

Tal said, "Come on, Joe, take it easy. I know you're mad. Let's just win the game, all right?"

"Tal," I said, "I just wanted to warn you, that's all."

Well, we ended up losing, in extra innings, so push never came to shove. But, as far as I was concerned, that was irrelevant. When I calmed down and thought it through, I still wanted out, even more.

The next day I was getting ready to leave for California when I got a call from Tal. He said that we really needed to talk and I reiterated to him what I had said to him the day before, that I did not intend to play another game for Bill Virdon. And then I was angry all over again. I blamed Tal for Virdon—because he had extended his contract during the season. "You let him destroy a whole season," I said. "We're just another team now and so I think it's time to move on. You told me you brought me here because you wanted leadership on the ballclub to keep you from blowing things down the stretch, but you blew it by letting that asshole push Art and me to the side just when we were needed the most. No," I told Tal, "I'm outta here. I signed a one-year contract and there's no way I'm coming back."

The pain of this was so great. There was so much joy in this season, so much that was just trashed by stupidity and vanity. I felt so good about what the players had done, I had wanted so badly to make this a real homecoming.

Once again, I had made friends in Houston, had played alongside guys I admired and cared for. I played for an organization I really liked. But I could not get past Bill Virdon. It was odd in a way because I think we were probably better—in the way the A's were when they ganged up against Charlie Finley—because there was this guy at the center of things a lot of the players on the club collectively disliked.

The breakdown I had with Bill Virdon might have cost me dearly but for John McMullen, the owner of the team. McMullen was new to me and, over the season I spent in Houston, had become a close personal friend. He is one of the game's great gentlemen, a person with real conscience and integrity.

John tried to talk me out of leaving, but he also made the way smooth for me to go elsewhere. He never put a knock on me that might have soured other ballclubs from wanting to do business with me; in fact, he wound up taking a lot of heat because he understood what had gone on and had actually tried to do something about it.

John had followed the managerial situation very closely during the season. He was, because he cared to find out, keenly aware of the chronic dissension between players on the team and Bill. He was determined to let Bill go when his contract expired at the end of the season. His feelings, within a tight circle at the top of the organization, were well known. In the middle of this, however, as the ballclub was taking and holding first place, Tal Smith, because he was the GM and in charge of baseball operations, took it on himself to extend Bill's contract. John, preempted from firing Bill, turned around and fired Tal. He never let the media know the real reason for letting him go, was willing to let himself look bad in the process so Tal would be able to work another day somewhere else. He asked me in the end to stay because he needed me there.

It was really hard to turn down a friend but I told John that if I stayed I would only be the bad guy and the center of controversy in the clubhouse. I loved the game, I said, and more than anything I did not want to walk away from it on a sour note. Too many players conclude their careers in ways that leave them feeling bitter, and that was not going to happen to me, I said.

John understood—and I was gone.

14

Home and Away

I did not want to finish my career just anywhere. I wanted to go out a winner. And I wanted to feel at home. When Spec Richardson, who had been the GM at Houston when I first played there and the guy who traded me to Cincinnati, called and asked if I would be interested in coming to the San Francisco Giants, my answer was a quick yes.

The Bay Area was my home. And I had been away for too many years. I wanted and needed to spend more time with my family. My daughters, twelve and nine, were growing up without me there for long stretches of time, and Gloria, who had postponed her own interests so she could raise the children in my absence, wanted now to go back to school and then into business. I needed to be home more.

In addition, the Giants were an interesting team to me. They hadn't won yet but they had a set of players waiting to prove themselves. And they had a black manager, Frank Robinson, at the helm. I knew and admired Frank from my playing days and I was more than interested in being there as he worked out what was still a historic role in major-league baseball.

When I went to spring training, I discovered, that Frank had not gotten over being fired by Cleveland, his first manager's post. By most accounts, his troubles in Cleveland came not from problems with white players but from those he had with black players.

A lot of the black guys there complained about the way Frank treated them. The story I heard was that Frank had gone out of his way *not* to show any favoritism to black players—to the point of possibly punishing them just because they were black.

When I got there, Frank didn't talk or communicate much with any of his players, black or white. He spent most of his time in his office and when he did come out he was usually sullen and impatient.

I had a couple of run-ins with him early, once in spring training, another time in the first weeks of the season.

In one spring game, I had the day off. Late in the game, Frank sent me in as a defensive replacement for Duane Kuiper. I was upset because I had specifically been given the day off and I was being dealt with as though I was just another roster number. I let Frank know it.

The second run-in was more serious. I had had a good spring and had started the season feeling strong and healthy. Opening day, Frank removed me for a pinch hitter around the seventh inning. He did it in spite of the fact that I had gone 1 for 3 that day because, he said, he didn't want me hitting against a lefty.

It wasn't the first time I had been pinch-hit for, certainly, and I would have had no trouble understanding it if it came later in the season when it was clear I hadn't been handling left-handed pitching. But it was opening day and Frank had no idea of what I could or couldn't do. He seemed totally oblivious to the fact that over my career I had *always* hit lefties better than righties.

After the game I went to Frank and let him know how pissed I was. I was barely out of Houston and here I was into it again. I told Frank I wanted him to understand that I had put in my years and I didn't appreciate being treated like a journeyman player.

"If I'm not hitting lefties two weeks, two months from now, fine, go ahead and lift me—but until I prove to you I can't hit lefties don't do that to me."

When Frank started to defend himself I cut him off.

"I tell you what, Frank," I said, "I don't need this. I'm on your side. But if you're gonna screw me, forget it." I turned on my heels and I walked out of his office. I didn't know what to expect—but I was never lifted from a game in that way again and I never had trouble with Frank after that.

For much of the season, or rather the first half of the season—because it was '81, the year of the strike, and there were two distinct seasons then—I did not think Frank was a good manager at all.

Having lots of time off, I thought about different managers I knew, ones I had played for and against. Naturally, I kept comparing Sparky with Frank. I remembered the way Sparky insisted on discipline *and* ordinary communication. The door was always open, "hello" was mandatory. Sparky, "the Minor-League Motherfucker," had certain advantages Frank Robinson, the superstar, did not. When Sparky didn't know something, he wasn't afraid to acknowledge it. There was one time he came to me to pick my brains about base-stealing. We sat together for hours while I pointed out to him what I knew.

I thought about Gene Mauch, a guy who had managed several rival teams, and was the best strategist I ever saw. He was the guy who was widely credited with the "double switch" (pinch-hitting for someone *and* simultaneously making a pitching change, switching their spots on the lineup card so the pitcher's spot would come up in the spot just used by the pinch hitter). Mauch was a fierce needler, knowing exactly when to stop (when a player lost his concentration but just before he was ready to fight)—and he was a generous teacher. At my first All-Star Game, Mauch and I were seated next to each other on the bus going to the ballpark. He explained, in detail, why I was a better second-place hitter than Sonny Jackson, another Houston teammate of mine.

"You're a pull hitter, Joe. You also take a lot of pitches. Because Jackson's a base stealer, too, that gives you a bigger hole to shoot for on the right side because they have to guard against him. He is helped out because he knows he'll have a few pitches to work with because of your bat control."

Mauch was an opposing manager who kept his eye on everything and wasn't at all shy in sharing what he knew—even with a player on an opposing team.

Chuck Tanner, the manager of the Pirates for many years, was another favorite. He was as color-blind as Sparky (he was the first manager to put nine black players on the field at the same time) and, like Sparky, he was both a disciplinarian and a friend. No one had better words about his players than Tanner. He was the game's eternal optimist. But he was in your face if you didn't do your job. Years later, when I first thought of managing, he gave me some advice:

"Walk through the clubhouse with one eye," he told me, "and then, above all, let your players play."

Like Sparky, Tanner's own major-league playing career was a modest one.

As well as being a superstar, Frank was a guy who came up in a system that didn't feature communication. Players in his day did what they were told. Frank played for years under Fred Hutchinson in Cincinnati. Hutch was a guy who filled out a lineup card, pushed his buttons, and expected his players to do what they were told.

Being away for many weeks gave me the perspective and the determination I needed to talk to Frank. Because we were friendly, because we were two old-timers who had shared similar experiences, because we were two Bay Area guys who were back home again, we were able to sit down together. One time Frank acknowledged how much trouble he was having and wanted to know how I saw things. That was my opening. I told him that one of the real deficiencies on the ballclub was that guys didn't know what to do in different situations, they didn't know *how* to hit, how to think in the field. I told Frank that he should go up to guys, individually, and tell them what he wanted from them.

"I'd talk to them," I said, "but you're Frank Robinson and you've done a lot more than I have in this game."

Up to then, he just wouldn't do that. But now, in the second half, he did. I don't know how it happened. I'd like to think I had a part in it, but I know that Frank followed no one's lead but his own. One day he was just there—out of his office, on the field, with the guys—and there he stayed. He was a fine manager in the second half, and a great manager in 1982 when we almost won the pennant.

Our ballclub changed, too. In the beginning, we were a team without direction, without character. You couldn't have predicted we would come together the way we did in 1982.

The difference in Frank helped everyone. It wasn't just that he was more outgoing, he was more into his players, more willing to let them take over and use all their abilities. You didn't need a bunt sign to bunt, another to run, another to hit behind a hitter. You could do it on your own—and that kind of play became infectious with us. We found ourselves as a team and we almost rode home to a championship.

In '82 we had Reggie Smith, who had come over from the Dodgers. When I played against him, I always thought he was a prima donna. One time when I was stretching and running before a game (I was the first guy in the big leagues to start doing that), I noticed Reggie and the Dodger players all running together. I hollered over to him, teasingly:

"You all are a bunch of hypocrites, you run together but you can't stand each other."

"Shut up, you don't like what we do, don't say anything!" he barked out, as though he had been mortally insulted.

As a teammate, I found Reggie to be all business, a good guy who played hard. But he was also very stubborn, every bit as stubborn in his way as Frank.

Reggie believed as an article of faith that with runners on first and third and no out, he had to hit a ground ball to be sure of getting the run home, even if it meant a double play. Nothing could change his thinking.

I argued with him once, told him that if he hit away and got the ball in the air, he'd still be likely to bring in the run. He wouldn't budge.

"Suppose I pop up, then what?"

One day we were on the bus and suddenly Reggie, in a very loud voice, started complaining about the shoddiness of travel arrangements on the Giants, how bush league it was to have only one rather than two or three buses. The Dodgers, he said, always traveled in style.

Frank told him to shut up. Reggie ignored him. I then got in the middle of it. When Reggie kept on screaming, Frank said, "Okay, that's a hundred bucks." Each time Reggie said something else, Frank upped the fine another hundred. After a few minutes it was getting totally out of hand. Neither of these guys would ever give in.

Finally I said, "Wait a minute," and I went back to talk to Reggie. I told him to calm down, as strongly as I could, and he did. Then I went back up the aisle to Frank and said, "Look, you can't stop him from talking, this is a free country."

Frank told me that was fine but Reggie couldn't get away with that in front of the guys.

"You're right, Frank," I said, and I went back to Reggie and told him that it was America and he had a right to say anything any time he wanted—but he really couldn't embarrass the team and Frank like this. Reggie laughed and said, "Okay." That was that. The next day, Frank and Reggie were pals. It was as though nothing had ever happened.

Jack Clark, then a young outfielder with us, was another "problem." He has played through his long career with one serious injury after another, which inevitably has kept him from reaching his full potential. That happens. I had tremendous luck in my career in that I sustained only one serious injury over twenty-two years. Jack had too many to count. But what was remarkable about him then, and afterwards, was that he never begged off; he played hurt.

Jack was and is one of the most easily misunderstood people in the game. He is one of a handful of guys I have played with who instinctively know what to do to win. They play to win, which means they know how to take over and carry a team when they have to. They *want* to hit in the ninth inning with the game on the line (there are a lot of people who don't), and he hit the ball as hard as anyone I have ever seen—and in those days he would always be willing to hit to right center if he didn't get a pitch to jerk. He had a powerful arm, was a good outfielder, had speed, and was always underrated—which didn't bother him in the least. So long as his team won.

Jack was a guy who also has had some trouble over the years because he has a way of talking, particularly to the media, where what he says can be misinterpreted. He's into winning, that's all, getting his teammates, his manager, anyone and everyone involved to pay the same kind of attention he does to getting the job done.

Jack got into it with Frank one day when we were in the thick of it in '82. We had just won a dramatic extra-inning game against the Pirates and we were all thrilled by it. When we got into the club-house afterwards, Frank ripped us for sloppy play. He said we didn't deserve to win, that we were lucky and shouldn't get too excited.

That was wrong. I had been around Sparky long enough to know that a manager never has to blame his players if things don't go the way he wants. Sparky always took the blame on himself for bad play. When he wanted something from a player he would very often ask another player to pass it along in the course of ordinary conversation. Once when he wanted to criticize a young player during spring training (he had nonchalanted a pop-up), he got on all his big guys during a team meeting on the evils of nonchalanting pop-ups.

Alone among the players, Jack Clark was the guy who could and would stand up to Frank. With Jack, unlike Reggie, who was basi-cally a quiet guy, letting others know where he stood—especially when it involved the team—was right in character.

Jack exploded when Frank came down on us like that, and he had plenty of support. We were all so happy at having pulled out a big game and Frank took it away from us. Jack was cursing and determined to go in and confront Frank in his office. Because I was Jack's friend as well as Frank's, I put myself in his way. I did not want to see a blowup between these guys—which could only make matters worse.

"Leave it be, Jack, I'll take care of it," I told him.

"No," he said, "I'm tired of you taking care of it for us, we should take care of it ourselves."

I kept talking to Jack until I finally prevailed on him. But while I stopped him from going into Frank's office I could not stop him from talking to the newspapers—which he did that night. And there it was in print the following day.

Jack let Frank—and every fan in the Bay Area—know that he and the team were tired of that kind of stuff from Frank, that we played our tails off and we didn't deserve to be criticized like that.

A number of writers took Jack's remarks as a personal criticism of Frank—which it really wasn't. In reality Jack and Frank got along fine. The criticism had to do with the situation—not the man—and Jack was speaking for all of us, not just himself. I wound up talking to Frank privately and I was satisfied that he understood where Jack was coming from. But he did not back down either. We weren't in this for one game, no matter how good winning felt, he said. We were in for the championship. We were that good, he argued, but we couldn't win if we made avoidable mistakes and refused to acknowledge them.

Jack Clark gave me a wonderful compliment. He said, "Every player should be lucky enough to play one year with Joe Morgan, and he'd be a better player for having done so."

Another favorite of mine on the ballclub was Al Holland, the relief pitcher. Holland was a totally fearless, high-wire artist. He craved the time he had out there, the tougher the better.

We were coming down the stretch that year in a tight three-way race with the Dodgers and Braves. The week before the end of the season we went into Los Angeles for a crucial four-game series. After we took the first three games, the finale was the biggest game we had all year. We wound up carrying a one-run lead into the ninth inning when the Dodgers rallied, loading the bases with two out. Al was pitching and Steve Garvey, one of the best hitters on the Dodgers, was coming up. This was another one of those situations where a visit to the mound from an infielder was automatic. I strolled in toward the middle of the field to make sure my guy was going to stay relaxed and focused.

Whenever I walk to the mound, the first thing I do is look the pitcher straight in the eye. I can always tell what I need to say to him by making eye contact with him. If a guy is unsettled or afraid, you'll see it in his eyes and the words you choose will be different than if you see determination and fire.

Al's eyes were twinkling, almost like he was Santa Claus.

"What the hell are you doing here?" he asked.

"Just wanna make sure you're all right," I said.

"Damn right I'm all right," he said. "Tell Garvey to get his ass in the batter's box and let's go."

And we stood out on the mound laughing. There were 50,000 fans screaming in the ballpark, we're smack in the middle of a pennant race, and we were holding up the game because we were having a private little laugh.

I went back to my position. Al, on cue, took care of Garvey to end the game. In the locker room, and then back in San Francisco, everyone wanted to know what we had been laughing about. What do you say, release of energy, summer lightning, Al Holland's great nervous system? I don't remember what either of us wound up mumbling to the press. But for me that moment will always be the one where I had a tiny glimpse into the heart of a truly great competitor.

We did not win the division, the Dodgers took us out on the last weekend in San Francisco, winning two of the first three games of our set. I had a great personal thrill in the finale by hitting a game-winning three-run homer to ruin the one chance the Dodgers had of catching the Braves. I hit the homer off Terry Forster, the Dodgers left-handed closer who had relieved Fernando Valenzuela, and when I finished my tour of the bases, Jack Clark picked me up in a bear hug at the plate. For forty-five minutes afterwards the fans would not leave the park. I had to go back out there from the clubhouse and then I was so moved by the cheering that I went from left field to right field along the edge of the grandstand, signing autographs. It was as though we had won the pennant—but all we had done was knock off the Dodgers (in San Francisco that is almost equivalent to winning the pennant).

By that final weekend, Frank, who was soon to be named Manager of the Year, had completely transformed himself. He was by then completely a players' manager, a players' champion.

Just before that last weekend—I have never seen another manager do this—he called several guys into his office, guys who had been there for him all year: Reggie Smith, Jack Clark, Darryl Evans, myself.

"Listen," he said, "I've got a problem. I really don't know who to start this weekend. You guys have fought hard all year, this is your race, you deserve to be in on the decision—let's talk about it."

And so we did, back and forth, until we came up with the weekend rotation. It was the finest vote of confidence a manager could have given to his players, even though it did not translate into a championship.

I would have loved to have finished my career in San Francisco—but it was not to be. Just prior to my second and final year in San Francisco, the Giants got a new general manager, Tom Haller. There is no point in detailing the complaints I had about him. Suffice it to say that Haller did not make a single move down the stretch to get the needed pitching help that might have meant the pennant for us. (And it was out there: Everyone in the clubhouse knew that Don Sutton, among others, was available for the taking—but Haller never made the move.)

The black players in the clubhouse, a number of whom found themselves traded or cut from the squad, also believed that Haller disliked black players. The combination—someone who wasn't smart enough or committed enough to do what he had to do to help the team win, and someone who was working out his own racial hang-ups—was enough for me to see the handwriting on the wall.

I had just one run-in with Haller, but it was enough. During our last visit to L.A. at the end of the season, I was scheduled to have lunch with a friend, Joel Lupkin, a businessman. He sent his secretary, a white woman, to pick me up at the hotel. Haller saw me leave the hotel with her—and said hello. That night, Frank called me into his office and said that Tom was concerned about my appearing "tired" in the Los Angeles series, that maybe the reason I hadn't gotten any hits in the ball game that night was because I had some lady with me.

"Wait a minute, stop right there," I said to Frank. "First of all, it's none of your business or Tom Haller's business what I do with my time. I'd respect you more if you didn't get involved. Second of all, you know why Haller told you, don't you?"

"Yeah, the lady was white," Frank said.

"Yeah. He saw me walking out of the hotel with Joel Lupkin's secretary and because she was white I had to be messing around with her. So you stay out of it and tell Tom that if he's got anything to say let him come to me directly."

At the end of the season, a local writer wrote a controversial column about Haller. It was entitled "Haller Prefers Vanilla." It was about the personnel moves Haller was making to whiten up the Giants. Bob Lurie, the owner, who was a terrific guy, had plenty of courage in hiring Frank, but he also wound up hiring (and later, firing) Haller.

Over that winter, Reggie Smith was let go and Al Holland and I were traded to the Phillies. Haller told the press that he had me traded because he had a better second baseman, Duane Kuiper, on the ballclub and therefore didn't need me. I told Bob Lurie what I thought Haller was really up to before I left—that he had gotten rid of three black guys who made a difference on the field and in the clubhouse. I offered to make a bet with Bob that the Giants would finish last in the coming season as a result. Bob wouldn't bet but he argued, "We're a good team."

"You were a good team before you got rid of Reggie Smith, Al Holland, and me," I said. "The only guy you have left who'll help you win is Jack Clark."

I was dispirited over being traded, but the move to the Phillies kept me interested in playing. Bill Giles, an old friend, was there and really wanted me to come. And so were a couple of old teammates—Pete Rose and Tony Perez. The Phillies already had the promise of being a winner. And there was an additional challenge: In a strange way, the Phillies represented another chance to go home again, and to go out a winner. I decided to go ahead.

The Phillies were referred to by many sportswriters that year as "the Wheeze Kids." But we were by no means ready for rocking chairs.

We got off to a terrible start that season, possibly because all of the older guys were battling cold weather in the spring. Pat Corrales, our manager, was let go at mid-season and was replaced by Paul Owen, a nice enough man but a guy who had absolutely nothing to say about anything—especially what was going on in the field. One of the coaches, Bobby Wine, actually ran the ballclub, telling Paul when and where to make all his moves.

With the warm weather we stopped wheezing and began winning regularly. We finished by winning about 50 of our last 80 games. The old guys all were hitting by then.

There was a long period of time during the season when I was no longer certain I could really be an effective player. Perhaps it had been all those moves, perhaps it had been an accumulation of too many years away from home, away from my family, maybe it was just age. I passed my fortieth birthday during that season. I knew there wasn't much time.

Age is a very strange thing for a professional athlete. The loss of physical skill is sometimes the last thing to go—sometimes it diminishes very little. I remember that Ted Williams, in one of his very last years, hit close to .400. The penalties are usually subtle. You recover from injuries more slowly. It is harder to stay sharp mentally.

I had been having problems concentrating for a while. I found myself in one period worried to an unusual degree about my daughters. I'd be in the midst of a game, in the batter's box, and I'd be thinking about them. They were growing up without me around. They were young women, they had difficult times to go through, what would happen to them? This was maddening for me on the ballfield but I could not stop it. For a while I saw a therapist to try and deal with the problem—but the problem was really not fixable in that sense because there was nothing I could do to make myself younger.

I did not have a great full season in Philadelphia but I had the best September of my career, just when it was needed most. I enjoyed my stay in Philadelphia.

It was fun to be there in the clubhouse. While the guys didn't hang out with each other much, they were a loose group of individuals, which made life through the long season a lot easier. There was laughter on this team.

Early in spring training, I became friends with Gary Matthews. Gary, or "the Sarge" as they called him, seemed to me a player who was capable of doing many things to help a team win. He hit well, could run, was a good defender—at least so I had believed, watching him over many years. With the Phillies, the Sarge usually was replaced late in the ball games for defensive purposes. I couldn't understand that and said so—to him and others. However, I was warned, "Just wait till the regular season."

Sure enough, once the season started, the Sarge played till the seventh inning and that was it. He was out of the game like clockwork. Having been removed late in games by Bill Virdon myself this sort of strategy just never sat well with me. But I also didn't understand what was really behind it.

Sometime during the summer, on a particularly hot and humid day, I went up into the clubhouse between innings to change my shirt. I happened to notice, as I passed, that a large beer cooler was standing open. That seemed peculiar to me. Damn, I thought, what's the cooler doing open? I went over to close it and I noticed that a lot of bottles were missing. I looked around the corner to see if anybody was in the lunchroom drinking—nope—so I just kind of forgot about it.

But then during these hot-weather weeks, when I often went to the clubhouse to change my shirt, I noticed the same thing—cooler open, bottles of beer missing.

So one day at a team meeting, Paul Owen, who had no control over anyone and who nearly always kept to the background, said, "Look, we know some of you guys are drinking beer during the game. You shouldn't be doing that. That's just not right."

An uncomfortable silence followed. I wasn't mad or even offended, I was amazed, but I was curious as hell about what was going on. A couple of teammates put me straight.

"Hey, why do you think they take Sarge out in the seventh inning all the time?" one guy said to me.

"What are you talking about?"

"About the seventh inning *he's feeling no pain out there*," another guy said.

"Oh man, no way," I said. These teammates of mine just laughed.

"Watch him, he disappears for a while, comes back out, and he can't see, man!"

After this meeting, the club decided to take some action. The next day when we came in there was a big fat padlock on the ice cooler. Okay, that solves that, I thought. Simple. We all went outside for our warm-ups and then for the game.

Around the seventh inning, it was once again time for me to go in and change my shirt. I went up the runway to the clubhouse and there, in plain view, was the cooler, standing open, its lock broken, a large, neatly lettered note plastered to the door, which read:

"DON'T EVER LOCK THIS BEER COOLER AGAIN!"

I couldn't believe it. I ran back to the dugout and got Perez to come back upstairs with me.

"Look at this shit," I said.

We both stood there laughing. So much for the strategy of late-inning replacements!

On this ballclub there was always an ongoing mix of outrageousness and professionalism. Perhaps because so many guys were older, there was an ability to stay focused while giving up little in the way of personal habits and idiosyncrasies. In style we might have been a little like the old Oakland Raiders football team, a bunch of guys with a renegade reputation, which they used to pump themselves up. So long as this was the case, there was no problem for me. In fact, it made my somewhat lonely life a little livelier.

I was very much impressed with our ballclub—but I also was able to stand apart almost as an observer—just because I was so alone. I had played against but didn't really know some of the ballplayers who were now my teammates. I got to see them in a somewhat different light.

Mike Schmidt, for example, a guy who simply terrorized the National League with his home runs and run production, was anything but terrifying up close. Mike was the only player I've ever seen who had all the talent in the world and none of the confidence to go with it. He might be the least confident superstar who ever played the game. In one game, he struck out in the first inning, came back and sat down on the bench and said, "I'm just not in the flow today."

"What do you mean?" I asked him.

"I'm just not in the flow," he said, obviously down on himself.

"You've got three more at-bats," I said.

But he really didn't. With that one at-bat his day was over. Another time, he got a hit his first time up and he came back just bursting with energy to play.

"I can feel it today, I can feel it!" he kept saying.

When he was like that the chances were that no one would get him out.

The Philadelphia fans didn't make things easier for him either. There was an absolutely schizophrenic relationship between them.

It was almost funny to watch. Schmitty would strike out, they'd boo the hell out of him. Next time up he'd homer and they would go nuts. There was one game in particular where he struck out three straight times and then won the game for the team with a last-of-the-ninth-inning home run. The guy had come up to the plate with the fans howling for his hide. He finished his tour of the bases with the fans wanting to storm the field and carry him off on their shoulders!

The very next day, he hit a home run in his first at-bat, a reprise of the night before. That should have won the fans over for at least a couple of weeks. But in his next at-bat, when he struck out, they were on his case all over again. It was very peculiar. I saw him hit three home runs in one game and still get booed when he struck out in his last at-bat.

The booing not only bothered him but, with his shaky confidence, it made him do things a little differently. He would often not go out on the field to warm up, for example. Instead, he'd stay in the runway leading to the dugout where no fans could see him and talk to him, and he'd throw a baseball against the wall again and again, getting loose.

As a result of all this, Mike was a truly great player but he was never the leader he should have been.

Steve Carlton, on the other hand, was a guy most people beyond the clubhouse thought of as strange and otherworldly. There might have been the suspicion that he was too sensitive for his own good. Actually, he was everything anyone could want in a pitcher.

He was a pure warrior. All of those martial arts exercises he did with Gus Hoefling to keep strong were also in keeping with the warrior spirit he brought to the mound. He was a total master—and probably an underrated one at that. I still think there are a lot of fans out there who don't realize he won four Cy Young Awards. (I started working out with Gus, too, but it didn't do as much for me as it did for Steve.)

In the clubhouse, far from being a guy who didn't like to talk, he was fun to be around, full of stories, many of them directed against himself, a good companion, a great teammate. The cold war he carried on with the media, which wasn't of his own making, never affected his attitude toward his teammates or the game. Unfortunately, it also served to give people a completely mistaken idea about who he was.

There was also a darker side to the ballclub—and I stayed away from it, really wanting to know as little about it as possible. Over time, a few stories had surfaced hinting about the possibility of drug use on the team. Some of those stories, concerning the use of amphetamines by several players, had surfaced before I got there. I had no interest in poking my nose into what I had assumed was probably no more than malicious gossip.

Coming and going to the locker room, I was just a guy going to work. I'd stop and talk with people I was used to seeing and who wanted to say hello or talk to me. There was a guy, I remember, whom I saw around all the time, nodded to, talked to—like he was a member of the Phillies' family.

One day, after I said a few words to him, Garry Maddox came up to me and said I was making a big mistake talking to the guy, that I should make it a point of staying as far away from him as I could. Garry said he was sure he was selling drugs—and he was down there all the time because he had a connection with a couple of the players.

I said to him, "Listen, if you know, and the club officials know, then why aren't they doing anything about it?"

"I don't have an answer," he said.

Neither did I.

In a far more personal way, I became aware of the troubles that were gradually surrounding Pete Rose. I didn't run with Pete while I was in Philadelphia. He lived in New Jersey with his wife, he just wasn't around that much.

On the road, though, we did have time together. But it wasn't quite like old times. Pete had some new friends, people I didn't know, and who, when I was with them, made me feel uncomfortable.

There was one guy in particular who seemed to go everywhere Pete went. One day in San Diego, I met Pete at a restaurant at around 3:30 in the afternoon before we went out to the ballpark. His friend—whose name I forget—was with him. The guy was big and slick-looking, a weight-lifter type. We were talking and Pete's friend felt loose enough to let me know about all kinds of pills he had access to.

I told Pete afterwards that his pal seemed really shady. Pete said that he was okay, that the drugs he was talking about were only steroids used for body-building. We got to the ballpark and Pete then brought him right into the clubhouse. Later, when we got out on the field, I told Pete that I didn't want his friend around me ever again.

"He's a crook, man—and if you don't know it, you're gonna find out," I said.

"Okay," Pete said. Whenever I spent time with Pete after that, the guy wasn't in his company. It didn't register until much later that what I was seeing was really a problem. Then the mountain fell in and my friend, the closest friend I had during the best years of my baseball life, was on the bottom of the pile.

I have tried to make sense of what happened to Pete and, also, what it was in myself that did not allow me to see enough to understand and, from understanding, perhaps to have been able to be a better friend and help him address his problem.

For years I asked no questions about gambling because I didn't think there were any questions to ask. Professional athletes, because their natures are so competitive, frequently get into wagering. Pete was just one of the scores of guys who regularly went to the track, for example. Pete and dog tracks? Sure. Pool a weekend card of football games? Sure.

The Phillies won 90 games that year in taking the National League East by 6 games over the Pirates. We knocked off the Dodgers in the playoffs, splitting in Los Angeles and sweeping them at home. But that was as far as we could go.

We lost in five games to the Orioles in the Series that followed. I believe we were the better club—but we lost. There are never any certainties in a short Series; any two teams that are relatively competitive can wind up winning, but it is also true that there is a way to play to win—and because we did not have decisive leadership in the dugout, it cost us dearly.

The first game in Baltimore, we were losing 1–0. I hit a homer in the eighth inning to tie it up. Then Garry Maddox hit another in the ninth to win it. Baltimore took the second game. Coming home with a split was fine, but right at that point, Game 3 became the criticial one for us. Steve Carlton, who had come up with back problems during the playoffs, had been held out of the first two games. It was doubtful that he could pitch but he said he wanted to give it a try.

Four or five innings was all that was wanted, said our dugout management-by-committee: "Just try to give us a few strong innings."

I hit a home run and Gary Matthews hit one to give us an early lead in the game. Steve, meanwhile, pitched great baseball. We got to the fourth inning, though, and his back started to tighten up on him again.

"Give us just one more inning," he was told.

So Steve went out there and got through the fifth. "One more," they said after that.

Steve was now in agony. Between innings, he went into the runway behind the dugout and lay on the ground, the trainer working on his back, trying to stretch him out. He went out and pitched—and then came back to the runway and to the pain that was just killing him.

I couldn't stand it. I told Paul that we had Al Holland, the best relief pitcher in the game, in the bullpen. "Why don't you use him?" I asked.

They let Steve go out there till he lost it—and until we lost. Far past the point where he was no longer effective, Paul stayed with him until two runs and the lead were surrendered and, worse, Steve left, obviously through for the rest of the Series.

I did not have a particularly good full season. I played injured for a while, my numbers were off, I was obviously getting no younger. But I carried the team in September, was player of the month. My contract had been for one year with an option for a second. After the Series, the day before I was scheduled to leave for home, Bill Giles called me into his office and told me that they were going to release me—and Pete Rose. I was almost ready to retire but I was not there yet, so this announcement really upset me. I wanted to be the one to say when and why I was leaving the game.

Like it or not, that was not to be.

15

———

You Can't Go Home Again

In 1982, during my last year with the Giants, my friend John McMullen, the owner of the Astros, contacted me about becoming a manager at Houston. I was flattered and excited by the offer. But, at the time, I was also torn. For a variety of reasons, I did not know if I wanted to manage.

I was interested in making sure that the *system* opened, that black people, at every level, had the same opportunity in baseball as anyone else.

And I was intrigued by the idea of managing, thought I could do a good job and, because John McMullen was a friend and a person I very much respected, I gave the offer a great deal of thought. I asked my father and my wife and Sparky what they thought—they all advised me to take the job. I was leaning that way and probably would have gone ahead but for a conversation I had with Billy Williams, the former Cubs' star, who was also a close friend. He asked me if I had gotten playing out of my blood. I told him I had not. He then suggested that until I had I would be making a mistake if I took a managing job. Even though I was on the verge of accepting John's offer, that pulled me back and made me confront the obvious in myself: I was a ballplayer and would be until the day I—and not someone else—said I wasn't.

At the same time I did not see how I would be able to go off to just any team in order to keep playing. Fortunately, I never had to make that kind of decision. At the time I was released by the Phils, I was told that the Oakland A's were interested having me play for them.

For a while I found it hard to focus on doing anything. I needed time to sort things out, to see what it was *I* wanted. After a few weeks, I sat down with Roy Eisenhardt, the club president.

Roy asked me to play right away. I said no. I intended to retire, and I even had the ball from my last hit in the '83 World Series because that figured to be the last hit of my career.

I was impressed with Eisenhardt. We soon acquired a fast friend-ship—which we have maintained to this day. Roy is probably as bright a person as there has been in the game. He had tremendous feeling for others, great ability to learn, and a modesty about him-self that belied just how much it was he knew. He, more than anyone, had been instrumental in lifting the A's out of the Charlie Finley doldrums.

He offered me not a one-year but a two-year deal to play with the A's. He sensed how much I wanted to play, and rather than trying to exploit that he presented me with an opportunity to leave baseball the way I wanted to. He hoped the deal would lead to my staying in the A's organization after I retired, he said.

I was still saying no, because that's what I had made up my mind to do. Finally Roy said, talk it over with your family. My wife and my parents said, play. So I accepted—gladly.

I did not play out my two years, however. The adjustment to the American League was difficult. The style of play was completely different. With the DH and with smaller parks, the game was slower, less exciting for me. I had to learn a new set of pitchers. Above all, I had to adjust to a new team in a new time.

The A's of 1984 were the remnants of the Billy Martin billyball brigade. There was a lot of wreckage there, guys who had been through a roller-coaster ride and who, management hoped, would now welcome a little peace and quiet.

Steve Boros was the manager, a guy almost diametrically opposed to Billy Martin in temperament. He was a nice guy who just didn't want confrontations. That was well and good if tranquillity was the name of the game but not so good if the goal was to take hold of a team and shape it.

Steve was unable to keep guys from coming late, generally coming and going as they wanted. On one occasion, we had a day game, a businessman's special, at 12:05 P.M. Several key guys, including Rickey Henderson and Dwayne Murphy, were not in the clubhouse as game time approached.

Ten minutes before we were supposed to start, Rickey and Dwayne showed up. And then, they lingered for a few minutes in the clubhouse arranging day passes for friends and family. Steve said nothing to them—not then, not afterwards.

In the first inning of the ball game, Dwayne pulled a muscle in his side swinging at a pitch and had to come out of the lineup. I got so angry, I went up to him and said that might not have happened if he had had time to warm up prior to the game. Steve never backed me up. Dwayne shrugged me off.

I had my own problems merely trying to contribute as a player. I had a good stretch of games through mid-season but increasingly I felt I was playing for myself. I never had the sense that what I could offer the ballclub from twenty-one years' experience in the game was really needed. One time I got together on the bench with a group of younger players, including Dwayne Murphy and Mike Davis, to talk about base-stealing. All of these guys had the ability to steal a lot of bases but there was no one on the coaching staff knowledgeable enough to offer real help to them. They had been taught automatic things like looking at the movement of a right-handed pitcher's back foot as a sign to go, taking leads of precisely four steps—things like that. I wanted these guys to think about things that were less obvious but that would give them a greater advantage: learning a green-light, red-light system based on a pitcher's first move, for example.

As I was talking, I noticed a couple of the guys swiveling around to catch a look at a few of the ladies in the grandstand. The guys were laughing. It was like they were in a high school class they didn't want to be in. That was enough for me. As far as I was concerned, school was out, the semester was over.

Even though I ultimately enjoyed myself through that season, I also gradually came to the realization that my time as a player really was over. I also realized along the way that Roy's commitment to me, though absolute, was complicated by front office politics.

Roy, because he was a friend, used to regularly come to my house to play tennis. One day, he came over with Bill White to play, even though I had to go in for a ball game. That day, I got a phone call from someone asking me if I had seen an article in the papers about Roy and me. No, I said, and I was told that I had better get a look at it because it was all about a meeting up at my house with Roy where, it was alleged, I urged him to fire Steve Boros.

The story was totally false but had obviously been planted by someone within the organization who did not have the same opinion of me that Roy had. Roy was as upset as I was and tried to find out who was behind the piece. He never did. Eventually, Roy himself was eased out of the organization; and though he has never blamed anyone and is far too much the gentleman to suspect that friends of his might have been after his job, the likelihood is that that was the case.

For me, though, the idea of a front office divided over my remaining in the organization weighed heavily in the decision I soon made: I told Roy that I did not want to go ahead with the second year of my contract. I wanted to retire.

The A's allowed me to go in style. They arranged for me to have a day. It was just fine, in front of my family and lots of hometown friends and fans. I was moved by the celebration, by the warmth and encouragement I got from my teammates and from the guys on the other side that day, players from the Kansas City Royals. I wished I could have helped bring a pennant to Oakland. That was not meant to be. But I was more than satisfied that I was stepping down the way I wanted to, by choice, feeling like a winner. My last major-league hit came that day, a double to left center.

At season's end, I sat down with Roy again. He made it clear that he and the Haas family, father and son, wanted me to stay. And then I told him about that story that appeared in the papers which almost certainly meant there were others in the organization who felt differently than he and the Haases. "There are people, high up in the organization, who don't want me there," I said. Roy said he was aware of that, just to forget about it. But I could not. I did not want to be the focus of dissension, for whatever reason, within the organization I would be serving. Also, I told Roy, if he didn't have a defined job for me (none was offered), he'd have to create one and, for sure, he wouldn't want to do that only to fire someone else: that wouldn't be acceptable to me either.

So there the matter was left—I was out of the game and, for the first time since I was a kid back at the dawn of creation, free to deal with the rest of my life.

I had a plan for my post-playing life, one that had been on the shelf for over twenty years. I went back to school and got a degree—something I promised my mother I would do all those years ago when I set out to be a ballplayer—and I went into private business.

I've always tried to look at things from a fresh angle. When I saw my playing career coming to a close, I gave a lot of thought to what came next. I was always interested in business; in college I was a business major. And I wanted to get into business as more than a figurehead for somebody else's car dealership or beer distributorship. I wanted to work for myself, to take on the responsibilities of meeting a payroll, planning and executing within a budget, working with others to make an idea grow into something worthwhile and productive.

A beverage distributorship was actually an attractive possibility. Other things being equal, the beverage companies like to have well-known people involved in the distributorships because of the public relations value it has, and I knew the right situation could be a very good business deal for me.

While I was still with the Reds I went to work in the off season for Ken Markstein, who had a Budweiser distributorship in the Bay Area. I did everything to learn the business: worked in the warehouse, rode the truck routes and stocked the shelves, made sales calls, and picked Ken's brains at every opportunity.

When I was with the Phillies, I took trips on days off to investigate different business possibilities. Through John McMullen I had made contact with Coca-Cola. After the Coke people met me, they said, "We would love to have Joe Morgan as part of the Coca-Cola family." One time in spring training I flew to Atlanta for a meeting with Jesse Jackson, who was working behind the scenes to facilitate minority business ownership.

Coke and I both wanted to do something, but it had to be the right thing. I wasn't interested in a little money. I had enough to retire on. But I was interested in a lot of money.

Coke offered Bill Cosby, Julius Erving, Brad Llewellin, and me the chance to purchase one-quarter of one percent each of the New York market. Now one percent of New York actually represents a good-sized business. But I wanted to build something of my own, that I could pass on to my kids. That's why I chose to go into business after my playing days, rather than take a baseball job. You can't pass a baseball job along to your children and grandchildren.

Recently Garry Maddox, a Phillies teammate, called me up. He said, "Joe, when you were flying off to meet Coca-Cola and Budweiser on your days off, that really impressed upon me that I should be thinking ahead." Garry now has a thriving business selling novelty items. I thanked him and told him, "Maybe you can help show the way to someone else now."

When I was playing in the Bay Area, Ken Markstein took me to meet Fred Kuehlman in St. Louis. He runs the Cardinals' baseball operations for the Busch family and is also an executive at Budweiser. They liked me, liked the way I had prepared myself to get into the beverage business, and they promised me the first opening in Northern California.

At the time I was set on having a business in Northern California. Today I'd be more flexible, because I can see that there were good opportunities elsewhere. A Bud distributorship opened up in Monterey, but the company and I agreed that it didn't have enough growth potential.

While we were waiting, I investigated Coors. Tom Louderback, the ex-Raider, had a Coors distributorship in Oakland, and he put me in touch with the Coors people. George Bush also wrote a letter about me to Peter Coors, the current CEO, in which he made clear that he wasn't writing the letter as a formal courtesy but because he really knew me well and knew I could be an asset to Coors.

People are often shocked that I am in business with Coors, because of the reputation the older generation in the Coors family had for being opposed to the civil rights movement. I knew about that company history, but I don't live in the past, I just use it as a reference point. When I met Peter Coors and the present generation of Coors management, I saw that I could work with them. And I felt that in doing so, I could change a lot of people's minds about black people in business. Coors is now donating to minority charities, and beyond that has instituted a program of "minority covenants" through which they help minorities get into Coors and other businesses.

In the sixties it really was necessary to raise a ruckus, to strike and demonstrate. But now a number of doors have opened in our society, and our role has changed. We have to walk through those doors, to keep them open for minorities, and to open new doors. Who are the real agents of change in our society anyway but those who seize opportunities and make something of them. Should Jackie Robinson have turned down organized baseball because it was all white and top heavy with bigots?

A Coors distributorship wasn't just waiting for me, though, so in the interim I established three Wendy's franchises in Oakland with the aid and encouragement of John McMullen. I bought the land, designed the buildings, did everything. One in downtown Oakland, one in mid-Oakland, and one in a neighborhood under a lot of stress from crime, drugs, and unemployment. That was an effort to do something helpful, and unfortunately the franchise couldn't survive as a business proposition. But I ran all three profitably until a Coors deal did open up, and then I sold the franchises to Wendy's. The third franchise has since been shut down.

The important thing about the Coors deal, the thing that really showed they meant what they said about opening their operations to minorities, was that they didn't redline me into a ghetto distributorship, they offered me the chance at the territory with the biggest growth potential in Northern California.

Today I'm almost always the only minority at business meetings, but I'm hopeful my example will help those who come after me. And I'm eager to make my business as successful as it can be. We've had several years of steady growth now, and maybe someday soon I'll get to add a Coca-Cola distributorship to the one for Coors. I check in with the people at Coca-Cola regularly, so they won't forget about me. After all, if I'm going to be family, I can't be bashful.

The crazy schedule of a professional ballplayer gave way to the long hours of building a business. There was a price to pay for that. My wife, having willingly devoted herself to being mother and half-father to our children, our children being nearly grown, now was interested in starting a business career of her own. It was hard for me to accept that, because I've always had a very traditional notion of the way families worked. But I did accept in the end because I knew what Gloria had been through and I knew just how bright and talented she was.

For a while we traveled parallel paths. Gloria began working as a fashion coordinator for a department store chain, eventually going into business for herself. She had her own fashion boutique which lasted until the Oakland–San Francisco earthquake in 1989.

My hours and Gloria's were different. Neither of us realized we were gradually going our own ways. Sometime after that, we separated and divorced.

For a long while, as separation progressed to divorce, I was hurt and confused. I was helped enormously by Bill Russell, with whom I had become close over the years.

Russ has been a friend like no other. During the time of my separation and divorce, when I was at my lowest, he was living in Seattle, 1,200 miles away. We talked constantly on the phone. Every couple of weeks, he jumped in his car and drove down to spend time with me. We'd play golf, sit around and talk, just spend time together.

Russell had gone through a divorce after a long marriage. He helped me understand both sides of the equation, Gloria's as well as mine.

Russ was and is a man of enormous pride and integrity, highly intelligent, full of fun, but also contradictory and even contrary at the same time.

During the '60s, when the Celtics were riding high, he and Wilt Chamberlain became fast friends. In the 1969 NBA finals between the Celtics and Chamberlain's Lakers, Wilt suffered a first-half injury in the seventh and final game (won by the Celtics). Chamberlain wanted to go back in for the second half, but the coach would not let him. Not knowing this, Russ blamed Wilt for dogging it, for not being there as a competitor when it most counted, when Russ was playing his farewell game as a pro. To this day, he remains on distant terms with Chamberlain. Because I like them both, I have tried to bring them together, but unsuccessfully.

For years, Russ has been just as stubborn about signing autographs. He won't sign because he's a person, not a number. He'll spend hours talking to perfect strangers—but no autographs.

I remarried three years ago. My second wife, Theresa, is white. In some circles that poses a problem. That doesn't bother us. But we have to be concerned a little bit for our twin daughters, because children of mixed marriages sometimes find it hard to be accepted by either side.

In our two families, acceptance was not easy. While I know it took time to be accepted in Theresa's family, she was not immediately accepted in mine either. My parents maintained from the start that this had nothing to do with Theresa's being white but with my having been divorced.

But time has eased that now. Ashley and Kelly are now two, and they are the light of our lives. I know they will make me as proud of them as I am of Lisa and Angela, my two grown-up daughters.

Theresa and I are real companions. She is as avid as I about tennis and golf. She was a serious amateur runner for years before she met me.

We have coinciding but differing tastes in music. I am a jazz buff (Miles Davis, Bob James, Wes Montgomery), she likes jazz with a beat but tends to Madonna and Michael Bolton. I'm into sound, Magnaplanar loudspeakers, surround systems, the whole works— she's into listening. I am an avid wine collector, and Theresa joins me going up and down vineyard country, meeting different growers like Margaret and Robert Mondavi, who helped me produce and bottle my own private Joe Morgan Cabernet.

Gloria and I worked through enough to be good friends today. My older daughters, who had a hard time during the divorce, have also remained close. In fact Lisa, my oldest daughter, works at my company and also has a business as a makeup artist. My second daughter Angela goes to Cal State/Northridge. She wants to be a judge.

For many years now I have been involved in AIM, Adventures In Movement, a program for handicapped children that uses music to help them experience movement in an enjoyable way. Billie Jean King and I have been national ambassadors for AIM since 1975, and Nancy Lopez joined us a few years later. For the last twelve years I have also had my own youth foundation to help kids in the Bay Area. My involvement with both AIM and the foundation has been really rewarding.

My baseball career is filled with great experiences that I'll always treasure. The only thing I'm disappointed in is that my number was never retired in Houston or Cincinnati. The time for that to happen was when I went into the Hall of Fame. I spent eight years with Houston, and eight with Cincinnati. I was the first Astro selected to start an All-Star Game, and I was the first Astro inducted into the Hall of Fame. In Cincinnati I accomplished things that very few players will be able to match. But neither team saw fit to retire my number. It isn't as if they haven't retired any numbers. The Astros have retired Don Wilson's and Jim Umbrict's numbers, and they're going to retire Mike Scott's and Jose Cruz's. The Reds have retired

Freddy Hutchinson's number, and they retired Johnny Bench's when he left the game. To have my number retired would have been the crowning glory of my Hall of Fame induction year. Now it would be meaningless, and I wouldn't attend the ceremony if either team did it.

I have kept in touch with the game as a broadcaster. I began broadcasting games for the Cincinnati Reds several years ago, then moved on to doing network color for both NBC and ABC, finally moving on to the work I do now for the San Francisco Giants, locally, and for ESPN nationally.

I enjoy broadcasting, and I've tried to become the best at it just as I tried to become the best at my position on the field. The key is a simple idea, to broadcast the game as you see it. But it's amazing how few announcers really do that. In the first place, most television announcers talk so much, you'd think they were working on radio. And a lot of announcers go into the booth pre-programmed about which players and aspects of the game to hype. Some announcers come to the game with their key comments already written out on a pad, inning by inning.

I've been lucky enough to have good teammates in broadcasting. ESPN's Steve Bornstein, John Wildhack, Jed Drake, producer Bruce Connal, and director Marc Payton all share my view that the game should dictate what is said during the broadcast. In my opinion, that's why ESPN's baseball coverage has been good for the fans. They have given my broadcast partner, John Miller, and me, and the other ESPN announcers, the freedom to announce the game as we see it.

I've also been lucky in doing local broadcasts for the San Francisco Giants. At the local level, broadcasters are hired and fired by the team, and they are usually expected to be cheerleaders. But like ESPN, the Giants have enabled my partner, Duane Kuiper, and me to call the game as we see it.

John Miller and Duane Kuiper both make my job as game analyst a lot easier. One reason John Miller and I work so well together, as evidenced by a Cable Ace Award in 1991, is that John has a great sense of humor as well as a great knowledge of baseball. Where I emphasize the serious side of the game, John sees the humor in it. John's dry humor even makes rehearsals go faster. Duane Kuiper has a similar ability to combine a sound knowledge of the game with a knack for showing its lighter side, to balance the serious points I try to make.

My broadcasting career has allowed me to keep up with the game, to keep up with old friendships, to make new ones. Sparky remains a deep and abiding friend. From time to time I see him when his ballclub comes through. Sparky took the Tigers to a world championship in 1984, becoming the only manager ever to win a World Series in both leagues. Free agency and front office upheavals have kept the Tigers back in recent seasons but Sparky invariably fields a team that does better than people expect. He still looks for his players to say hello to him, he still walks through the clubhouse to stop off and talk with anyone, he still acknowledges his big guys and encourages his youngsters. He tells me he's changed his mind and that he's now glad I didn't go into managing because I'd be eaten up by criticism and that shouldn't happen to a Hall of Famer. When he tells me that I worry about what he's up against. Sparky will one day be in the Hall of Fame as a manager. He's been at it now for twenty-three years. But because he's still active, he knows all too well that he can be fired at any time. Only he's fifty-nine now, not forty-five. Baseball has been his life.

I see Johnny Bench frequently. Our paths cross as broadcasters; we frequently are together in celebrity golf tournaments, card shows, and the like. John is a low-handicap golfer who, if he ever got his short game worked out, could compete on the Senior Tour (I have a five handicap and no improvement in my game would get me to that level).

We have become closer friends today than we were when we were teammates. A couple of years ago, when Theresa was pregnant with the twins, John and I were at Don Drysdale's golf tournament. John's wife, Laura, asked me if Theresa and I had names picked out yet.

"Theresa had her choice, Kelly, picked out right away," I said. "I've spent months looking for mine."

"How 'bout 'Ashley,' " Laura said. I was thunderstruck.

"Perfect," I replied. The three of us laughed and raised a glass together. When I got home I told Theresa, who liked the name as much as I did.

Broadcasting and investments have allowed John to have an active and comfortable life. One day we were talking on the golf course.

"You know, Joe," he said, "when we were ballplayers we thought we earned a lot of money. We did, actually. I earned enough, for example, to buy a beautiful condo. But you know what? A utility infielder today earns enough to buy an entire community of condos."

While neither of us actually carry on like old-timers, we inevitably share the times we had as players, wondering about different teammates in the present, about where the game is headed. Both of us run into Tony Perez when we broadcast. Tony, who had been a coach with the Reds, is about to become the team's manager. John and I are both happy for him but I also worry because Tony was hired only for a year and a couple of his coaches, named not by him but by the Reds, had been rivals for the managerial job. Still, Tony is as forceful and as positive as ever.

Then there is Pete. In the days before Pete's banishment was announced by then commissioner Bart Giamatti, Pete was publicly proclaiming his innocence of all charges made against him. He maintained his innocence even to his lawyer, Reuven Katz, a close friend of John's. Katz, in his turn, had put his own reputation on the line insisting that what Pete had said was so. When Pete, at the last minute, accepted the deal with Giamatti (which thereby tacitly acknowledged the charges that he had gambled on baseball), he had left Katz out to dry—and John could not forgive him for that.

We both appeared on NBC's "Today" program shortly afterwards. I found it hard to say anything about Pete, because my feelings about him were so mixed. Bryant Gumbel asked John if he thought Pete was ignorant of what he was doing, arrogant, or just didn't give a damn.

"All of the above," John answered.

I see Pete less than I would like, though we have remained in touch. Since our time together on the Phillies, it was inevitable that we would have less to do with each other. But I was powerfully affected by what eventually happened to him. His downfall was tragic because everything he represented on the field had been so positive. His style of play and his attitude toward the game—no matter what later critics have said—were exemplary. Pete played the game, always, for keeps. *Every* game was the seventh game of the World Series. He had this unbelievable capacity to literally roar through 162 games as if they were each that one single game. There is still a Pete Rose Way in Cincinnati. There are no streets named after any other Cincinnati sports personalities.

I honestly knew little about the extent of his gambling and less about those associations he cultivated in his last years as a player. When we were teammates, Pete was not a compulsive gambler— he was a compulsive baseball player.

The charges of gambling that ultimately came down against Pete, of course, had to do with his betting on baseball—not while he was a player, but afterwards. I was as disturbed as anyone, perhaps more so, by what eventually surfaced. I called and spoke with him several times during his ordeal to ask him how things were going and his answer invariably was, "Joe, I'm going to beat this thing." Pete's attitude was that he was going to go at these charges nose-to-nose, the same way he went at the game and at everything else in life.

I believe, solely on the basis of what I've read—and I've read pretty carefully—that Pete bet on baseball and that, as a consequence, he let baseball down in a big way. Anyone in the game, particularly anyone like Pete, who has a real sense of baseball history, has to be sensitive to just how destructive any baseball link to gambling can be. The action taken against Pete was therefore not only justifiable but inevitable. And yet, I think it all could have been different.

If only Pete had been able to ask for help from baseball. My suggestion to him was to say, "I think I may have a problem. I don't really know how to deal with it. I want help." Baseball—and America—would have opened their hearts to him. But Pete could no more have done that than he could have apologized for the way he played the game. Full speed ahead, helmet off, hair flying. What was a virtue in one place was his ruin in another.

Still, baseball also let Pete Rose—and America—down by the way it handled his case. There was never a finding that Pete bet on baseball, even though enough investigative work had been done to make the case. Instead there was a "compromise." Pete accepted a lifetime ban in return for no finding of specific guilt. Immediately after the agreement, though, Commissioner Giamatti announced to the media that while the deal didn't say so, he indeed thought Pete had bet on baseball.

Pete was outraged. He claimed the commissioner had stabbed him in the back.

And while Giamatti may have betrayed the agreement he had signed, there was also the question of the "compromise" itself. By not making a specific finding on the charges that had been aired for months in the press against Pete, it left the whole case hanging. It left to speculation and assumption what was never spelled out.

Pete eventually did jail time for tax fraud. His whole life has been shattered. Recently, he has begun to rebuild and, hopefully, to heal. He has a radio talk show which started small in Florida but has since become syndicated nationally. He has become quite popular. When I talk to him, he has even begun to sound an occasional, faint note of self-criticism. "You know, Joe, I'm sure I was part wrong, but I still don't see why they . . ." Etc., etc.—that kind of thing.

At the time of his banishment, though it hurt me to say it, I believed that it was right for Pete to be kept out of the Hall of Fame. My belief was based on a sense of the damage he had done to the game. The damage remains but Pete has now paid for that dearly. The only question remaining is whether or not he now should be allowed to take his rightful place in the Hall of Fame.

My own answer, unequivocally, is that he should. In the time Pete was a player, he gave his heart and soul to the game, he epitomized its fierce competitiveness, its joy, its beauty. He made baseball better merely by his walking on a field. The batting titles, the MVP award, the consecutive-game streak, the records for most hits and most doubles ever, even the hot-dogging which went with it, all belonged to an achievement the likes of which we will not see again. If baseball can ever find a sense of forgiveness, it will reverse itself and vote him into the Hall of Fame.

The collective wisdom of baseball, though, is very much at issue these days.

EPILOGUE:
From the Booth

Over the past two decades, the game of baseball has prospered as never before. Revenues, driven by mammoth television contracts, have soared, and so have payouts. Different owners have sworn they were yoked to money-losing operations in this period but the fact is that when teams are bought and sold, their asking price alone suggests how much value has accrued in the game in recent years. When George Steinbrenner bought the Yankees from CBS in 1973, the reported purchase price was a little over $10 million. The current value of the Yankees, according to a number of different trade sources, is well over $200 million. Other teams, in poorer markets, have price tags of $100 million and above. The two newest expansion teams, the Colorado Rockies and the Miami Marlins, each paid start-up fees totaling around $95 million.

It is equally true that as much as the game has recently been awash in money, it has also been on the verge of drowning, as the turmoil of the last year or so has clearly shown.

Whatever the outcome of baseball's current labor problems, there will be long-range problems that will continue to eat at the vitals of the game until real solutions are found.

The economic problems of the game—player salaries, television revenue, pension arrangements, merchandising agreements—remain at the center. Most fans and many owners complain bitterly that the bidding wars for different players have gotten completely out of hand and they point to the players and their union as chief culprits.

But when owners, who complain about high salaries, turn around and pay more than a king's ransom for Cal Ripken Jr., even as his numbers and effectiveness decline, then they have nothing to complain about. Whatever greed exists among players is there because different owners fall all over themselves trying to outdo the other owners in securing desirable players. They create the system of greed and they have only themselves to blame when its bitter fruit becomes obvious. The owners can insist all they want that they need a chief executive office rather than a commissioner to defend their interests, but if, individually, they continue to undermine each other by paying more and more money to each new free agent, then they, not the players, must face the mirror when they talk about greed.

The owners, of course, know all this but they keep bidding the price of free agents up. The reality, at present, is that they don't know what to do to stem the tide except to declare war on the players. The likelihood of success coming from this sort of collective effort is about as great as it was when owners decided that collusion was the way to go. The penalty from that past folly, pending an arbitrator's decision, will be in the hundreds of millions of dollars.

There is an economic reckoning coming. When Peter Ueberroth left baseball, he told the owners he'd made them more money than they could ever lose. But the television contract he negotiated between Major League Baseball and the networks will end in 1993. The past four-year contract with CBS and ESPN totaled $1.5 *billion*—which meant that every major-league team got a payout, each year, of around $24 million. That in itself was more than enough to cover payroll costs and more than enough to allow the game of salary drive to move into overdrive.

A new television contract will surely reflect the failure of the old. The networks, especially CBS (which shelled out $1.1 billion for its rights and then seemed ill prepared for programming), will never enter into a similar arrangement. ESPN has already announced its intention to buy out its broadcast options after the 1993 season. The likelihood is that baseball coverage in the future will be divided between different major networks (as professional football is) and cable.

This will be bad for fans. Baseball is different from football because there are so many more games. Football is played only once a week; baseball is played day in, day out over a six-month season and therefore it demands more attention. Aside from each team's local broadcasts, there should be one national broadcast network and one national cable channel to preserve a sense of continuity over the season.

ESPN's coverage has shown why a single national cable channel is a good idea. It has made fans around the country more aware of all the players and teams. Before, the broadcast networks showed mainly the New York and Los Angeles teams. Fans never got much of a look at the teams in smaller markets. Now that they can see all of both leagues on ESPN, they've been able to appreciate a Ken Griffey Jr. in Seattle or a Sandy Alomar in Cleveland and vote them into the starting lineup for the All-Star Game.

The total revenue for baseball from whatever package is worked out next will almost certainly be less than the last one: meaning a smaller pie for owners, and more money pressure where an abundance of pressure already exists. With a smaller pie, stronger owners (like the Tribune Company which owns the Cubs as well as the rights to the local TV contracts of several other teams, including the Yankees, Dodgers, Angels, White Sox, and Phils) really will be in a position to dominate weaker owners.

Money may or may not be the root of all evil in baseball but solving the money problem will only begin to allow solution of even trickier problems, chief among them being a complete absence of trust between owners and players. A decade and a half of labor struggles has left players and owners locked in adversarial combat. They speak to each other through lawyers, arbitrators, courts of law. A union on one side, a "Player Relations Committee" of owners on the other, the possibility of cooperation for mutual benefit is virtually nil. An owner can count on the fact that any public statement he makes regarding labor relations will be greeted with suspicion or hostility. Likewise, proposals from players and their representatives are taken by most owners as terms for unconditional surrender.

Caught in the squeeze of this ever-increasing and destructive combat are a range of other problems that continue to be neglected at peril to baseball's long-term survival.

During this decade baseball will mark the fiftieth anniversary of Jackie Robinson's first season in the major leagues. Much has changed since then but racism is still around.

Several years ago, when former Dodger executive Al Capanis appeared on "Nightline" and said that black people "didn't have the necessities" for upper-level jobs in baseball, he actually helped point out just how much racism there still is.

At present, there are no black owners in the game and only a handful of executives, chief among them Hank Aaron, vice-president for player development of the Atlanta Braves. When the Braves made it to two World Series in a row, we heard a lot about Bobby Cox and John Schuerholz and nothing about Hank Aaron, who clearly played a pivotal role in the organization's rise as the executive in charge of finding and nurturing their great young talent. Obviously, Hank had "the necessities"—and so do hosts of others.

On the field, there are similar problems. With the naming of Don Baylor as manager of the expansion Colorado Rockies and Tony Perez as manager of the Reds, baseball now has five black managers, the most at any one time in the game's history. With the Blue Jays winning a world championship last season, there was another milestone. Cito Gaston became the first black manager to guide a World Series team and the first one to win. But success should not hide the fundamental and persistent problem that minorities still have anything but an equal opportunity to gain jobs as managers or even as third-base coaches (reserved for "thinking" types).

For anyone who doubts that discrimination still exists when it comes to placing black people in the dugout or on the coaching lines, consider this: The few black managers who have won jobs in the recent past have all been stars or prominent players. There are no black equivalents of Earl Weaver or Sparky Anderson or Buck Showalter, guys who had little or no major-league experience as players. Ever heard of Erwin Bryant? He was a second baseman several years back in the Red Sox chain. He was as knowledgeable, as promotable as anyone around. He has as much chance of managing the Boston Red Sox as he does of being elected president of the United States.

Another argument used to keep the door closed is that too many would-be black candidates haven't had minor-league managing experience. The flaw in that line is that white ex-players who have never spent a day managing in the minors routinely get named to pilot big-league teams. Phil Garner and Lou Piniella all came to the dugout without wasting an hour on rickety buses and dusty fields down below. Chris Chambliss, on the other hand, has been managing successfully in the minors for years and he's still waiting for a call.

What bothers me most in all this, after the human cost, is just how much baseball loses by its ongoing hang-up with color. Before Jackie Robinson, when baseball was all white, the game was played in a certain way. From 1947 to the present, the game has changed— its style and its character are different. In many ways, particularly with the emphasis on speed, it's a more exciting game.

If the doors were really open to black executives, coaches, and managers, there would be a similar kind of change. Fully recognizing that individuals from any group are individuals, there is nevertheless an element in black life, in the everyday culture of the black community, that translates into the personality of individuals. I can't find a name for it but I do know that whatever it is would make the game attractively different. I happen to know and admire

Cito Gaston, the Jays' manager. For the years he has led that team, he has been under intense pressure to produce. The strong likelihood, voiced by many in the media, was that if he had not delivered a world championship last season he would have been fired (another subtle but real difference: Tony LaRussa and Jim Leyland, respectively named Manager of the Year in the American and National Leagues last season, had both, like Cito Gaston, failed to get their teams into the Series during the past couple of seasons—their jobs were never in doubt). Cito responded to the extra pressure he was under by being a far more conservative manager, less willing to take the risks he might have if he felt freer to be himself. If Cito had had that freedom, his team might have been that much more exciting. The NBA had a certain style before—and after—the arrival of black people in large numbers at every level of the league. The same would be true in baseball.

The way black people have historically brought about change is by activism. I don't know that that could or should happen within baseball. For one thing, because baseball is so predominantly white at the highest levels, there simply will have to be an element of understanding, of enlightened self-interest, as there was when Branch Rickey first realized that breaking the color barrier meant, beyond any moral questions, increased levels of revenue and talent for all of baseball.

I happen to be friendly with Al Davis, the owner of the Los Angeles Raiders. I became friendly with Al when the team was in Oakland. He is an intense, win-at-all-costs kind of guy but he is a great owner because he understands, before anything, what makes a team. Not only has he been unafraid to hire a black head coach (Art Shell who is a very close friend of mine), but he understood from the start that his players, all of them, black and white, always had a home on the Raiders. They could go elsewhere, retire, do other things, but they would have a home waiting for them in the organization—and not just in "community relations." Al is one of those guys who changes the way people wind up thinking about themselves. There are all too many minority guys who believe that it isn't realistic to think of a future with an important job in big-time sports, that it's like a hitter saying he's going to try to hit .500 next year. An owner like Al Davis makes it possible to think realistically about real goals. His organization and his sport are better because of it.

An obvious alternative to either activism or someone else's benevolence, however, is black ownership. Currently there is only one black-owned professional sports franchise, the Denver Nuggets basketball team. There are, to be sure, black people wealthy enough to buy into a team. But the cost of ownership now is so great that, even with open acceptance, bringing an ownership team together from the black community would be difficult. Not impossible, but difficult.

At the core of the hiring problem, and all the others, is this business of cooperation. So long as owners and players stand on opposite sides of the dollar divide as mistrustful of each other as the Hatfields and McCoys, there will be no intelligent resolution of problems surrounding free agency, television, drugs, expansion, race, and so on.

Can there be a resolution? The example of the NBA suggests there can be.

Over many years, the National Basketball Association, faced with financial turmoil, flagging fan interest, exploding player salaries, along with all the difficult social issues, evolved what was essentially a partnership between players and owners (everything from television revenue to merchandising agreements would be administered and shared together). Team salary caps, drug policy, and front office hiring all were worked out. The NBA, to be sure, still has major problems but it remains something of a model.

But in order for baseball to begin to learn from the example of the NBA, it will first have to learn how to get along with itself. It will have to find a way past the barricades between owners and players to something like real cooperation.

Several years ago, I was interviewed for the job of National League president. I sat in a room with a committee of owners outlining much of what I have been saying here. The league owners eventually chose Bill White for the post. Bill, who is a friend, will soon be moving on, having been unable to do much more than settle problems with umpires and be a ceremonial leader, even though I know he tried.

When baseball commissioner Fay Vincent was forced out of office last fall, the owners' reasoning was that he had done too much, that he overstepped himself in interpreting the provision in his job description that allowed him to act "in the best interests of baseball." Vincent, on several issues—like divisional realignment in the National League, intervening in the brief owners' lockout of players during spring training in 1990—was seen as too independent, too ready to side with the players.

Vincent's liability was twofold. He was not a baseball man, someone really familiar with the problems of both owners and players; and he was not, by nature of his office, able to do very much apart from the spotlight of publicity. The baseball commissioner, even more than the two league presidents, is a ceremonial leader of the game. There were too few people, on either side, who trusted him when he sought to do anything that involved more than being a figurehead.

The case of Steve Howe is a good example of that. When Fay Vincent visited me in the broadcast booth one night, I turned to him during a commercial break and told him how upset I was about the revolving door baseball was operating for Steve Howe. At that time he had tested positive for cocaine six times. What message does that send to kids? That if you have ability you can get away with anything? Every time you get caught, just look sorry and promise not to do it again.

Vincent told me he wanted to suspend Howe, but that he had no support within baseball, and that if he acted unilaterally he would be liable to a suit from Howe for infringing his livelihood. When Howe tested positive a seventh time, Vincent did act to suspend Howe from baseball for life. But baseball wouldn't support what was clearly the right decision.

News stories about Steve Howe almost always emphasize what a nice guy he is. I understand that feeling. A few years ago, Pete

Rose and I were in the Atlanta airport at the same time as Barbara Bush. I introduced Pete to Mrs. Bush. Much later I was at a White House reception for Little League. By this time Pete's troubles were public knowledge. When Mrs. Bush asked me about Pete I told her, "He's really a wonderful guy." She stopped me right there, "Most alcoholics and drug addicts are nice people. But that doesn't excuse what they do."

Baseball can't seem to learn that lesson, at least when profits are involved. The perception among baseball people is that Steve Howe can still pitch. When Pascual Perez had his drug troubles, the perception seemed to be, "He's washed up, let's unload his salary."

Vincent's removal, which really represents the demise of the office of commissioner as we know it, underscores for me just what is needed to get baseball to finally begin to stop the bleeding.

What a commissioner cannot accomplish in the present atmosphere, a less visible figure might. The idea of acting "in the best interests of baseball" is as important today, perhaps more so, than when the commissioner's office was formed following the "Black Sox" scandal of 1919. But it is clear that with both players and owners at war, the commissioner, who is hired by owners, not players, and who is one of the most visible people in the game, cannot do much without incurring someone's wrath.

Harry Edwards, the sports sociologist, put it very well in a recent conversation we had. Peter Ueberroth was able to be an effective commissioner because he had vision, energy, and commitment. Without all three we will not have an effective leader in baseball.

When Bart Giamatti was commissioner, there were signs that he had the vision, the energy, and the commitment to lead the effort to solve baseball's problems. I had the opportunity for some thorough conversations with him, when he was just about to leave the National League presidency to succeed Peter Ueberroth as commissioner. Giamatti was a key member of the committee to choose a new National League president, and they were interested in my taking the job. I was tempted, but only because of the chance to work with Giamatti. Later they offered the job to Bill White.

What impressed me about Giamatti was his deep love of the game. "I love baseball so much," he told me, "I want to do everything I can to help it." Then he added, with a glint in his eye, "Besides, if I wasn't doing this, I'd be back at Yale grading papers."

That was a laugh, because he had been president of Yale and probably hadn't had to grade papers in quite a while. Our conversation took place over breakfast at the Yale Club in New York. We were both feeling each other out a little. We talked about everything in baseball, including Steve Howe and the Pittsburgh 7, as the papers were calling the group of Pirates and ex-Pirates who were found to be involved with illegal drugs there. Toward the end of the conversation, Bart said, "I know we could work together. But there's one thing I'm concerned about. The newspapers reported that you had a problem with my suspending Pete Rose for thirty days for bumping an umpire. That troubles me."

He was testing me, I suppose. Pete's troubles were just about to boil over, he knew how close Pete and I were, and he wanted to know if I could be objective. As I told him, I had no problem at all with Pete's suspension, except that it was too short. I told him that I had been brought up in the game to believe that if you bumped an umpire you might be suspended for life. The umpire has got to be untouchable, or the game begins to erode.

It would have been interesting to work with Bart. But I really wanted to establish my business and build that for the future, so I had to say no. It was a terrible shame when Bart died, but the cause wasn't a surprise. He chainsmoked all during our four-hour meeting at the Yale Club, and we sat in a little alcove because he didn't want to bother other people with cigarette smoke. Later that day, when the full committee interviewed me around a conference table, Bart sat off to the side for the same reason.

Whether the office of commissioner is that of CEO for the owners or something else, it is clearly in baseball's best interests to create a separate position that would allow for the sort of confidence building and trust between owners and players that must occur before any real movement toward cooperation can take place. Such a figure could act as an intermediary or roving ambassador between both sides, out of the limelight, away from publicity, able to promote, suggest, implore, reason, argue, wheedle, do whatever is necessary to get both sides to see that they have overriding *mutual* interests that must eventually be dealt with. The ambassador would need enough authority to call both sides to a meeting room, and keep them there.

If baseball created a position of this kind it would have to do so carefully and forcefully. The position should not be a ceremonial one. It should have the sanction of both players and owners. The right to examine any and all financial records on either side, should be clearly spelled out. Therefore, it would be essential not only to create such an office but to make sure it is filled by a person who really would be able to gain the trust of both sides. That would almost certainly mean that the candidate could not be simply a prominent person, a politician, say, or a figure from show business—but someone from the baseball world, someone whose experience in the game was wide-ranging and deep enough to elicit trust on both sides.

A designated intermediary could have a real and beneficial impact in many areas. Take the matter of arbitration.

As matters stand now, this annual exercise is conducted in a purely adversarial fashion. The rules and procedures require both players and owners to submit their different salary proposals. Representatives of the ballclub and, usually, the player and his agent then have at it before an arbitrator who by agreement must choose one of the two proposals on the table.

An offical intermediary cannot change the arbitration system per se but he can help both sides make sure they understand that beyond whaling away at each other they have needs that are real—and mutual. If the intermediary knows the ballclub's financial picture, he can perhaps make it possible for a player to hear what he might otherwise not be willing to hear; likewise he can point out to an owner just what it is, beyond numbers, that makes a particular ballplayer important enough not to trash him and, possibly, not to contest him through arbitration.

On the entire subject of negotiations between the Players Association and the owners covering the range of issues involved in the Basic Contract (minimum salaries, television and merchandising rights, pension and welfare benefits, etc.), the intermediary can be a troubleshooter long before the trouble begins. There was a major strike in 1981, smaller actions and lockouts at other times. The labor scene in baseball in 1993 with its big unresolved issue of television revenue suggests that the future will, if anything, be even more rancorous than the past.

The intermediary, well in advance of negotiations, can help both sides have a better, clearer understanding of the needs of the other, to face honestly, rather than selfishly, what is and isn't possible.

Even before economic questions are settled, the intermediary can help in a whole range of areas, continually reminding players and owners that they have a history to live up to and a history of problems to keep in mind. The intermediary can be an advocate for making sure the system of player development (not just the minors but college, the amateur leagues like Babe Ruth and American Legion, and neighborhood and industrial leagues) is more responsibly supported. This does not mean finding money where none exists. The intermediary can help find ways and means to bring in outside support from public and private groups.

He can work with clubs to show them, in detail, what others have accomplished or are trying to accomplish in community relations. The Oakland A's, for example, have had a strong community relations program for years. The Haas family has poured money and organization into programs for youth, underwriting the costs of tickets and so on.

Similarly, our designated facilitator can help evolve a coherent and mutually acceptable drug policy, something that takes into account the need for both enforcement and rehabilitation. The ability to work behind the scenes would possibly enable the intermediary to head off trouble before it got out of hand. If a player has a drug problem, the intermediary might help the club, the league, and the player work it through after the headlines wither. He might even intercede before there were headlines.

Finally, the intermediary might be just the person who could help in the area of minority hiring. If he did his job of confidence building well enough, if he knew the ropes well enough, he might be able to help both owners and players agree that it was in their common interest to work for genuine equality of opportunity across the board. If baseball ever understood—as the NBA apparently has—that that was necessary for the long-term survival of the sport, there would be no need for committees and commissions to deal with the language problems of an Al Campanis or a Marge Schott. The comfort level that allowed such language to flourish would be gone because there would have been no room in the game for the thinking that produced it in the first place.

What I have learned over a lifetime in the game is that striving is really everything. I am living proof that you don't need special advantages to be a success. Baseball has taught me that tough times go away, tough people don't. That is a lesson that baseball itself could use right now.

Our game is old and it has a history. Its past is both a glory and a shame; its possibilities, right out of the heart of our democracy, are only as limited as we are. My old friend Monte Irvin once said that baseball has done more to move America in the right direction than all the professional patriots with all of their cheap words.

That remains as true today as ever.

Play ball!

Postscript

Before I close this book I want to mention some friends around the country:

the Aim family, Dayton
the Azeoff family, Montreal
the Alesia family, Chicago
S. Antonio, California
the Bass family, Boston
the Bernier family, Montreal
the Berry family, Pittsburgh
Dr. H. Brelsford, Houston
the Busch family, California
J. Buchman, California
the Bush family, the White
    House, and now Houston
B. Behymer, Kentucky
B. Cholak, Cincinnati
H. Chandler, Kentucky
the Collet family, Dayton

B. and R. Connolly, Cincinnati
the Croxton family, Cincinnati
the Cabell family, Houston
the Chin family, Cincinnati
the Dawson family, San Diego
T. Davis, California
J. and L. Deutsch, Florida
B. Elkus, Cincinnati
J. Forrest, Atlanta
B. Frank, New York
J. Gaines, California
D. Geddes, New York
J. Geiger, Dayton
B. Giles, Philadelphia
A. Green, California
J. Hightower, Houston

the Harrison Family, Houston
R. and B. Hacker, Cincinnati
the Hazzard family, Los
    Angeles
D. Hawke, New York
B. Hayes, Cincinnati
H. Hinzmann, New York
the Hulick family, Pittsburgh
J. Jackson, Chicago
S. Jackson, California
H. Kalas, Philadelphia
J. Kitagawa, Hawaii
K. Kane, Texas
S. Korb, Cincinnati
E. Ladd, Houston
J. Lang, New York
C. Levy, Cincinnati
S. Lenenberg, Pittsburgh
C. and J. Lenton, Houston
J. and F. Lupkin, California
A. Maye, Los Angeles
E. McKibben, California
J. McMullen, New York
R. and M. Mondavi, Napa

the Joe Morgan Beverage
    Company family
J. Mott, California
T. and M. Massa, New
    York
M. Miller, New York
A. Nizetich, California
C. Norket, California
P. Pascarelli, Philadelphia
P. Roussel, Houston
the Reich family, Pittsburgh
W. F. Russell, Seattle
the Shell family, Los Angeles
SKYLO, California
C. Sifford, Houston
W. Stargell, Atlanta
K. Sweitzer, Cincinnati
G. Thorne, New York
S. Uslan, California
the Voss family, Dayton
S. Richardson, Kentucky
B. Wendell, California
R. and M. Weaver, Cincinnati
J. Zerheusen, Cincinnati

Life on the road was difficult. But these friends made it easier. People come and go, but friends are forever!

Thanks,
Joe